HIKEOLOGICAL ESCAPE

Discovering Spirituality and Purpose on the Camino Santiago and the Pacific Crest Trail

CHRIS "WINDSCREEN" HOMAN

Library of Congress Control Number: 2025915142

ISBN: 979-8-9995684-0-3 (Paperback)
ISBN: 979-8-9995684-1-0 (eBook)

Editor: Sam Fletcher
Book design: Melissa Vail Coffman

To my family, who raised Chris.
To the trail, who raised Windscreen.

CONTENTS

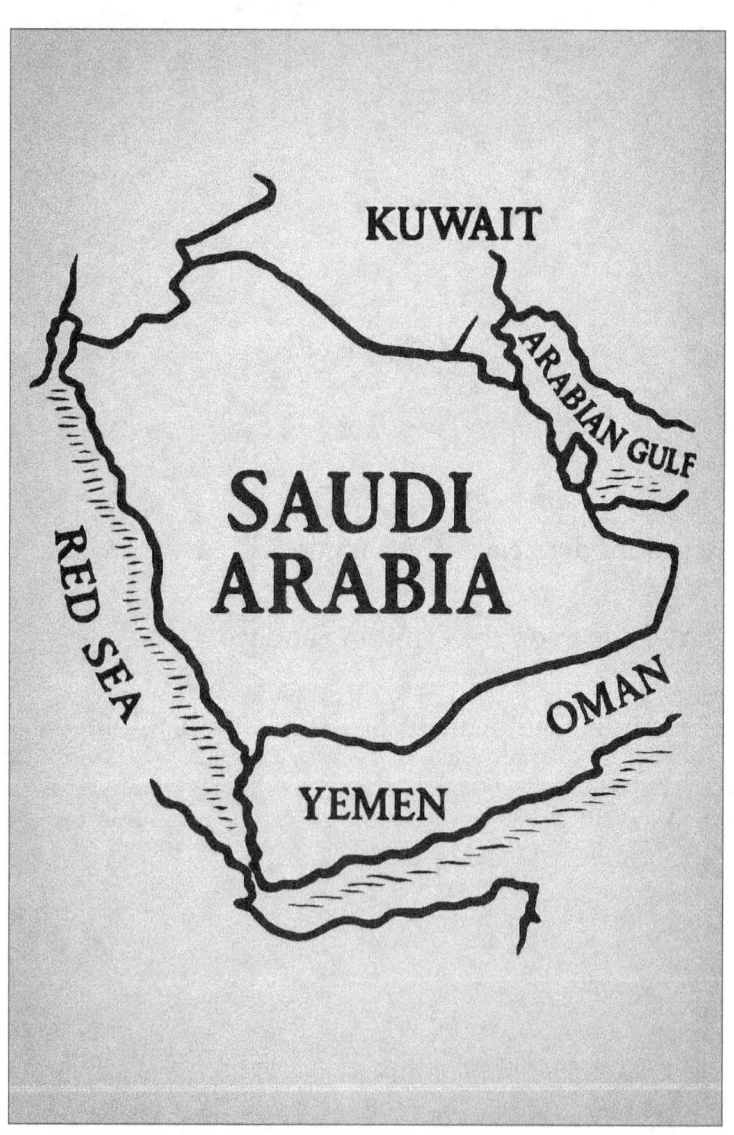

PART 1

An Infidel Leaves the Kingdom

"If you are different from the rest of the flock, they bite you."

—Vincent O'Sullivan, The Next Room

"Religious zealotry therefore became the anchoring fabric weaving fractious fiefdoms together into a Kingdom." —Qanta A. Ahmed

1

A knock pulled my focus away from the workbooks I'd been going over with my students. My eyes adjusted to the sunlight mixing with the classroom's artificial lights as I wondered if it wasn't one of my American colleagues who had a quick question, or someone was stopping by to remind me about an upcoming meeting. Maybe it was Leo, bored and looking to chat about *Game of Thrones* or *Breaking Bad*. Instead, I saw my boss's face with a look I'd never seen before—half-apology, half-heartbreak.

"Can I bother you for a moment?" he asked, his voice low enough to avoid disturbing the room.

I nodded. "Digayga," I said to the class in Arabic, letting them know I'd be back in a minute.

The students pulled out their phones at once to ping off text messages, while a Miley Cyrus song began. I closed the door behind me.

"Hey Chris, sorry for the interruption." A furrowed brow had replaced Paul's usual calm and humorous demeanor.

"It's always good to chat with you, Paul. What's up?"

"After work tomorrow, swing by my villa at 1500 for a half hour. I have something to discuss with you."

"You got it, boss. Is everything okay?"

Paul smiled professionally and patted my arm. "See me tomorrow afternoon."

I closed the door after entering the classroom and let my eyes adjust to the overly white interior lighting. My mind wandered about what Paul had to tell me. Overseeing our cadre of Americans instructing Saudi students in their twenties to become qualified F-15 mechanics wasn't an easy task, but I thought Paul was better at it than his predecessor.

I hadn't done anything wrong, had I? Throughout my many years as an ex-Air Force contractor in the Middle East, I'd seen more than a few people, deservedly and undeservedly, lose their jobs. There'd been whispers among my American colleagues lately about budget cuts, reshuffling, restructuring. Overseas contract jobs are nothing if not hotbeds of rumors, the bigger the better. I had developed a thick skin around what people claimed to know. Whispers didn't carry the weight of a visit from the boss before the third cup of coffee, so I began to concern myself with the possibility of change.

A few days prior I had told Waleed, one of my Saudi colleagues, about my atheism. We'd been waxing philosophical, and when he asked me if I believed in Allah, I confessed to Waleed I thought all of humanity's faiths were myths.

"I tend to think the universe is indifferent . . . it's '*ghayr mabal.*'" I translated. "Please, don't tell anyone this, Waleed."

"I won't," he promised, knowing how much trouble I'd be in if the Command staff or the Saudi Arabian religious police had heard what I had just admitted to Waleed. God help me, even when it could get me fired, or beheaded, I still wanted to. It wasn't even to rebel or be edgy, but because it formed me. Living without the promise of heaven to tidy up the loose ends while people walked around me with certainty in their religiosity astonished me. In places where doubt is dangerous and where conformity is currency, part of me thought my compulsion to shine a light on it wasn't reckless, but moral. I told myself it was the soul's immune response to hypocrisy, to forced silence, to the spiritual litter swept under gilded rugs.

As far back as I could remember, religion had been the scaffolding around my identity. Even way back to kindergarten, my classmates and I sang "I've got the joy joy joy joy down in my heart" in Mrs. Lolley's music class, at top volume as though we meant to keep Satan at bay. As critical thinking replaced the power of song to fight my demons, it leaked out in my conversations, metaphors, and journal entries. Even in the Kingdom of Saudi Arabia, I feared that repression of truth could be its own kind of slow death. That's why I gambled wildly one sunny afternoon when we were the only two left at work, Waleed and I had a truthful chat about religion and faith. I got the feeling that our conversation had been a first for him. While neither of us were about to convert the other, we did agree that if there was a divine truth out there, it would surely prefer to be wrestled with honestly than worshipped blindly, right? I wanted to hold onto the trust in sharing something so direct. So verboten. After taking a second to see what was before me, I realized if Waleed had said anything about my atheism to the Colonel or any other important person, the Royal Saudi Air Force wouldn't have permitted me to continue teaching. I would have been hauled out and questioned at the Command level, never to return to teach aerospace electrics in Saudi Arabia.

While this was about something unreligious, I could see on Paul's uncharacteristically humorless face that it was something big. Even as I finished teaching that day's coursework, I began to think about what I would do if I were to lose my job.

"Relax," I told myself. "You're overthinking things again."

I'd spent the last couple of years working in one of the most under-stimulating countries on the face of the planet. I'd managed to save enough money to get a Toyota Tacoma upon returning home, but I wasn't sure I could dilly-dally for long between jobs. I could choose to stop renting out my home in Albuquerque and live in it myself if I wanted. When I thought about finding work on Albuquerque's flight-line, I reminded myself working in the United States would mean having only two weeks off a year. I was delighted at the thought of being so much closer to loved ones at home, but having a normal job in America would render my love of traveling unrequited. My life would be unfulfilled.

What if I could only find a suitable job in Iraq? What if that was the only place left where I could find work that paid enough to keep the wheels turning? The thought gnawed at me. When I took contracts there years prior, I told myself it was just temporary—a bridge, a paycheck, an adventure. But the truth was that working in a combat zone gave me something I didn't know I was craving: the illusion of purpose. Stay alive, fly around on helicopters, and repair perimeter camera systems. The tension had been constant, but in a strange, brutal way, it was simple. There was no room for existential spirals or lingering questions about my life direction. I didn't overthink my place in the universe when avoiding incoming rocket-propelled grenades. While I missed the simplicity of those years, I promised myself I wouldn't go back. Not unless there was absolutely no other option. I had spent enough time holding my breath, living in borrowed time and borrowed clothes, pretending danger was just another Tuesday. I wanted to live in places where I could fully exhale. I forced myself to consider other paths, even if they were riskier in different ways like lying about being religious, or betting on dreams that didn't come with hazard pay.

If I applied for another contract in Saudi Arabia or elsewhere in the Middle East, pay and time off would be to my liking, but I would continue missing loved ones back home. What if an aircraft electrical job opened up in Afghanistan and tugged at my spirit of adventure so I served the dreaded military industrial complex? Would I succumb again to the temptation of a guaranteed paycheck even if it meant flirting with danger and death?

I carried my questions to Nassim Compound where my western

colleagues and I lived in company housing. I wanted to talk to my friends and see if they knew more than I did about why our boss wanted to see me, but I kept it to myself. The worrying frazzled me, so I went to bed after a gym workout.

That night I had a dream I was back on the Appalachian Trail, sweat-slick and wild-hearted, when a hiker named Face Jacket had just given me a trail name: Windscreen. I liked how cool and sleek it was, like something that slices through the elements without flinching. I remembered how glad Face Jacket was when I laughed after hearing it, how it stuck, and how it made me feel like part of something ancient and alive. I missed being that stripped-down version of me, the one who didn't care about anything but the next ridge, the next sunrise, the next laugh around a smoky fire. I loved who Windscreen was.

As I brushed my teeth to delve into yet another day in the grind of normal life as an American in Saudia Arabia, it occurred to me that if I was at a crossroads, I would either remain in Saudi Arabia, apply to work in a combat zone, settle for premature mediocrity in America, or follow this dream. As I weighed my options I realized I already knew what I wanted to do.

I rang Paul's doorbell and took a deep breath.

"Hi, Chris," my boss said as he opened the door wide and ushered me in.

"Looks like a party!" I said, seeing Scott, Paul's Assistant Manager, working from a laptop from his couch. Paul gestured for me to make myself comfortable on the couch across from them.

"I would prefer that it was a party, Chris. Something's come down from head office stateside. The contract for next year has been modified. There's just no easy way to say it, the company's making cuts, and your position is in the company's making cuts, and your position—"

Paul's voice caught. He cleared his throat and tried again.

"Two electrical-environmental trainer positions are subtracted from next year's Royal Saudi Air Force training program. I hate to tell you this; I have to let you go. Jimmy, too. You guys have the least amount of time in the company. It's not fair at all."

"The needs of the many outweigh the needs of the few, right?" I said, raising an eyebrow.

"Precisely. Is that something you learned in college?" Scott asked.

"It's something he heard on Star Trek," Paul interjected before I could answer.

Both managers chuckled while I stared at the floor, slowly digesting what was happening. This was it—I was getting laid off, like a decommissioned starship. Right there on the couch, I felt something surprising . . . not dread, not panic. Relief. I had been quietly craving an eject button from this job, and now they were pressing it for me.

"It's not what I want," Paul continued, snapping me out of my thoughts. "If I had any say in this, you'd stay. But they've made their decision and—"

I slumped deeper into the couch cushions and exhaled like someone just cancelled a dentist appointment I forgot I made.

Paul and Scott exchanged a look. "Are you going to be okay?" Paul asked.

"How long do I have before I need to leave Saudi Arabia?" I asked.

"By the end of January. So about three weeks," Scott said. "Same for Jimmy."

I sat forward and looked at them both. "Just to satisfy my sense of professionalism—was this because of anything I did? Was it the puns?"

"Are you kidding? The training plans and teaching materials you've been writing are above reproach, and you're excellent in the classroom," Scott replied. "Rest assured, Chris, this isn't on you."

I let out another long, theatrical sigh. "Okay good. I'd hate to have been fired because I was bad at my job."

"No one knows about this yet," Scott added. "Not the Colonel, not the rumor mill, not anyone."

"Not even Jimmy?" I asked. I was honored they told me first. This wasn't punishment, this was how contracts work. This is how *life* works.

"If I had to let someone go, I would pick me, too," I said with a smile I couldn't hold back. "I've been thinking what would happen if I lost my job. I know what I'm doing next, now I've got severance and a deadline."

"You got another job in the works." Scott guessed.

"You're planning an adventure." Paul chimed in.

"A hike." I confirmed.

"A hike? Really?" Scott asked, looking confused.

"Actually, two hikes. The Camino Santiago and the PCT . . . the Pacific Crest Trail."

Paul and Scott looked at me as if waiting for a punchline.

"The Camino Santiago is an ancient pilgrimage in Northern Spain, and after that I'll fly to the States where I can start the Pacific Crest Trail. It's like the Appalachian Trail, except it goes through California, Oregon, and Washington State. It might take me six months. Five if I'm lucky."

Paul laughed, wide-eyed and pleasantly surprised. "That just might be the best reaction to being laid off I've ever heard."

"Damn, Chris. People usually hate being laid off," Scott chuckled, eyeing me like I'd just thanked him for setting my house on fire.

"What can I say? Some people want a white picket fence, some want a corner office, some want a collection of Lamborghinis. Me? I just want to hike and see the world."

Paul nodded. "And now you can."

"And now I can," I grinned, like the universe had finally handed me a hall pass.

There was a knock at the front door.

"That'll be Jimmy," Paul said, glancing toward it. "I'll let you know how things will play out, but I wanted to give you as much notice as possible."

"I appreciate that. Really. And hey, thanks for not firing me over email," I said, shaking his hand.

Paul's face shifted back into Serious Mode as he braced himself to drop the hammer on Jimmy, who wasn't going to be excited about having his job taken away.

I gave Jimmy a solid pat on the back as we crossed paths at the door. "Good luck, man," I said, keeping my voice soft but steady.

Then I practically skipped down the street, whistling 'I've Got a Golden Ticket' feeling like I'd just won my way into a chocolate factory instead of getting the boot from a Saudi military training gig.

The sun sets on my Saudi Arabia experience

An F-15 photobombs one of my Saudi friends

2

A few weeks prior to my meeting in Paul's villa, I accompanied one of my students, Sameer, as he stood in front of ten board members as the final part of his all-important final, the skills knowledge test (SKT). At the SKT a board of higher-ranking airmen, officers, and highly placed civilians fire random technical questions at students before they pass the course and progress as certified technicians from the classroom to the flightline. It can be nerve-wracking for any student, but Sameer was beyond flummoxed that morning. His voice shook as he gave slow replies. He answered questions wrong he knew the answers to, like how many kilovolt-amperes the F-15 main generators put out, what caused the unsafe landing gear light to illuminate in the cockpit, and how many minutes of breathable oxygen there were in the event of a primary bleed air system.

After the test, I went to bat for him. I told the board Sameer knew the material. He was just rattled from sitting in front of a firing squad in thobes. To the Saudi board members, I probably looked like another American trying to cover for his guy, the educational equivalent of shouting "He's just nervous!" at a karaoke bar while someone butchers Bohemian Rhapsody. I wasn't wrong. Sameer was capable. He needed support, not a roasting.

Despite my best efforts—and my calm, well-reasoned arguments delivered in my best "please don't make me grovel" tone—they gave him low marks and told me to bring him back in one month to retake the SKT test. That'd be great, except I only had a few weeks left in the country, which meant I had my work cut out for me, because I wasn't about to leave even one loose end. I came into this with a mission: teach with heart, finish strong, and maybe—just maybe—help Sameer pass without needing a priest (or imam), a lawyer, or therapist on standby.

I sat one-on-one with Sameer five days a week after regular classes to dive deep into the electrical and environmental systems of the F-15—which sounds a lot more glamorous than it was. He wore a confident smirk in front of his classmates, the way twenty-year-olds do when they're bluffing their way through life with the emotional toolkit of a confused golden retriever. But I wanted to help him move past the façade, to develop the kind of confidence that wouldn't disappear the second someone in a uniform raised an eyebrow at him. Saudi elders—even the kind ones—had a Jedi-like ability to make the brightest students stammer, sweat, and forget their own names. And I got it. I'd been there. When I was around Sameer's age, I tossed and turned the whole night before my own panel review, practically cuddled with my alarm clock, and still almost managed to oversleep. Nerves don't care how prepared you are—they show up uninvited, wearing combat boots and shouting motivational slogans in the worst way possible. I wasn't just teaching systems—I was coaching courage, grounding him in something deeper than rote memorization. I didn't need him to strut; I needed him to trust himself.

Sessions like these were where my light grasp of Arabic shone. I knew just enough to understand when Sameer was asking me something he felt embarrassed not to already know, and just enough to reply without accidentally proposing marriage or ordering a goat. It helped ease the tension. We'd laugh, clarify, and get right back into getting to know how cockpit pressurization works.

After a couple of weeks, Turki joined us. The three of us marched through the syllabus like a squadron—nose to tail—starting at the avionics cooling section near the jet's nose, working all the way back to the final stage valve that taps air from the engines. We covered it all: landing gear limit switches, cockpit pressure controllers, and every easily forgotten component in between. Honestly, there were days I felt like I needed a pressure controller myself.

I'm fairly certain neither of them cracked a book outside our sessions—this was Saudi Arabia, not Hogwarts—but by the end of the month, both Sameer and Turki could've walked a panel through those systems with the poise of seasoned techs. It wasn't magic. It was sweat, repetition, a little camaraderie, and just enough humor to keep us from losing our minds over valve diagrams.

The morning of the test showed up in its Sunday best—bright blue sky, sunshine so hopeful it might've been trying to sell us something. I was excited. Today, I'd get to watch two of my students graduate, and as any teacher knows, that's our version of walking the red carpet. Myron, another instructor in my field, also had a couple of students testing that day. I offered to drive us all over to the Base Training Wing—about ten minutes away. Nobody knew I was getting laid off soon, which made the car ride feel a little like driving a parade float toward my own retirement party.

Once at the Training Wing, Myron went to round up his students while I met Turki and Sameer in the hallway outside the boardrooms.

"How do you feel, Sameer? Turki?"

"I feel great, Mr. Chris," Turki said with a grin that was either confidence or sheer adrenaline.

"Good," Sameer said, not making eye contact, his fingers working nervously at the gold watch on his wrist like it held the answers to the test.

Then came the bark from inside the boardroom: "Sameer Al-Moutairi!"

Showtime.

I patted Sameer on the shoulder. "Hey man, you got this. Let's go."

Then, out of nowhere, Sameer turned to Myron and said, "Mr. Myron, will you come in the room with me?"

It was like getting dumped at prom . . . right outside the gym doors.

Myron looked at me like he'd just been handed a live grenade. "Have you talked with Chris about this?"

I blinked at Sameer, trying to process. All those extra sessions. All that effort to help him feel ready. The long hours explaining final stage valves with my pigeon Arabic and interpretive dance hand gestures. And now he wanted a last-minute switch-hitter?

"Mr. Chris, Mr. Myron is older and has more time in this," Sameer said gently, as if he were offering me a Band-Aid after running over my foot.

I wanted to yell, "Are you fucking kidding me?" But yelling in the Training Wing tends to make your badge melt and your career end faster.

So instead, I smiled and said, "Mafi mushkila." No problem.

I'd nurse my ego later—preferably with carbs and sarcasm. Sameer needed his head in the game, and I wasn't going to let my bruised pride become one more thing he had to overcome. Myron nodded awkwardly and followed him into the boardroom.

The door clicked shut, leaving me alone in the hallway with my dignity . . . and just enough time to question all my life choices.

"Who do you want to join you for your SKT board?" I asked Turki.

"You, Mr. Chris," Turki replied, like it was the most obvious thing in the world.

"Good. You have twenty minutes until you're up."

"I will go outside to smoke. If they call me, please tell me."

"I will," I assured him.

While students lit up outside, I paced alone in the corridor that smelled of bureaucracy and nervous sweat. I tried not to dwell on Sameer choosing Myron over me. Sure, I'd been his private tutor, cheerleader, and part-time life coach—but hey, why take your emotional support raccoon to the dance when there's a silverback gorilla in a lab coat?

Instead of spiraling, I focused on what still needed doing before I left Saudi Arabia for good. Nobody here knew I was leaving, but I'd already told everyone back home, from my siblings to the guy who sold me my hiking boots. After walking out of Paul and Scott's villa, I'd shifted gears fast—mapping out France and Spain, hunting for budget flights, obsessing over train schedules, and pinching pennies from my 'Dream Truck' fund like a squirrel hoarding nuts for a new life in . . .

"Turki Al-Assiri!"

I turned to see Sameer and Myron walking toward me with matching grins like they'd just cracked the Da Vinci Code. Sameer was glowing.

"I passed, Mr. Chris!" Sameer beamed, the gold on his watch catching the light like it, too, was celebrating.

"He didn't even need my help!" Myron said, giving me a congratulatory pat on the arm.

I smiled, nodded, and offered a sincere, "Well done, Sameer. You earned it."

"You ready?" I asked Turki as he strolled in, trailing enough nicotine to give the hallway walls a buzz.

"I am," he said, like someone who had already lit the fuse on his own fireworks show.

I followed him into the boardroom, took my seat, and watched as the panel fired off their toughest questions like intellectual artillery. Turki held his own, only pausing once to ask for clarification on what powered the emergency generator. I reworded the question, as permitted, and he nailed it on the first try.

The board gave their nods of approval, and when they told him he passed, the look on his face was pure electric joy—the kind of grin that makes all the overtime and coffee breath worth it.

"You did great," I told him as we stepped out. "Now go put those planes in the air!"

He grinned. "Yes, Mr. Chris."

After Myron's students high-fived their way back to class and the cigarette haze cleared, I stood there a moment longer. Between the smoke, the pride, and the quiet sense of completion, it hit me: I was finally on my way out. But damn, what a note to leave on.

Putting planes in the air.

The heaviness of being successful was replaced by the lightness of being a beginner again, less sure about everything. It freed me to enter one of the most creative periods of my life." —Steve Jobs

3

"Let's go to The Camel, Leo!" I yelled from my room while I swapped my instructor polo for a shirt that said, 'Definitely not fermenting alcohol in my apartment.'

"Okay!" Leo hollered from his bedroom, always down for whatever passed for drinks in our desert dystopia.

Alcohol was illegal in Saudi Arabia, but a bunch of us had taken up moonshining. The hooch we made on Nassim Compound was nobody's first choice, but it beat separation anxiety and cultural disrespect better than herbal tea ever could. Brits had been brewing the stuff here since the Empire wore red coats. Our compound, like most, had a little makeshift party zone—the Camel—where we could all gather to dance like the music-loving heathens we were.

Even I tried my hand at fermenting juice into wine a few times in my own apartment. Results varied wildly—one batch gave me a decent buzz; another stripped the paint off my inner stomach lining. I looked forward to staying in my lane and tasting quality wine and whiskey again.

The Camel had just opened when Leo and I walked in, but we weren't the first patrons.

"Hey Chris, hey Leo," Myron said, raising his pint like a medieval bard.

"Congrats on today, Myron," I said, signaling the barkeep to pour a couple of drinks from the totally legal tap.

"You as well. How about Sameer, huh?" he replied.

"Yeah, man. Had he talked to you at all beforehand?" I asked, still trying not to sound too salty.

"No, man, it was just as surprising to me. I'd be pissed too if a student had done that to me."

"Well, we got through it. This round's on me," I said as the barkeep slid two pints across the counter. Myron and I clinked glasses.

"Did you hear about the meeting tomorrow?" Myron asked.

"Nope," Leo said.

I took a sip of my drink. I already knew what the meeting was about, and this wasn't the kind of beer that made shocking news better.

"Let's play darts, Leo. You in, Myron?"

"Nah. I'm having one beer to celebrate, then heading to my villa. You guys have fun."

"Let's play, Chris," Leo said, already fiddling with the dartboard like he was warming up for the Olympics.

After winning three games in a row, Leo yawned. "I'm headed to bed, Chris."

"Good night, Leo." I said as we disappeared into our rooms. I glanced at the clock and realized it was lunchtime in Dallas. Perfect timing to drop a bombshell, I thought as I grabbed my phone and called my brother.

"You're leaving Saudi and going to Spain?" Andrew asked as if I had just told him I was joining the circus.

"Yeah. Then I'll stop through Dallas to see you before I go to California and hike the PCT."

"Man, you really love wearing muddy socks. Are you going with anyone?"

"I don't know anyone who can—or would want to—hike with me. Why, you wanna take up hiking?" I asked with a chuckle.

"Yeah. You can carry me on your back like a hiking baby. Jeez . . . send me your flight plans, and I'll take time off work—" he said, right before the line dropped.

I stared at my phone. How luxurious it would be to have reliable internet and phone reception, I thought, like a prehistoric human imagining indoor plumbing.

I laughed at the idea of Andrew hiking the PCT with me. His idea of a workout was a morning bike ride followed by a hot shower and a moral victory. Definitely not trudging through rain and blistered optimism for hundreds of miles.

It was a shame I couldn't think of anyone who might want to hike the Camino Santiago or PCT with me.

Or . . . could I?

Two names popped into my mind like they'd been waiting in the wings, arms crossed, waiting for me to notice them.

I looked up Face Jacket's number and texted him: "Wanna hike the PCT?"

After I hit send, I grinned and pulled up another set of digits.

I'd met Francessca three months prior on a beach in Boracay at a café where we could drink coconut milk straight from the source. One coconut turned into a couple of drinks. A couple of drinks turned into nights filled with dancing, laughter, and just the right amount of reckless romance. At the end of the trip, we promised we'd see each other again. The sun was setting and the rum was flowing, but I meant it. I just didn't know if she did.

She picked up on the second ring.

"Oh my God, Chris. Are you really going to spend a couple of months in Europe before flying back to America? I can meet you at the Brixen train station."

"Let's do that," I said, smiling at the sound of her energy.

A beautiful woman, a European summer, and a hike I'd dreamed of for years? I had prepared myself for Francessca to manage a polite "maybe next year" or an "aww, that's sweet"—so hearing her say yes was a happy surprise. She'd just finished teaching English in China and was between jobs, living at her mom's house. We confirmed the dates I'd fly into Austria and meet her in Brixen—a German-speaking town nestled in the Italian Dolomite mountains. We'd take the train into France together and begin the Camino Santiago. She even had a backpack I could borrow, which was perfect because my current one smelled like jet fuel and landing gear grease.

"Tell me when you will arrive here. I can show you around before we travel to the Camino," Francessca said, her excitement building.

"I'd like that. Is there anything you want from Saudi Arabia? A prized camel?"

"Just you," she said, then hung up.

I melted into the bed and drifted into dreams of forests, lakes, and Francessca.

F-15—Mission ready

Last picture I took from my Saudi workplace.

4

Despite my excitement to leave Saudi Arabia, I geared up for a painful goodbye. I had packed lightly when I left Albuquerque, so getting everything into a large suitcase and two carry-ons wasn't difficult. As expected, my last days in Saudi Arabia were as hectic as the inside of my head. Outprocessing the Air Base, preparing documents to leave the country, planning a European adventure with Francessca, and keeping the PCT hike in sight had my mental and emotional dance cards full, in the best way.

After two weeks, everyone in the company had heard about the cutbacks. My colleagues were on edge, but grateful to still have jobs. They were sad I was leaving, and I had to admit I would have preferred a bit more time to say bye properly, but that's contract work. I would miss the friends I made, but I wouldn't miss the musicless-ness, the social biases, the closed-mindedness, or the litter.

The litter was the thing I'd miss the least. Roadsides and high-ways flooded with plastic bags, fast food wrappers, soda cans, even construction debris left to rot in the brutal sun. Deserts and pic-nic areas that should have been pristine were strewn with leftovers from family outings. Plastic plates, Styrofoam, baby wipes, water bottles, and hills of overstuffed trash bags populated the landscape. Urban areas, even around mosques and residential zones, had trash cans overflowing, or worse—unused.

I saw everyday my students view public spaces as "not their responsibility," so they, and everyone else in Saudi Arabia, treat shared spaces like a temporary zone—use it, trash it, move on. It reminded me of what the United States was like when there wasn't enough awareness about the long-term effects of litter or the concept of shared public stewardship. While there were laws against littering, they weren't enforced, and people knew it. Even the Saudis I worked with on the Air Base assumed someone else would clean up after them—usually poorly-paid foreign workers—so they never thought twice about tossing trash. It pained me every time I visited the Red Sea beaches, always carpeted with bottles and food waste. The sense of disconnect from land and community sent the message: "I don't care. This isn't mine."

It was especially ironic in a place that placed such importance on ritual purity and cleanliness in daily life. The contrast I saw daily between personal hygiene and public filth was stark. That social outlook toward litter—the casual neglect, the assumption that someone else would take care of it echoed the way many Saudis avoided doing menial tasks and "undesirable" jobs, especially when foreigners like me were around. It wasn't about trash, the way I saw it, I'd been looking at a deeply ingrained cultural hierarchy. Living inside that structure as a foreign worker, educated and aware, was revealing and infuriating. The same unspoken code towards littering applied to daily tasks like cleaning, fixing, building, organizing, sweating in the sun—anything that felt like manual labor. Foreigners were slotted into that "someone else" category without hesitation. The way I saw it, there's no shame in needing help. But hiring help wasn't the same as devaluing humanity through dependency and dismissal. I didn't mind the workload—I minded the class-based dehumanization. My Saudi colleagues were making messes and allocating the most unpleasant jobs to foreigners like me with the unspoken confidence that we were there to absorb it both emotionally and physically.

It's not that they hated me. It was that I wasn't even considered. Let's be real—money doesn't equal respect. While I'd signed a decent contract, what I learned after arriving in Saudi Arabia was also that I was to perform like a high-functioning ghost: always available, always competent, never too visible, and never emotional. That's not employment—that's outsourced servitude dressed in professional clothes. Every time I did grunt work alone and completely, it felt to me like another form of littering. On my last day working with the Royal Saudi Air Force, several of my Saudi colleagues told me I'd be missed. I thanked them, but I wondered to myself if they weren't just going to miss another disposable utility.

Little things kept catching my attention, like how I wouldn't have time to eat a fresh batch of ratatouille if I made one, how I wouldn't get to sample the most recent batch of wine I was fermenting in the dining room (please don't tell the Saudi religious police), and how I wouldn't be around to mull over the new season of *Game of Thrones* with Leo. Before I knew it, my last night in Saudi Arabia was upon me. After packing up my room, I joined Leo at The Camel and ordered a pint.

"You really don't mind taking me to the airport tomorrow? I can always take the shuttle," I asked as Leo handed me three darts.

"You can shuttle your mouth," he replied.

"I'm going to miss losing at darts to you." I laughed.

"Oh yeah, I'm sure you'll miss drinking weak piss-beer with Leo from all those waterfalls and mountaintops. Maybe I'll quit this job and go with you."

"Joy would kill you if you went hiking six months. Besides, you can admit it, you think it's crazy to intentionally trudge through wind, rain, and mud for hundreds of miles."

"Maybe you *are* crazy, but in a cool way." Leo's dart sailed to its intended spot on the board right as Jimmy walked in and ordered a beer.

"Bags packed, ready to go?" I asked, noticing the exhausted look on his face.

"Finally," Jimmy replied. "I hear you can't wait to get outta this place. Don't you like having a job?"

"Yeah man, but I like traveling more." I patted his back.

"Well, good for you, I guess. *My* bills don't just pay themselves." Jimmy said unenthusiastically.

"Good thing I saved up for a rainy day." I patted Jimmy's back. "I asked Paul for a reference letter. I bet he'll write one for you too."

Jimmy perked up a bit. "That's a good idea."

"Here's to landing on our feet." I clinked Jimmy's glass.

"Chris, are you going to socialize all night or throw?" Leo asked, brandishing the darts.

"Watch me do both."

Twenty-four hours later, I gave Leo a final hug outside the airport.

"Saying goodbye is the fucking worst," I confessed.

"Post plenty of pics, Chris."

"I will," I said, getting my backpack on. "Better not stick around too long, or someone will sideswipe you. Drive safe."

"You too, Chris. Drive safe."

"I will."

My mind wandered back to when I first applied for the job in Saudi Arabia almost two years earlier. Back then, it was just another pin on a world map—exotic, mysterious, and vaguely threatening in the way places are when you know nothing about them except what cable news and action movies have taught you. I wasn't looking for meaning; I was looking for a paycheck, a change of scenery, and maybe a few stories that didn't involve job applications and microwaved dinners. Two years later, I had the paycheck and the stories—still working on the meaning part.

Everyone around me at the airport moved with purpose—like they had meetings to attend or lives that made sense. I sat in a plastic seat that could've been molded by Satan himself, wondering if I was destined to drift from contract to contract like a tumbleweed. I pressed play on my earbuds—Chantal Kreviazuk's "Leaving On a Jet Plane," to match my emotional state. Uncertainty sat beside me like an old frenemy, but at least now I had the good sense to make it shut up with music. There wasn't much of it in Saudi Arabia. For generations, Saudi culture treated music like it was a gateway drug to total anarchy. Towns and malls operated in monastic silence, interrupted only by the call to prayer and the occasional honk from a driver expressing his divine right to cut across five lanes of traffic. Music never escaped the privacy of headphones or a living room speaker—a personal, hidden indulgence rather than a shared public joy.

That was part of why I craved something different. Not just the music, but the feeling of walking through a place that celebrated living out loud—where songs drifted from cafés, church bells rang unapologetically, and no one looked at you sideways for smiling at strangers. Soon I'd see Francessca. Soon I'd be walking the Camino, chasing something better than direction—beauty, even belonging.

Music in the soul can be heard by the universe." —Lao Tzu

5

When I landed in Europe, Beethoven piped through the streets like some kind of soul rehydration. It felt like gulping red wine after crawling through a desert made of dust, sand, and discarded Dunkin' Donuts bags. (Yes, Saudis love Dunkin'—and, throwing the cups out of car windows is a national pastime. You haven't lived until you've watched a Lexus SUV gracefully glide past a mosque while flinging a Big Gulp into the wind.)

Still, I kinda missed it. Not the garbage, but the people—my students, the spontaneous Arabic lessons over capsa, the tiny victories that made the job feel less like a contract and more like a purpose. Even if I never fully understood the culture, or they understood mine, there was a rhythm to it. A weird, offbeat rhythm that grew on me.

With a skip in my step, I spirited myself from Vienna's airport to Brixen's train station, boarded the cozy train, and leaned my head against the cool window as Austrian snow-covered mountains gave way to Italian snow-covered mountains.

I arrived in Brixen and stepped off the train into crisp winter air that carried aromas of fresh pretzels and warm coffee. A Beethoven sonata drifted out of the public speaker system like a soundtrack queued just for me. I greeted Francessca with a kiss—one I'd been looking forward to since we said goodbye in Boracay.

She gave me a guided tour around her Brixen stomping grounds and we visited Bozen to see Ötzi, the 5,000-year-old preserved prehistoric man discovered in the Austrian Dolomites.

"Poor guy. He never knew the taste of coffee," I whispered with a deadpan seriousness usually reserved for war memorials.

She stared at Ötzi for another long beat, then nodded. "Don't joke. Hypothermia is dangerous."

"I was just kidding. You're right."

"Let's get back to the house and do a thorough gear check," she said, giving my arm a businesslike squeeze.

The next morning, we launched into a series of buses and trains that eventually dropped us in Munich. At the Hofbräuhaus, we ate like German royalty—pork shanks, spaetzle, and pilsner that blew the socks off the bathtub hooch I'd been sipping in Saudi. I was halfway through praising the texture of the spaetzle when she checked her weather app mid-conversation.

"The Pyrenees are getting a lot of snow. I'm worried the Camino might not be walkable."

"Let's check with Camino headquarters before we change or cancel plans, okay? Maybe they'll suggest we start on the Spanish side instead."

"I don't want to get stuck or lost in the snow."

"We don't want to end up like Ötzi," I said dryly. "Risk . . . risk is our business. That's what this starship is all about."

Francesca looked at me like I'd lost my mind.

"It's from Star Trek," I told her.

"It's just . . . weird. Like, why are you so into a show with people in pajamas talking about made-up space crap? You know that's not real, right? Like, none of that matters in real life."

"If you say so," I mumbled.

We spent the night in a comfy pensione, resting and trying to get in the right mindset for the next day's journey: bus, train, another bus, and finally, one last ride to Saint-Jean-Pied-de-Port.

The first bus driver suggested we jump on the Camino at Pamplona instead, far away from the snowy Pyrenees. Francessca liked the idea of starting the Camino farther west, deep into Spain, but I wasn't keen on carving out such a large chunk of the trek. We headed stubbornly toward Saint-Jean Pied-de-Port as Francessca's weather reports showed more snowstorms circling overhead. Sensing Francessca's rising panic, I called the Camino headquarters before our second-to-last bus.

A lady's soft voice answered the phone. "Bonjour?"

"Bonjour. Comment ça va aujourd-hui?" I said.

"Very well, thank you. How may I help?"

I guess all my high school French did nothing to disguise my American accent.

"Two of us are enroute to start the Camino, but we are worried about the weather. Is it safe in Saint-Jean Pied-de-Port, or should we—"

"Oui. It is safe to start the Camino here. What time will you arrive?"

"Our bus will get in at 5 o'clock tonight."

"Bon. Please come to the Camino headquarters building. It is just a short walk from the train station if you follow the yellow signs."

"Merci beaucoup!" I said, then hung up and turned to Francessca. "We're good to go."

We both exhaled in relief, and I felt a flicker of genuine anticipation crack through my travel fatigue. The bus hummed its way down winding French streets with all the grace of a swan ballet.

I turned to Francessca. "You know, back in Saudi, my daily commute felt like a live-action video game with no reset button. Driving there is like . . . interpretive dance with cars. You've got guys

Face Timing their cousins while going 120 kph, kids who look like they just passed second grade behind the wheel of a Lexus, and not a turn signal in sight. I once saw a family of camels in the bed of a pickup—not even strapped down."

She raised an eyebrow, not sure if I was serious.

I was.

"Austria and France feel like the Autobahn for civilized beings. Back there it was every man, boy, and feral goat for himself."

Francessca offered a small nod, eyes back on the window. I smiled to myself. If nothing else, the Camino was already shaping up to be less treacherous than my morning commute.

We had a couple of hours left until our destination and a bit of sleep promised to massage away fears about the weather. My mind swam between the past and the present. I nodded off as emotions from three years ago chased me. The funk of aimlessness, impatience, and unfulfillment descended upon my soul that came with the search for employment. I started to sweat as it all came back to me in dreams.

I'd been applying for dozens of jobs a day even before finishing my master's degree, knowing how rare likable jobs are—especially the kind that pay you more than exposure and a branded tote bag. After months of ghosted applications, rejection emails that sounded like polite breakups, and the occasional "We'll keep your job application on file (read: bonfire)," I finally decided to hit pause and hike the 26.2-mile Bataan Death March with my Air Force brother, Chad.

The Bataan Memorial Death March brings out the best in everyone. It's hard to be a cynic when you're sweating through your shirt at mile 17 and someone hands you a banana to keep you going. It's the rush of endorphins, it's that weirdly joyful punishment that comes with walking for hours through a desert with veterans and hikers—but I welcomed the break from job-hunting. For one magical, sand-in-my-socks day, I wasn't refreshing LinkedIn or doubting my life choices. I was just one sweaty, happy masochist among many.

After the march, I returned to the job hunt like a war-weary soldier reentering battle—just with less armor. The march had made me feel alive again, and that was addicting. That kind of clarity hits differently after spending years buried in textbooks, under term papers, and between USAJobs and Indeed.com.

What was I afraid of, really? Being broke? Powerless? Unseen? All of the above? Fear had metastasized beyond rent money. It was spiritual now—like a full-body imposter syndrome that had its own zip code and a soundtrack of late-night inner monologues.

Then, one afternoon, as I was jogging past the Sandia foothills—my phone rang.

"Hello?" I answered, trying to sound not out of breath. (I was.)

"Mr. Homan?"

"Speaking."

"I have your aircraft maintenance instructor application, and it looks like you're exactly what we're looking for. Are you interested in contract work in a city called Khamis Mushayt in the Kingdom of Saudi Arabia?"

Cue angel choir. Cue sudden urge to Google "Khamis Mushayt" while still pretending I totally knew where that was.

"Yes sir, I am." This was the call. The one I'd been hoping for since grad school, since the first rejection, since long before I pretended to like networking. I recognized the HR equivalent of finding an oasis after wandering the desert of underqualified applicants.

"Excellent. Do you have a valid passport, and would you be available to fly out by the end of this month?"

"Yes and yes," I said, resisting the urge to shout from the mountain.

And just like that, life pivoted from unemployment doom-scrolling to international adventure.

Camino Pellegrino—Mission ready

6

"We're almost there." Francessca whispered, bringing me back to present-day France. "You were talking in your sleep—is everything okay?"

I wiped a trickle of drool from my chin and looked up to see the dry cobblestone walls of St. Jean Pied-de-Port as the bus pulled slowly into its spot. I struggled with knowing my true emotional state. What are my goals beyond the Camino and the PCT? What happens when the fun is over and I have to look for a purpose again? My mindscape was like a war zone. Used to changing locations, I didn't know the peace of belonging somewhere. Would I always choose to work jobs in places where I might die? Is this break between jobs going to lead me to revelation or will my sense of purpose continue to outpace me?

"I'm ok," I replied, squeezing her hand.

After so many hostelers and bus drivers warned us the Pyrenees were dangerous and impossible to traverse, it was a joy to set foot in the hamlet of St. Jean Pied-de-Port.

We put on our backpacks and followed the yellow shells and arrows to the Pilgrim Office, where a pair of women greeted us with open arms.

"Bonjour!" I greeted them with a big hug.

"Bonjour!" replied the lady with a voice I recognized from the phone. "You made it."

Although the mountain weather was harsh, the Camino ladies informed us we would follow a designated Camino Bypass safely around the snow-packed parts of the Pyrenees, so we could get to our first albergue in Ronceveaux at the French-Spanish border.

"Oh, that's awesome."

"Yeah, it's so *awesome*." Francessca repeated, poking fun at my American choice of words.

One of the ladies poured each of us a cup of tea while the other gathered us close to show us our Camino passports, or *credenciales*.

"Hold onto this until you get to the Camino Office in Santiago, then they will take it in exchange for your official certificate," the lady said as tea warmed us up. "Isn't that right, Europe?"

A dog collar jingled from the far corner in reply, catching our attention. Relaxing by the heater was a brown St. Bernard whose kind eyes looked at us with approval.

"Does Europe mind being loved on?" I asked.

"He thinks it's awesome," Passport Lady said, smiling at me. I went to work rubbing Europe's ears, making them flop about as he leaned his head in my direction.

"Here, also, are your conches." Tea Lady passed to us a large shell, each with a red string tied to go around our necks or on our backpacks.

"Now you are pellegrinos, what you call pilgrims. I've stamped each of your credenciales to officially commence the start of your Camino. If Europe will let you follow me, I'll take you to your first albergue, what you call a hostel, and you can settle in for the night."

"*Merci*," I thanked them both, eager to practice my French even if it was just a couple of words at a time.

"Merci, beaucoup," Francessca replied in a more authentic French accent than I was able to accomplish.

I gave Europe one more head rub before leaving the office. With our shells around our necks, Francessca and I followed Tea Lady a short way to a narrow cobblestone lane lined with shops.

Tea Lady unlocked the albergue door with a big church key and pushed open the heavy oak door. I half-expected ghosts to escape their hold and fly out to torment the world. We walked into the stone-floor kitchen, past the bathroom, and into a dormitory with several bunk beds where Francessca offloaded our backpacks.

"You can use the kitchen and utensils. Please leave the please clean for the next pellegrinos. You two are the first ones here, but I think there will be others arriving later tonight. This time of year, there aren't many people on the Camino, so you will have room at the open albergues along the trail. They won't start filling up for another month, maybe not until April, whenever the weather becomes warm. Down the street are some food stores and restaurants. Welcome to Saint Jean Pied-de-Port."

With that, Tea Lady left us to return to being a beacon to others in their time of newness and uncertainty. Francessca and I then toured Saint Jean Pied-de-Port's town center, poking our heads in shops and enjoying the street music. We decompressed fully from one journey as we mentally geared up for the next. There was a sense of civilized nobility around us that had been present for hundreds and hundreds of years.

It was as if this town existed just for pilgrims, those who traveled far and wide to hike the Camino Santiago, looking for spirituality, God, truth, or something else. Since the 9th century, according to legend, the long-lost remains of Saint James the Greater (one of Jesus's original apostles) were discovered in a field in Galicia, Spain. Locals called the spot Campus Stellae—"field of stars"—which evolved into Compostela. A shrine was built, word spread, and suddenly Christians across Europe had a new holy destination to walk to, especially as Rome and Jerusalem became dangerous or expensive. Towns grew wealthy feeding and fleecing the pious.

The scallop shell, now the iconic pilgrim symbol, got popular because it was a practical spoon and proof you made it. Pilgrims often walked for penance—forgiveness of sins, a dead relative's salvation, or because they were doing something naughty and a church official handed them a walking stick and said, "Go repent, far away." The 1990s saw a surge thanks to books, documentaries, and word-of-mouth. Then came Paulo Coelho's "The Pilgrimage," and later Emilio Estevez's film "The Way," which shot the Camino straight into the mainstream. believers, seekers, atheists, heartbreak survivors, retirees, and yes—fit couples who may or may not break up in week two can walk dozens of routes, the most popular being the Camino Francés, starting right where Francessca and I were shopping for provisions in the small French town of Saint-Jean-Pied-de-Port.

We got a baguette and some cold cuts and a bottle of wine for dinner. Porridge for breakfast. Bottles of water and snacks for the journey. Sorted. We knew the Camino would never be more than a few hours' walk from food sources, so we could pack lightly.

When we returned to the albergue, one man and three women were rustling through their backpacks as they chatted in Korean.

"*Annyeonghaseyo,*" I greeted them from the kitchen.

All four turned to me and smiled.

"Camino tomorrow?" the guy asked me.

"*Hai!*" I replied. Wait, that's Japanese. "*Ye!*"

More laughter and happy eyes.

"We, too. Hungry now. Getting food in town," the guy said.

"See you," Francessca said as we started preparing our dinner. "We're hungry, too!"

Francessca and I finished eating our first meal on the Camino Santiago just as the heavy oak door of the Camino albergue heaved open and the four Korean pilgrims blew inside with the wintry night wind. We chatted a bit, but yawns were upon us. It wasn't long before we tucked ourselves into our sleeping bags for the night, eager to begin our day before sunrise.

The albergue in Saint Jean-Pied-de-Port

"When you want something, all the universe conspires in helping you to achieve it."
—*Paulo Coelho*

7

That night in the first albergue, I dreamed I was back in my first week in Saudi Arabia—jet-lagged, sun-dazed, and blinking like a mole seeing daylight after grad school. I was realizing, to my relief, that my students were selectively curious—they weren't always interested in aircraft electrical systems, but they were fascinated by my life, and my reproductive history. Saudi inquisitiveness wasn't shy. There were fascinating cultural nuances to decode, like when to shake hands and when to just nod solemnly. Some of my colleagues, bless their barbecue-stained American hearts, struggled to see past the surface. They treated every difference as a personal affront—like the whole country was conspiring to not be Texas. Complaining was the lingua franca of the expat compound, and it was Olympic level. These were people who could find something to hate about the sunrise. I often felt like the last man standing between open-minded curiosity and a Black Hole of Whining.

It took conscious effort not to drift into the whirlpool of negativity, especially when it came disguised as "just being honest." I found refuge in brushing up on F-15 systems, working on my rusty Arabic, and tuning into the bright spots—like a student's breakthrough or a conversation that surprised me with its depth.

My job was to train Saudi airmen on the F-15's electrical and environmental systems until they could work independently without electrocuting themselves or each other. Simple, noble goals. Being an instructor combined three things I actually enjoyed: tech stuff, language, and teaching.

Not every American I worked with impressed me, but I liked the gig enough. I could picture staying in the job for a year or two, longer if I didn't get a hernia from eye-rolling at grown men who thought "taco" was a spice.

In Saudi Arabia, being over 30, unmarried, and childless is like being a unicorn—but not in a good way. More like, What is this strange animal, and why is it smiling alone?

"Mr. Chris, why don't you have a wife and children?" Sameer asked me one day, innocently.

I took a breath. "Well, Sameer," I said, "I think there are ways to live a meaningful life beyond bringing more kids into an already overpopulated world. Some of us are here to teach, explore, and occasionally sleep in on weekends."

I gave him a wink. "Plus, I think it's okay to have sex without wanting children."

The room erupted in giggles like I'd just told them a joke about camels and French kissing.

"Read the Quran and you will believe it." Abdulmajeed advised me. "It is mandatory for us to get married. Marriage is good."

Part of me wanted to stand my ground and recite to them all the ways it is rewarding to march to the beat of my own drum, but I could tell that conversation would be for another day. My students had in their minds a set way of living a noble life, and it wasn't how I lived mine. I was almost envious of their bulletproof certainty, but trying to get them to think with a more open mind was a challenge.

Abdulmajeed was one of those rare people who could solve complex systems in his head but couldn't imagine why someone would want to live a life different from his own. He was brilliant, charismatic, and surprisingly fun to teach—so long as I didn't mind him routinely telling me that my worldview was wrong, my goals were misaligned, and my hobbies were a Western cry for help. He had the confidence of a man who knew exactly where the center of the universe was—and believed it was located squarely beneath his own prayer rug.

"Of course, it is," I replied to yet another unsolicited sermon. I suddenly felt like the last agnostic standing at a revival meeting. This wasn't the time or place to unpack the existential implications of hiking solo or listening to Pink Floyd without a chaperone.

"Tell ya what," I said with a grin. "Let's get back to learning how not to wire these F-15s backwards. One wrong splice and we're not debating theology—we're explaining to a colonel why his $80 million jet is now a flaming lawn dart."

Another day, my students and I were standing outside to witness a solar eclipse. Abdulmajeed turned to me as we saw the shadow of the moon against the sun and asked, "Mr. Chris, do you know why this eclipse is happening?"

"The eclipse intercepts the light from the sun to Earth," I answered.

"It is caused by Allah to frighten and intimidate the bad people around us," he informed me with the worldliness of a someone who never left home.

I thought twice about responding with the sarcasm and humor that came to mind first. Instead of being snarky like I wanted to, I simply replied, "Makes sense."

It took some mental gymnastics for me to wrap my head around the idea that thousands of adult students could look at science—real, grounded, volts-and-amps science—and still treat it like it was magic. But there I was, trying to teach aircraft maintenance to a group of men who believed electricity was less about physics and more about divine will.

My job was to train these guys to Western standards. That meant not just teaching how F-15 systems worked, but also trying to instill a basic appreciation for not electrocuting themselves or their coworkers. A tough sell when some of them believed that if Allah wanted them to get shocked wiring an anticollision light, then who was I to stand in His way?

So, every day, I played the role of safety prophet, issuing commandments like "Check the circuit breaker before touching that wire" and "Thou shalt not power on the jet while someone is under it." My students mostly smiled, nodded, and then did whatever they were going to do anyway—*inshallah*.

The classroom wasn't much better. If a test was coming up, they'd assure me there was no need to study. "If Allah wants me to pass, I will," they'd say with total conviction, as if the laws of electrical theory bent to celestial favoritism.

"But Allah also gave you a brain and a workbook," I'd remind them. "Maybe He wants you to use both?"

Every afternoon, they'd lobby to leave class early, insisting they'd absorbed enough. I kept smiling, kept explaining, and kept checking wires like my life (and theirs) depended on it. Because, in a way, it did. "Guys, even I had to study this material extra hard when I was your age, and English was my first language. To pass this course, you need to study. Hard."

"We know, Mr. Chris. But today we are tired. We have been working hard this morning."

"We've been working for an hour. If not now, when?" I asked. "Let's review the section together, and let me know when something doesn't make sense."

For someone who wasn't even sure what exactly made up his own cultural identity, I was becoming increasingly confident of one thing: whatever it was, it sure as hell wasn't Saudi Arabian.

This became glaringly obvious every time I handed out a quiz. Back in the States, cheating occurred in hushed tones and subtle glances—the stuff of furtive notes and guilty conscience. In Saudi, though? Cheating was a group sport. I'm talking full-volume conversations, answer-swapping like it was a potluck, and the kind of teamwork that would make Olympic relay teams jealous. It was like I'd walked into a trivia night at a confident café.

"Gentlemen, please—no talking during the quiz," I'd say for the tenth time, waving my arms like a crossing guard at rush hour. They'd nod solemnly, and then not even two minutes later passed around answer sheets like appetizers.

Then there were the phones. I had students more committed to their WhatsApp chats than to the basic laws of electricity. I tried diplomacy first: asking nicely, reminding them how rude it was to scroll through TikTok while I explained pressurization systems. But after the fifth time in a row, I started collecting phones like a disappointed camp counselor. Part of me expected one of them to ask when snack time was.

"Mr. Chris, why don't you let us talk during tests?" Saed once asked, his eyes wide with sincere confusion. Mind you, this was the same Saed who cheated with the flair of a Vegas card shark and had yet to submit a clean test in silence.

I almost laughed—until I realized he was completely serious.

"Doing the work on your own proves that you know it," I explained patiently. "Which is kind of the point of getting certified."

"But I will always have my friends to help me if I forget something," he replied, as if we were all just studying to become part of an aircraft maintenance group chat.

"And what if you're alone on the flight line and the cockpit's lost pressurization?" I asked. "You gonna FaceTime a friend while the pilot passes out?"

"I will fix it, God willing."

"Right," I sighed. "And until then, you're fixing it my way, which means no talking during tests. If you don't like that, I'd be happy to take you to the Colonel's office and let him explain it."

In Saed's defense, the students didn't take kindly to the no cheating policy we teachers upheld. Could it be Saudi students expected to cheat in our classes because they had always happened through-out their academic lives? This explained why so few students could string together enough English to form a coherent sentence, despite having passed two mandatory years of basic English. This wasn't high school. This wasn't compulsory. This was a military institution where students pretended to become proficient. I wouldn't empa-thize with cheaters here.

I returned to my villa on Nassim Compound and began to think about how I could make students like Saed try harder, and none of them worked. I could tell after a few months that some students were only going through the motions without making any real effort. I know how to recognize when a person wants something so bad they won't rest until they get it (been there), and I know how it feels to be so bad at something the only solution is to practice relentlessly (been there, too). A good teacher would know how to reach these students. If I wasn't good at my job, then what was I?

Feeling dispirited at work, like a piece of litter

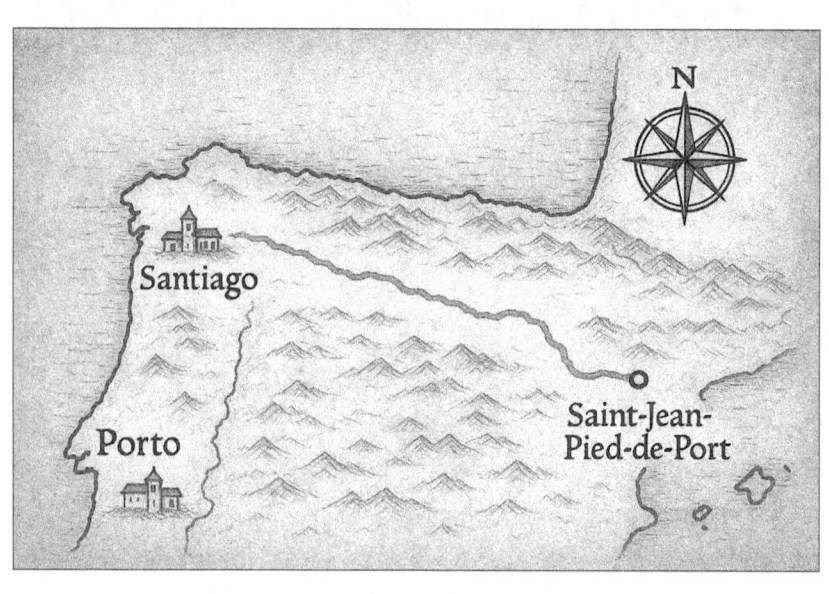

PART 2

A Pilgrim on the Camino Santiago

"But I don't want comfort. I want God, I want poetry, I want real danger, I want freedom, I want goodness. I want sin."

—Aldous Huxley

Pilgrim? Hikertrash? Both.

8

I woke up Francessca gently as our Korean friends began to wake up, hoping she was as eager to meet the Camino Santiago as me.

"It's so early," she mumbled unimpressed.

"We're crossing the Pyrenees today. The Pyrenees!" I said, barely able to contain myself.

"I know, I know. Ok, give me a second . . . go get breakfast," Francessca directed.

"You want anything?"

"Yeah, I have some yogurt . . . I'll have that."

I kissed her on the cheek. "OK, I'll leave you to it."

An hour later all six of us walked out into the pre-dawn February chill. We put the warm albergue behind us as shell-shaped signs guided us towards our future. The four Koreans walked at a relaxed pace together while Francessca and I enjoyed a more ambitious pace toward the sunrise. Our pace warmed us up, and I couldn't take my eyes off the gentle snow falling on the green and golden fields. At lunch, Francessca wanted to take a longer break than I did, but she encouraged me to press on to Ronceveaux (*Roncesvalles*, if you prefer the Spanish).

Walking by myself all day gave me a chance to process a little of what I wanted to do with the rest of my life. Even though I found no real answers, I enjoyed putting some mileage under my feet. Part of what I love about arriving someplace new is the opportunity to see through new eyes and let the differences wash over me. I couldn't help but cherish cultural values I connected with instantly like freedom of choice, individual expression (except Islam or beige . . . *yikes* . . . better think on that), technological innovation, and social progress.

Immersing myself into the European landscape felt comfortable. I didn't have to lie to anyone here (hold on . . . did I *have* to lie in Saudi Arabia, or was it simply easier for me to lie?). I was again in a part of the world that honored the right of everybody to do and get what they want as long as they don't infringe on the rights of other people (right?). I didn't need to hide what my religion was, nor would I have to suppress my thoughts on human rights or society in general.

I was in constant pursuit of the next source of pleasure, a never-ending cycle of striving toward fleeting happiness. My chase contributed to overconsumption and environmental degradation. My spending elevated a culture that prioritized instant gratification over long-term well-being. I wanted to better recognize when I was on that futile hedonic treadmill and, for the first time, I felt like I wasn't. But then, I wasn't really doing anything sustainable; this adventure was only a break from my normal. How could I make my normal life healthy like my hiking life? I yearned for the clairvoyance of my hiking life to spill into my normal life. On trail, I never doubted who I was. On trail, I was Windscreen.

Trail names like Windscreen and Face Jacket are badges of honor in U.S. long-distance hiking, part alter ego, part trail mythology. On the Appalachian Trail I was reborn. I shed my 9-to-5 skin and became a dirtbag legend who consumed miles for breakfast and Pop-Tarts for dinner. Trail names give permission for people like me to adopt the anarchic vibe. On the Camino de Santiago, the culture's older, more ritualized, and more European. People go there for spiritual or religious reasons. Here there be pellegrinos instead of trail rogues. The vibe is less "discover your wild self" and more "walk, reflect, grow." Your name is your name—simple, grounded. Being in cities or towns every night, surrounded by regular society means that there isn't the feral energy where nicknames emerge. While someone might pick up a nickname on the Camino, it's rare, and it won't carry the same mythic weight as it does in the American backcountry.

Hiking the Camino wasn't in any way going to be the same as the Appalachian Trail was, or the Pacific Crest Trail would be. Similarly, the person taking these steps wouldn't be the same person found on those other trails. Windscreen has never been bigoted or accidentally racist. Windscreen wouldn't lie about his religion on a work visa for a Saudi contract. Windscreen, since he was born, has always known what his life was for. Chris Homan seems to still have to find these things out.

When I descended from the Pyrenees into Ronceveaux, I eagerly made my way to the well-marked albergue. The host greeted me with a stamp for my passport and an invitation to stay for the night for just three *euros*. I grabbed a warm shower easily enough since no one else had arrived yet and put on fresh clothes as I laid mine over the radiators to dry out from the rain and snow. Then I waited for Francessca by the fireplace in La Posada, the albergue restaurant. I journaled, ate a late lunch, and drank a large beer (for calories, of course).

As I finished my plate, a hiker came in with an energetic grin and asked the bartender where the albergue was. His clothes were fresh from truck-splatted slush.

"Are you hiking the Camino?" I asked.

"Yeah, everyone told me I should start here, in Roncesvalles. I'm Rodolfo, from Brazil."

I shook Rodolfo's hand. "I'm Chris, from the US. I hiked here from Saint Jean Pied-de-Port not long ago. Welcome to Roncesvalles. There's a bunch of bunk beds in that albergue." I pointed out the window to the building where my stuff was.

Rodolfo thanked me and went to see the host. A couple of hours later, Francessca and the four Koreans arrived with chattering teeth and saw about getting washed and warmed up.

That night, the host invited us pellegrinos to attend Pilgrim's Mass. My first instinct was to graciously dodge it—religious ceremony has never really been my idea of a fun time. I was more in the mood for pasta and a long exhale. But Francessca, ever the spiritual romantic, gave me a pointed look that said, Only a fool would ignore the holiness baked into every cobblestone on this trail. She wasn't aggressive about it—just quietly certain, in that way people are when they've already had the argument with you in their heads and won.

The priest's voice rang out in rich, deliberate tones. Between the Spanish and the Latin, the ceremony felt more like ancient theater than church—and honestly, that helped. I grew up Catholic, so incense and unintelligible language gave me the illusion of profound wisdom.

Francessca, on the other hand, soaked in every word with wet-eyed reverence. I glanced over once and caught her lips moving silently with the prayers, her hands folded like she'd done this a thousand times in a past life. She had. Her faith wasn't aggressive or evangelical—it was quietly radiant, the kind that made me feel like a tourist not just in Spain, but in the whole experience of belief.

Around me, the pews were full of bowed heads, clasped hands, and quiet awe. I looked around and felt something. Not faith, exactly. Not clarity. But a kind of reverent weight I couldn't ignore. It was beautiful. It was also confusing as hell.

Afterward, Rodolfo, Francessca, and I shared a couple bottles of wine with SuBin, Hansoo, Kay, and Sue. The conversation spun through God, countries, and Camino origin stories. Most people seemed driven by love for the divine—or fear of it. I was here because I love hiking and I wanted to experience Europe. At least, that's what I kept telling myself. Francessca didn't call me on it, but she didn't need to. Her eyes said, "You're chasing something, too."

The next morning, we left Roncesvalles under a sky that looked like wet steel. The Camino clung to the roadside more than I liked, but at least my fingers weren't frozen. My pack was the lightest of the group, so I moved fast, floating ahead like I'd done this a hundred times before. Hiking was my comfort zone, God, not so much. I often found myself ahead of everyone, slipping into the meditative rhythm that long trails reward. But I'd pause, always, and look back for them. Francessca's face, always seeking meaning. The others, laughing or trudging. I didn't want to be alone, not really.

I liked thinking the locals appreciated my American habit of tossing out friendly hellos and trying to spark a laugh, even if my sense of humor didn't always translate. I wasn't reverent the way Francessca was. I didn't need faith to feel moved. Just motion. Just light. Just people.

And that was already starting to feel like a gap between us neither of us could quite name—but I could feel it, humming beneath our steps. I liked hiking bigger distances than most pellegrinos, but I liked being part of the group and so did Francessca. I think she regretted telling me to hike at my own pace, because it meant we only saw each other three times a day at planned stopping points. Hansoo and I found an albergue in Villava we liked, and we settled in to cook dinner and get rest from the blustery wind. I kept an eye out for Francessca, but none of us saw her walk by. With so few albergues open this early in the season, it was easy to figure she went on three more kilometers to stay at the Jesus y Maria albergue in Pamplona's city center. Sure enough, she messaged our group to let us know she had done exactly that. I decided I would head out early in the morning and have breakfast with her and welcomed Rodolfo when he asked if he could accompany me.

We shopped for groceries so we could make dinner. It turned out Hansoo was quite the chef, and he let me help at his side as the others played Billy Joel songs and picked out a bottle of wine to open first. There is something that comforts me whenever I prepare the vegetables for cooking *ratatouille*, the act of it makes me feel as if I'm at home. At the cutting board, I am a madman operating toward deliciousness. I savored slicing lengthwise into zucchini, piercing tomato skin while it bleeds, and cutting into a bell pepper's hollowness to pluck out the seedy flesh. There is nothing else in my life that makes me feel like a serial murderer quite like when I'm making ratatouille.

We made the most of the space and freedom we had before people started inevitably pouring onto the Camino. We had plenty of beds to choose from, plenty of space to hang our clothes to fully dry, and even a spot for me to curl up and read as the others snored nearby.

I'm usually the only morning person wherever I go, but having a buddy to hike and chat with in the cold mornings was pretty cool. Rodolfo was as upbeat as me, and we taught each other a little from each other's languages by the hour. He talked often about his love of his son and of Brazil. He suggested I visit his country sometime, and I knew I would.

We booked it to the Jesús y María albergue just before sunrise. Francessca was already awake, lacing up and packing with the energetic urgency of someone trying to put a hard night behind her. She seemed a little miffed that we hadn't coordinated to meet up, but she didn't press it. Instead, she introduced me to Alise, a petite German woman she'd bonded with overnight. I shook Alise's hand, trying not to feel replaced. When I greeted the other guest in the room, a scruffy older guy hunched over his pack, he barely looked at me.

Francessca leaned close and whispered, "He's even weirder than you."

I gave a dry chuckle, pretending I didn't feel a little stung. "Weird" had always been part of my charm, but in her voice, it was starting to sound like a warning label.

"You have everything?" I asked as she zipped up her pack.

"Yeah. Let's go." she said, and off the three of us went.

Pamplona greeted us with wide avenues and proud, ancient stonework. The city shimmered with a kind of old-world confidence that invited you to linger, sip something strong while basking in its age and relevance. It felt alive in a way Riyadh never had—the sound of street musicians and the sight of couples holding hands seemed almost radical in comparison. The Saudi marketplaces I'd grown used to were hot, loud, and segregated by invisible social walls. Here, life mingled. Even the clothes felt liberated—casual, breezy, unapologetically secular.

As dazzling as Pamplona was, I wasn't sorry when the Camino led us back into the folds of the countryside. My soul stretched out over the green hills and rolling farmland, relieved to shed the city's density. The breeze was clean, the air was thick with the smell of damp earth and something simple. I could've walked for weeks.

We ended that day's hike together in Puente la Reina, joined by a mix of pellegrinos headed in the opposite direction. There was camaraderie in comparing notes: which albergues were open, which towns were worth a detour, and which boots caused blisters. It was a good day for everyone.

Until dinner.

We were shopping for provisions when I noticed Francessca freeze mid-aisle, pale as paper. Her hands trembled as she opened and reopened her bag, rifling through it with increasing panic. I didn't need to ask what was wrong. She slumped to the floor, her voice cracking with disbelief.

"All my cash is gone."

I crouched beside her as she cried, holding her close, my heart knotting. She had taken out eight hundred euros before leaving Munich, enough to coast through the Camino comfortably. Now it was just—gone.

The violation was raw, intimate. She kept shaking her head, trying to fathom that another pilgrim—a fellow traveler—could do something so cold. I stayed by her side, absorbing her spiraling rage and despair.

"I wouldn't have been robbed if we'd stayed in the same albergue last night," she said quietly, eyes hollow.

I blinked. It wasn't a direct accusation, but I couldn't tell if she was blaming me, or blaming the sequence of events that led to an empty purse.

I didn't know what to say, so I settled for kindness. "Let me know if I can help. You know I want to."

Her face, so gorgeous, even twisted in grief, softened. "Thank you," she whispered.

Inside, though, stress curdled into something heavier. I hated seeing her like this. I also hated that, again, I was the one managing the emotional fallout, the logistics, the comfort. I offered to loan her money—of course I did. What else could I do? But something in me started to wonder just how much of myself I'd keep pouring into a connection that already felt increasingly one-sided.

"Maybe next time don't carry so much cash?" I said as gently as I could, trying not to sound like I was scolding a child.

"Yeah . . . that wasn't such a great idea," she admitted, wiping at her eyes with her sleeve.

"We should at least report it. Let the albergue know what happened, warn others."

She nodded and called Jesús y María. She described the guy she suspected, and the staff recognized her description at once. When the staff told Francessca that others had also been robbed, it soothed her a bit. She called her mother in Brixen soon after, switching into Italian so quickly I couldn't follow even if I had wanted to. Her voice shifted: weary, childlike, leaning hard on home.

I gave her space and stepped outside. When I returned, she was still on the phone. I crawled into my bunk and lay there in the dark, listening to the distant hum of voices and footsteps from the hall.

Midnight came and went. She stayed on the phone. I drifted into sleep alone, feeling a little bit useless.

Once asleep, I was back in Saudi Arabia.

"Teacher, what does 'motherfucker' mean?"

"It's an impolite word we won't use in this class," I replied, holding my laughter.

"Oh, okay. Like *haneeth*."

Haneeth was a word I hated hearing; it seemed to mean both "faggot" and "slut," based on how my students would use it in conversation.

"Not really," I responded, "but it is disrespectful word for you to say here."

While there were certainly moments when Saudis ignored me, there were also moments that reminded me of the difference I was making in these students' lives. Such moments rewarded me more than money could. Teaching was the best part of my day, but talking about movies ran second. A close third were those moments I could talk about religion.

"Are you a Christian, Mr. Chris?" Anas asked me.

"Yes," I lied. "Why do you ask?"

"Can I ask you something about your faith? In Islam, we believe true faith means submitting completely to God. But I've read in Christianity, faith is more about believing in Jesus as the Son of God. Do you think faith is more about what you think or what you do?"

I sighed, eager to honor my student's curiosity without giving myself away.

"That's a really thoughtful question, Anas. In Christianity, faith is often seen as both—belief in God and Jesus, but also trying to live in a way reflecting that belief. Some people emphasize one more than the other, but ideally, they go hand in hand."

"But how do you know your faith is correct? In Islam, we have the Quran, which we believe is the unchanged word of God. What gives you certainty in Christianity?"

"Well, I think faith isn't always about certainty. It's about trust. People find distinct reasons to believe—some through individual experiences, others through studying scripture or history. But faith, by its nature, isn't the same as scientific proof. It's more of a conviction in something greater than yourself. I guess my point is I don't want to make you believe something you don't, just because it's what I tend to think of as sensible."

"But what if someone doubts? In Islam, doubt can be dangerous for the soul. What happens if a Christian starts to question their faith?"

"In many Christian traditions, doubt is actually seen as part of faith. It's something people struggle with, but it can also lead to a deeper understanding. Some people even say questioning is how you strengthen your belief."

"I've never thought about doubt like that. Have you ever doubted your faith?"

"At times, sure. I think everyone wrestles with big questions about life, purpose, and existence. But those questions don't always lead to losing faith; sometimes, they make it stronger."

"So, do you believe in God the same way I do, with absolute certainty?"

"Faith means different things to different people. Some have absolute certainty, and others see faith as a journey where they're always learning and discovering more. What about you? Do you ever think about faith in a different way?"

"No. I was raised Muslim, and I've always believed in one God with no doubts. But talking to you makes me think about how people see faith differently."

"And that's what I enjoy about these conversations. We don't always have to agree, but learning how others think can help us understand our own beliefs better. Some people take comfort in a godless universe. They argue since we are all going to die anyway, and even the sun itself will eventually fizzle out someday. Nothing matters except what we want to matter. Remember, I don't want to change your mind, I just want to know what you see, think, and feel."

"So, if I want money, I can steal money to make my life better," Anas said.

"I suppose so, if you can live with the truth of what you did."

"Stealing is wrong because God says so. Islam emphasizes virtuous deeds—helping others, honesty, and generosity. Even though you are not Muslim, you still are a good person. Goodness isn't about religion, but also about how we treat each other. But, Mr. Chris, if you truly believed in God the right way, you would be even better."

"You mean if I became a Muslim?"

"Yes."

"What if your faith is wrong and mine is right?"

"It isn't," Anas replied, looking in my eye with the certainty of faith I've never known.

"One thing about being in this world is there is always room for improvement. Sometimes life isn't what we think. Maybe neither of us are right." I trailed off softly.

I spent the first seven years of my education at Good Shepherd Catholic School, but in high school I contemplated how my spiritual depth went against dogma. "Atheist" was the most honest way I knew to describe myself. It had been important to Dad for me and my brother to learn under Catholic instruction, and now that he was no longer alive I wasn't keen to disrespect what he believed. Or what *anyone* believed. I wish people (and work visa application forms) could accept that hiking and traveling are my sacred rituals. The trails have been my spiritual journey, each step a prayer connecting me to the Earth. The mountains, my temples, standing tall and majestic, whispered ancient wisdom to me in the rustle of leaves and the rush of the wind. Each hike I embarked on was a unique pilgrimage that helped me to deal with the noise and ridiculousness of everyday life. The beauty of diverse cultures and the stories embedded in every corner of the globe and the wild serenity of the outdoors helped me to find truth and moral prudence. Hiking and traveling weren't only my passions, but they were spiritual callings that nourished my soul and connected me to something greater than myself.

I stirred awake the following morning and saw the Camino stretching out towards morning sunshine. Rodolfo was the first to leave the albergue to meet the day. Joachim, a Ugandan hiker we met the previous night, headed out shortly after him. Normally I would have begun early, but instead I waited for Francessca to wake up.

"Hey," I greeted her gently when she came into the albergue kitchen for breakfast.

Francessca walked over to me and hugged me. "Thank you for offering help to me last night. I want to stay on the Camino."

I hugged her back and exhaled deeply. I had hoped she would not cancel her adventure.

"My mother said she can transfer money for me to complete the Camino."

"I think your mother is awesome."

"She is," Francessca agreed. "So, I've pulled myself together and now I'm ready to get on trail."

There weren't any steep uphills or knee-jarring downhills. The Camino was gentle and relaxed. I don't know if it was getting out from under the threat of uncertainty from the stolen money or if it was the beautiful Spanish vistas, but I felt solace with each mile crossed.

Europe delighted my eyes, and the small towns the Camino wended through from time to time were quaint and idyllic, like they were created all those centuries ago just for me. Despite the beauty around us, Francessca's glum threatened to weigh us both down. Ready for a proper night of sleep, we stopped for the day at Estella, while Rodolfo left word he would press on to Los Arcos, twenty kilometers farther up the Camino. Our Korean friends were five kilometers behind us, and I wasn't going to leave Francessca alone at the albergue this time.

After all, the Camino was supposed to be a place where people found enlightenment.

Sometimes life is a motherfucker, even on the Camino Santiago.

"And wine can of their wits the wise beguile, make the sage frolic, and the serious smile." —Alexander Pope

9

Part of the Camino's appeal to the masses (pun intended, duh) is its religious character. Dogma and ceremony seemed baked into every populated junction, not just as rituals but as signposts nudging the soul toward confession and introspection. I couldn't take five steps without passing a crucifix, a chapel, or a fellow pilgrim who asked—gently, with soft eyes—what brought me here, as if they were really asking what god brought me here. I couldn't always tell if they were motivated by kindness or by that missionary impulse that feeds on subtle hierarchy: welcome the outsider, but only if the outsider's story eventually folds into yours.

Maybe it was neither. Or both.

In Saudi Arabia, I never once met a social justice warrior. Belief in God wasn't a suggestion—it was a legal and spiritual mandate. Atheism was both crime and sin, and feminism was something whispered about in private, if at all. Back then, I kept my thoughts tightly wound and doubly hidden. Now, on the Camino, I could speak them out loud—even if I knew they'd make some people flinch. At least I didn't have to fear jail for them.

What started to hit me was how so many people along this trail seemed to view their religion not as a path to truth, but as the truth itself. Absolute. Immutable. I'd been on the receiving end of that before—from the devout Muslims in Saudi who saw me as an outsider, a guest, but never an equal. Now I was wary of falling into the same rhythm with devout Christians who, with all their warmth, still gave me the same sense that I was a "project" to be saved. Across the world, the irreligious remain tolerated only so long as we keep quiet about it. Still, I was learning to hold space—for their convictions and for myself.

I was playing a quieter part in the cosmic orchestra, but it was still mine. That thought gave me peace, even if the world around me often refused to.

I started to wonder: is religion really about truth . . . or is it about anchoring ourselves in something unchanging while the world lurches forward? I had to admit, the pilgrims who believed fully and passionately moved with a kind of gravity I didn't possess. I never found that level of certainty in anything. But I didn't envy it, either. Not exactly.

One thing I did love about the Camino was the way it made room for passion—for believing in something, anything, deeply. For elevating your path, your questions, your own rhythms. I wondered if I'd feel more powerful if I was more convinced, one way or the other, about the godliness or godlessness of it all. But somehow, I knew I'd always live in that tension. And I was okay with that.

Anyway, I had more immediate questions to wrestle with.

Francessca had been quiet, still holding some unspoken resentment over her robbery. It wasn't fair to assume, but the energy between us had subtly shifted—like we were walking in sync out of habit rather than harmony. I didn't know if she blamed me or just needed someone to attach her anger to. Either way, it was wearing on me.

We reconnected with our Korean friends, which lightened things. I hiked alongside Hansoo while SuBin, ever bright, took it upon herself to cheer up Francessca. That gave me a bit of breathing room—and her, some space to feel seen by someone new.

At lunch, I sat next to Francessca and gathered the nerve to voice what had been gnawing at me.

"Can I confess something to you?"

"Okay," she said, turning toward me with cautious curiosity.

"I feel guilty we separated the night you stayed in Pamplona. It bothers me to think you might not have been robbed if I'd been there."

She wrapped her arms around me, and I melted into it. The hug felt real, but part of me noted how rare they were becoming.

"You're not to blame at all," she said. "You've been a big help, and I appreciate what you've done. You don't need to stay by my side all day—you can enjoy the Camino at your own pace. I'll be okay. Let's just try to meet up at the end of the day."

"Deal," I said, squeezing her hand.

By the time we left Puente la Reina, I noticed a subtle shift in how I was carrying myself. Not just the pack on my shoulders—but a kind of internal weight adjustment. Something had been loosening inside me. Walking hour after hour massaged my mental knots into something more pliable. Maybe it was the unavoidable intimacy of being in a place where no one cared about what you did for work or where you lived—only why you were walking.

Francessca, on the other hand, seemed increasingly tethered to the events of her robbery. She smiled when prompted, but it didn't reach her eyes. I tried to meet her where she was emotionally, but I was starting to feel like a first-aid kit she'd forgotten to put away. Necessary, but not particularly comforting.

She didn't say it outright, but I could feel her tallying up the moment we separated and the consequences that followed. She had every right to grieve the theft, but what I couldn't shake was the implication that I should've prevented it. I was all for partnership, but I wasn't looking to be someone's emotional seatbelt—fastened only when things got bumpy.

I slowed down when I got hungry and offered to share a banana with Francessca. "What are you looking forward to most about reaching Santiago?" I asked between bites.

She shrugged. "Honestly? A shower and some food that isn't tuna out of a can."

I laughed, but it was automatic.

"You?"

"Clarity, I guess," I said after a pause. "I came here thinking I wanted a physical challenge, a break from life. But lately it feels more like . . . I'm learning how to let go of things. Or learning what's mine to carry, and what's not."

Francessca stared into her cup. "Sounds deep."

It wasn't dismissive, exactly. But it wasn't an invitation to go deeper either.

By the time we crossed into Estella, I'd begun hiking ahead again. She said she preferred to take it slow. "Go on ahead," she told me. "I'll catch up."

At first, I resisted. Then I realized: why?

Walking alone, I noticed things I hadn't before. The symmetry of vineyards stretching to the horizon. A patch of purple wildflowers dancing in the wind like they were performing for no one. A man playing an accordion on the edge of a hill, just for himself. I noticed how my mind wandered more freely without having to stay attuned to someone else's moods.

I cared for Francessca. I wanted her to have a beautiful Camino. But I was beginning to see the difference between caring for someone and being responsible for someone else's experience. I couldn't walk the Camino for her. I couldn't fix the hole the robbery left inside her. And if I was honest with myself, I didn't want to try anymore.

When we regrouped at the albergue in Estella that night, she was polite but distant. I asked if she wanted dinner, but she said she'd already eaten.

"Okay," I said simply, not pushing. "See you in a bit."

I didn't feel relief or regret—just a quiet recognition that the Camino was changing me. I smiled, but something in me paused. I was hearing, for the first time, that this relationship wasn't anchored in "us" as much as in planning, convenience, and goodwill. As generous as that could be, I couldn't shake the sense that I was giving more than I was getting—and starting to notice.

With Francessca's understanding and blessing, I hiked with a skip in my step, free to enjoy the perfect weather all the way to the city of Logrono, where I explored the town until the albergue opened at 1700. The city was so clean and sophisticated, I must've looked homeless and destitute to the city folk who noticed me, and I felt more like hikertrash than ever. When the parochial albergue opened its doors, I gaped in awe at the high arches and elegant architecture, my eyes traced along every wall that reached elevated ceilings. Francessca, Hansoo, SuBin, and I happily paid five euros each for a generous dinner as well as a satisfying breakfast the following morning. That night, we all surrendered to sleep, feeling safe in each other's company. Safer in transit, oddly, than I ever felt in the wild unprofessional workplace I dreamed of that I had just spent two years working in.

"I get nothing from studying these books!" Turki snapped, rubbing his temples with both hands. "We don't get more money if we get high scores, and we don't get promoted. Why should we study this much, Mr. Chris?"

The air-conditioning did little to cut through the desert heat, and the textbooks in front of them looked like ancient stone tablets—unyielding and joyless. I wanted to shout, "Because this is your damn job!" But instead, I pulled from the ever-optimistic part of myself that still wanted to believe in the mission. I reminded them this coursework wasn't arbitrary—it came down from their military's upper brass, and like it or not, it mattered. With the clipped confidence of someone who's had to play both cheerleader and disciplinarian, I encouraged them to push themselves, to be their best. Hell, I hated dry textbooks when I was their age too. Back then, I just wanted to live a life worth something, one without the boredom and futility that institutional education sometimes feels like. I had figured out that if I studied hard and passed early, I could free myself sooner. But these guys weren't wired like me. Not culturally, not socially, and—frankly—not personally. They saw effort through a different lens.

"If Sameer just studied twenty questions a day, he wouldn't have to cram the night before the test," I told the class.

It made sense to me. It was logical. Tactical. Military, even. But logic was not the common currency in this classroom.

"If you study hard now, you'll succeed," I offered one more time, like a prayer I hoped would stick.

"In sh'Allah," Sameer replied, pulling out his phone, already disengaged. God willing.

"Don't blow me off," I said, half-smiling to keep it light, half-serious because I was tired of the dance. "Hard work makes a lasting impact."

"I'm not blowing anything off," he said coolly. "If God wants me to pass, I will pass. If He doesn't, I won't. It's not up to me."

There it was again—that cultural current I couldn't swim against. Fatalism masquerading as humility. I didn't want to start a theological showdown, so I held back. Heaven helps those who help themselves, I thought but only muttered, "Just study the first twenty questions. I'll help you tomorrow if you need it."

He nodded, sullenly. Whether he actually believed in divine determinism or just wanted a few more hours of phone time, I couldn't say. The result was the same: reluctant compliance.

Later that afternoon, Turki told me he would send a genie to visit me.

"A genie?" I asked, amused. "Well, sure. What can I do to help?"

He was serious. "Real genies aren't like the ones in movies. They don't grant wishes. They trick you. They hurt people sometimes."

I raised a brow, not mocking, just intrigued. "And how do I meet one of these?"

"I need something of yours. A sock or something personal."

The class murmured in Arabic, some laughing, others entirely solemn. I took off a shoe, peeled off a sock, and handed it to him, rolling it neatly. "Be my guest. I'd love to meet a genie."

I never met one. But I still liked that they believed I might.

Every day, I gave these students tasks. Every day, they resisted. I reminded them of our shared goals—my job, their job—and we repeated the cycle like a ritual. There were moments I swore I cared more about their professional success than they did. Selfishly, I didn't want to retrain a batch of students who failed out. I didn't want their indifference to stain my record, my work, my sense of efficacy.

I wanted my job to mean something. I wanted my presence in Saudi Arabia to amount to more than PowerPoints and review quizzes. But the cultural and religious barriers were real. I wasn't just fighting apathy—I was swimming upstream against generations of fatalism, against divine intervention. Still, I showed up, I adjusted, and I delivered. Because I'm a professional. And professionals get the job done—even when no one else in the room seems to care.

I carried a growing weight: the quiet, unspoken fatigue of someone who had tried hard in a system that never really wanted him to succeed. I tried my best to motivate students who treated effort like a joke and education like a punishment. Their indifference and superstition weren't personal, but I'd taken them personally anyway. I couldn't help it. I had wanted so badly to matter. I felt that even when I gave my best, the people around me didn't feel like meeting me halfway. I told my Saudi students that challenging work makes a lasting impact, but effort, when unreciprocated, turns into exhaustion.

Instead of focusing on F-15 electrical and environmental systems, my students wanted to convert me to Islam. My atheism was a secret liability—a punishable offense, a threat to the order. Normally I was free to admire other people's faith without craving it for myself, but at work I felt like I was always on trial for having a different faith. I realized one day that I'd been angry that I had kept giving parts of myself to systems, jobs, and people who weren't equipped to hold them. But now, step by step, I was taking those parts back.

One afternoon, as Turki groaned dramatically over a vocabulary quiz, I found myself pacing at the front of the room like a captain whose ship was going down. I felt directionless. Teaching in Saudi Arabia wasn't some great calling. It wasn't even a stepping stone. It was a placeholder. A way to keep the lights on while I figured out what the hell I was supposed to do with my life. I had thought the desert might offer clarity—some sort of wisdom in the vastness. But all I found were sandstorms, awkward silences, and bureaucracy that made Kafka look like an optimist.

There were nights I lay on my bed staring at the ceiling fan, imagining it spinning fast enough to tear itself loose and crash into me. Not out of any real suicidal fantasy—more like a wish for something to happen. Some plot twist to pull me out of the slow drip of meaninglessness. But it never came. Just the same day again. Even in the drag of it all, I accepted that if I was going to make it through this stagnant chapter of my life, I needed to stop waiting for external validation or a cosmic green light. I needed to stop being Picard, noble and burdened with protocol, and start being Kirk—chaotic, charming, winging it, and still somehow saving the day.

So, I leaned harder into humor. If I couldn't change the system, I could at least laugh at it. When students skipped class and showed up the day before the final, I'd greet them like prodigal sons. "Welcome back! Should I kill the fatted calf or just let you copy the review sheet?" When someone asked if I believed in genies, I answered, "Only when I'm grading your exams—because some of you will need serious magic to pass."

After months of employing humor, encouragement, structure, compromise, even bargaining like a Bedouin merchant at a spice market, nothing stuck. These young men were not interested in learning or the merits of academic discipline. They were interested in two things: air-conditioning and their phones. Everything else was negotiable—especially effort.

My life's meaning wasn't going to arrive on a camel with a scroll. My job didn't have to be noble. It didn't even have to make perfect sense. It just had to be mine—owned, laughed at, carried like a weird relic from a strange part of the galaxy. I knew I wouldn't be Saudi Arabia forever. This wasn't the mission. It was just the episode before the character arc kicks in.

As we prepared for another day on the Camino Santiago, Francessca put on a brave face. I could tell she wasn't over her misadventure, but I hoped she wouldn't have to keep making such an emotional effort so we could fully enjoy our time together.

I began to feel more spiritual here than I ever had under any dome or minaret. Not because I found God, but because I found space. Space to ask questions without fear. Space to believe that not knowing was holy, too. The Camino wasn't just a trail. It was a reckoning. Not a spiritual rebirth, but a gentle undoing of everything I'd assumed I had to be. Teacher. Uplifter. Fixer. Companion. Always the one to reach first.

It was okay to walk ahead sometimes. It was okay to stop trying so hard to be worth keeping. I thought as the sun rose over the next ridge, it was enough to simply be.

Francessca, for all her brilliance and beauty, didn't seem to notice when I got quiet. Or she noticed but didn't want to dig. Either way, I began to drift internally. I still enjoyed her company, and I cared for her. I began to wonder what the future had in store for mine with Francessca. We seemed to enjoy traveling, we had similar moral philosophies, and we were attracted to each other. Despite these things, I noticed my style of humor annoyed her more than it used to, even before she was robbed in Pamplona. I didn't know if I was being sensitive, or if we were losing our chemistry.

We continued to encourage each other anyway to Najera from Logrono. The weather turned brisk and there was some light snow, but a sustained pace kept us warm. The host of Najera's albergue, Louis, offered a warm bowl of vegetable soup when I arrived, so I offered to share the bottle of red wine I picked up in town. After so long in Saudi Arabia with only homemade hooch available, the taste of wine from these Camino vineyards made me feel bohemian and as carefree as Jack Kerouac.

It was liberating to be unlimited by deadlines and not setting my alarm clock. I basked in the Basque landscapes and upbeat people I met on the Camino. Francessca commented she was spending less than she budgeted, and I noticed how that gently lifted her spirits a bit.

After spending the night at the albergue in Najera, freezing rain stung my face and arms all thirty of those kilometers to the Granon albergue. Despite my brisk pace, I was shivering through my entire body when I opened the unlocked albergue door into a cold hallway with a stone staircase that would not have been out of place in a castle. I shed my outer layer under a sign that beckoned pellegrinos to go upstairs after taking off shoes.

I headed up the staircase barefoot and found a warm loft that looked like it could have belonged to Mr. Tumnus in the *Chronicles of Narnia*. I placed my articles of soaked clothes by the heater and changed into my indoor clothes after a quick cold shower. The weather forecast promised more weather like this, so I took time to enjoy the warmth and silence. After spending so much time in the Middle East, I accepted it would take time for me to acclimate to such chilly weather.

I journalled, did some yoga, and relaxed by the crackling fireplace until Francessca and our Korean friends arrived. My gear was warm and dry, so I made room by the fire for their gear. Our albergue host invited us to attend Mass after dessert, and we accepted. The mix of Spanish in Latin in the mass again made me feel closer to history. While I might not have subscribed to the biblical edicts, I liked how everyone receives strength from every sermon, no matter what part of the world they are from.

That night we got word from Rodolfo that he made it to an albergue in Belrado. We missed his Brazilian charm and beaming face, and we could tell he missed all of us also.

"Chris, why don't you cover some miles and try to catch him before he leaves Belrado so we can regroup?" Francessca suggested.

"I like that idea," I replied.

The Koreans chimed in, and we unanimously decided I would surprise Rodolfo tomorrow morning at his albergue and persuade him to wait there for us.

I loved the idea of getting an early start to a big day. I liked the idea of surprising him in his albergue. I liked the idea of us all taking a carefree day to put behind us the actions of a thieving bastard.

I breathed in the brisk air and freezing rain as I took off from the Granon albergue, feeling like I was the first person awake on the planet. The Camino was tough to follow in the starry darkness, but I kept my wits and stayed on the path. Kilometers flew.

"This is the way." —Din Djarin

10

"Chris! You're . . . here!" Rodolfo's face lit up with child-like surprise, as if I had just apparated into his albergue like a benevolent wizard.

I couldn't help but laugh as he hugged me like I'd just returned from war.

"I am," I said.

"And Francessca?"

"She and the rest will get in later today."

"What? Why?"

"Because we missed you. And also, it's time to party again."

This was enough logic for Rodolfo to spontaneously declare a zero day. He pulled out a dusty bottle of wine he'd been saving for "a rainy day."

By lunchtime, our ragtag crew—Francessca, Hansoo, SuBin, Kay, Sue, and even Joachim—arrived like characters re-entering the frame after an intermission. It felt like the Camino was putting on a reunion episode just for us. We hit the tavern, sang bad karaoke with too much conviction, and took turns buying rounds like we were celebrating the end of finals in a college town rather than the middle of a semi-sacred pilgrimage.

Dazed and under-caffeinated, we limped to a café in Villa Franca for espresso and eggs. From there, I peeled off with Rodolfo and Joachim to trek to Ages. Francessca and the others took their time. Honestly, I didn't mind the split—it gave me the space to breathe and the freedom to belt out 'Don't Stop Believin'' across the mud-slicked path like some demented Journey prophet.

By the time we collapsed into a cozy albergue, soaked in mud to the knees, our spirits were high and our standards for hygiene terrifyingly low. We showered, grabbed beers, and rejoined the group chat. That's when I saw Francessca's message: "The trail today was disgusting. I hated it."

My smile faded.

Rodolfo glanced over. "What is the matter, Chris?"

"Francessca doesn't like the mud," I muttered.

Rodolfo frowned. "She seems angry about many things. Even Hansoo and SuBin asked me why she is always so negative."

I sighed. "She's still reeling from the robbery. She's just not the type to see magic in the mess. We're still getting to know each other. Honestly, it feels like we're happiest when we're apart. She wants a serious partner. I want someone who laughs when the sky opens up and ruins our shoes."

Rodolfo patted my shoulder. "You need another beer. I will get it."

"As Captain Picard once said, 'It is possible to commit no mistakes and still lose. That is not a weakness; that is life.'"

Rodolfo blinked. "Who?"

Joachim chuckled. "He's quoting Star Trek again."

Despite all the weirdness, I loved the Camino. It gave me permission to be curious. To improvise. To get lost on purpose and trust that wherever I ended up, I'd learn something about myself. I didn't need a detailed plan—just a strong enough instinct to follow the yellow arrows and see what surfaced. I wanted to share that outlook with Francessca, but her compass was calibrated differently.

Rodolfo and I hiked 27 kilometers into Burgos, a city with enough history to give Rome a run for its ego. I wandered through its streets feeling slightly out of sync with the world. Not a tourist, not a pilgrim, not really anything. Too weathered for a gap year. Too unburdened for a work sabbatical. Too clean to be mistaken for a drifter. I was just . . . walking.

Francessca eventually arrived, and we were friendly. No tension, no spark. Just a gentle understanding that something had quietly shifted.

That night, we ran into Joachim again at cathedral mass. The candlelight and Latin murmurs moved me. We shared wine at dinner, and the wind outside howled like a ghost trying to get in.

The next day, Rodolfo, Francessca, and I set off again—this time under a bright blue sky. Francessca hiked alone. Rodolfo and I took our breaks every ten kilometers, content in our muddy shoes and shared jokes. But something in Francessca was pulling away. After dinner in Hontanas, I sat next to her.

"Hey. How're things?"

She rubbed her foot. "I'm not enjoying these distances. I think I need to jump ahead. Maybe take some time off the Camino."

"I think that's a great idea," I said, hand resting on her shoulder. "Let's agree on a place to meet, and I'll do my best to be there."

No heartbreak. No drama. Just a mutual nod to truth: we wanted different things from this journey. I wanted to sing in the rain and dance through mud. She wanted stability and safety. Neither was wrong, but trying to force harmony between two different melodies only created discord.

Was I a shitty partner for feeling relieved? Maybe. Probably. But also—I was grateful. Grateful for the laughter, for the mistakes, for Rodolfo and Joachim and our off-key 80s songs. Grateful for the realization that relationships, like hiking boots, only take you as far as they fit. And grateful for the Camino—for being the kind of place where losing your way is just another way to move forward.

It was Thanksgiving Thursday's and I wanted to talk to the students about Thanksgiving. Thanksgiving's mission was to gather best friends and loved ones, prepare some magnificent food, relax over whatever beverages suit you best, and indulge with television, chess, conversations, movies, or songs. No pyrotechnics, costumes, or presents needed. To simply acknowledge gratitude for everything we have in life is such a simple and healthy premise. With no politics to split friends apart, no rivalries between relatives, and more than enough food and drink to satisfy even the portliest of gluttons, what isn't to love about Thanksgiving?

Since none of my students had even heard of it before, I took the time to explain what Americans traditionally did. I searched the internet to find images of what Thanksgiving meant to me, and they were all ears when I explained what stuffing and cranberry sauce was.

"What is turkey, teacher?"

"It's like a chicken but bigger," I said.

I showed images of apple, pumpkin, and pecan pies topped with ice cream. At first I wasn't going to show any pictures of alcohol to my all-Muslim class, but then I figured *what the hell* and showed the students snifters of brandy and glasses of wine. All at once the class was interested in what whiskey was like.

"Do you like whiskey, teacher?"

"I do. It is a shame it is forbidden here. In small amounts, whiskey is good."

This sparked more interest about Thanksgiving and America, which became a vehicle to expand on our lessons. Each student saw the sincerity in my eyes as I gushed about my favorite day. I couldn't help it, I couldn't hide it, and I didn't want to. Nor did the students want me to. I began to think about how much I missed my brother Andrew. I'd seen so little of him in the last several years, and I wanted us to be closer. I missed him all the time, especially at Thanksgiving.

To celebrate the end of the workweek, my colleagues, neighbors, and a few friendly expats all converged on the Camel Club in the heart of the Nassim Compound, our little oasis in a kingdom of sand and paradoxes. The theme was "bring something homemade, something purchased, or just something resembling effort." I brought two heaping trays of my "so-garlicky-you'll-lose friends over it" mashed potatoes. Honestly, I should've called them "smashed garlic with a suggestion of potato." Five full bulbs, no regrets. I was there to make an impression.

The potluck was simple. Comforting. Almost pure. It was one of the few things that felt familiar, like a seasonal tradition untouched by bureaucracy or favoritism. People smiled. They passed dishes. They said thank you. It felt . . . human. Which, after a week in the Saudi school system, felt like vacationing on another planet.

At work, the rules were more like suggestions for the foreign hires and outright punchlines for the well-connected locals. I discovered quickly that even the printed, laminated policies had an escape hatch labeled wasta—that mystical social lubricant, that cheat code for skipping the line. Wasta, as I came to understand, was not just about influence. It was ancestry-powered gravity. If your family name carried weight, then gravity bent in your favor.

And the students? They'd tell you. With pride. Loudly. Often mid-sentence, mid-class, or mid-nap. "My uncle works in the ministry." "My father owns half of Jeddah." "I will not fail."

And they were right. Not because they studied. But because the system bent for them like it owed them rent.

As a foreigner, my authority was like a sandcastle at high tide. I could make things look respectable, even professional, but by morning? Washed out. Forgotten. My role boiled down to two things: assign grades and not take anything personally. I'd grade tests filled with the same exact phrasing across multiple answer sheets—and when I brought it up to the department leads, I faced a kind of dead-eyed indifference that made me question if I'd just spoken in another language.

"We will talk to them," the sergeant said, already looking past me.

"You mean . . . nothing will be done about it?"

"It is not for you to worry. Just teach them."

"Even if they only show up once a week and copy off each other?"

"Yes."

"But that's not teaching."

"You are not here to change the system."

That line. That was the quiet border I crossed most often—not between nations, but between hope and futility.

Driving home that day, I faced the usual highway warfare. Saudi roads were a kind of gladiatorial arena where the concept of "right-of-way" didn't exist. Turn signals were aspirational. Horns were gospel.

I pulled into the grocery store just to breathe. Just to feel like I had agency over something. The air conditioning was cold. The fluorescent lights buzzed like static in my skull. I wandered the aisles longer than necessary, not to buy more garlic—but because inside that grocery store, no one was grading me, honking at me, or ignoring me for their cousin's connection to the Royal Saudi Air Force.

And that's when it hit me. The order of things.

If I couldn't change the entire system, I could at least reorder the test questions. I could make them think. Or, failing that, confuse them enough to accidentally learn something. If nothing else, I could hold the line in my own little trench of pedagogy, even if the war was unwinnable.

I got creative. If they wanted to copy, I'd let them copy . . . but I'd start changing the order of the questions. Same quiz, three versions. Like the SAT had a lovechild with a shell game.

The next test, I handed them out with a smile.

"Don't copy each other," I warned.

The room was quiet. Suspiciously so. I watched as the usual side-eyes, nudges, and cheat-code glances unfolded—only this time, chaos crept in. The answers didn't line up. Question 3 on one paper was Question 7 on another.

I graded the tests immediately. Two students passed. Two.

I marched the stack straight to the department sergeant and dropped them on his desk with a note: "Because of cheating, only two students passed. Let me know if you'd like me to continue pretending this is teaching."

I knew what would happen next: nothing. I wasn't even mad anymore. I was just . . . resigned. The kind of resignation that makes you start baking absurd amounts of garlic potatoes and going full Gandalf on student assessments. I didn't come to Saudi Arabia expecting gratitude. I had hoped for meaning. Some small sense that what I was doing mattered. What I found instead was a culture I admired in parts, feared in others, and couldn't quite ever fit into.

Teaching aircraft electrical systems to students who barely showed up. Waiting on paychecks that might or might not arrive. Watching smart kids fall behind, while well-connected ones coasted on fumes. Still—I kept showing up. I was naïve. I was stubborn.

Why couldn't everything be as innocent and straightforward as Thanksgiving?

"Here comes the sun." —*The Beatles*

11

On the Camino de Santiago, priests often appeared like roaming checkpoints of grace—offering blessings, encouragement, and a faint sense that someone was watching out for you, even if they didn't know your name. After three weeks of hiking and hostels, I found myself reflecting on how different this felt from the environment I had just come from. I had traded the stark authority of Saudi mosques for the soft, warm ritual of Catholic cathedrals—and with it, traded the company of devout Muslims for Catholic pilgrims seeking something more . . . intangible.

I was doing the same.

As I trekked through Basque Country, I found myself wondering if it was me who hadn't fully come to terms with reality—me, who had tried to fit into two vastly diverse cultures and still found myself orbiting just outside both. Faith, it seemed, offered different masks of comfort, but I was beginning to see through all of them.

What struck me most wasn't religion, though—it was the windows. European homes invited the outside world in. They framed hills, trees, winding roads, and parks.

Parks!

I couldn't remember seeing a single park while living in the Saudi city where I taught. My old commute from the expat compound to King Khalid Air Base had originally sounded like a dream: exercise, fresh air, simplicity. But Saudi Arabia made it comically clear—if you weren't in a car, you didn't belong. There were no sidewalks. No bike lanes. No wandering. Anas, one of my brighter students, once told me that single men weren't even allowed in parks. "They might be too . . . excited," he said, apologetically.

A guy trying to enjoy trees alone is just a hormone bomb waiting to detonate. I tried not to laugh, but it made me feel like the punchline of a joke told by a place that didn't realize it was joking.

I left Hontanas early that morning, hands frozen but heart light. I needed to make peace with something that had been tugging at my mind for days: my cooling romance with Francessca. The stars still dotted the pre-dawn sky, and as I walked, I let their quiet sparkle distract me from the cold. It was a beautiful kind of ache—one that pulled at your fingertips and the edges of your memory at the same time.

By the time I reached Fromista, the sun was up. These were the moments where self-efficacy felt tangible: I had gotten myself here, through fatigue and frostbite, not because I had to, but because I chose to. That choice was mine. That path, mine. That aching blister on my heel? Also, mine.

After lunch, I pushed on another four kilometers to Población, where an open albergue waited for me with open arms and a surprised Rodolfo greeted me with laughter and a glass of wine.

A little later, Francessca arrived, her face soft with road-weariness, accompanied by a new companion: a chipper German named Detlef who seemed like the human embodiment of a protein bar—nutritious, enthusiastic, and always prepared.

"How are your feet treating you?" I asked her in the shared kitchen, trying to sound neutral but friendly.

"It's hard to tell," she said. "Detlef thinks I should slow down or skip the next hard part. Maybe hiking isn't my thing." She half-laughed, half-sighed.

"The Camino provides!" Detlef beamed. He handed her a knife. "Can you slice the tomatoes?"

"She doesn't like tomatoes," I said, stirring my own simple meal. "But I've got extra sauce."

"I hope you like onion," he said, looking at her with a hopeful grin.

"I wish we had garlic," she murmured.

I slid half a bulb across the table to Detlef. "Here. For the cause."

He grinned. "You're the man!"

I just smiled and went back to my spinach and eggs. It was a meal I had made a dozen times before, but I didn't need to impress anyone tonight. I was tired. I was hungry. I was at peace.

Francessca watched me cook. "Still doing your same pace?"

"Yup," I said. "Same rhythm, same sore feet, same uphill battles. Like jazz with blisters."

She chuckled. "It's funny how the Camino sorts people into their own rhythms."

"Yeah," I said. "Some people you think you'll walk with forever, and then the path changes."

She paused, glass of red wine in her hand. "Right . . ."

Detlef asked me what I was making, and I explained it in the most unsexy way possible. "Spinach, eggs, garlic, and vibes."

Francessca smiled. "That's his go-to."

"We're doing pasta," Detlef added, nudging her. "Well—I'm doing pasta. She's supervising."

"I opened the wine," she said, mock-defensively. "Very important contribution."

I laughed. "Enjoy dinner. I'll keep you posted where I end up. Wanna meet in Santiago?"

"Let's. And thanks for the pasta sauce and garlic, Chris," Francessca said.

"My pleasure."

I meant it. No heat. No subtext. Just genuine warmth between two people who cared about each other enough not to ruin it by forcing a square peg of romance into a round hole of mutual respect.

On the Camino Santiago, priests offered a sense of protection to those of faith. It had been three weeks since I traded the company of Muslims for the company of Catholics. As I processed the contrasting expressions of faith, I couldn't help but ask myself if I was the one who was not coming to grips with reality as I made my way through Basque Country.

As a Christ-skeptical heathen, I no longer reach for the dusty academic answers, when asked why I celebrate Christmas. Yes, the Church piggybacked off Saturnalia to secure followers, not to mention market share. Jesus likely wasn't born in December. I used to explain all that. Pedantically. One day I realized I was doing it mostly to hear myself sound educated, which is just another flavor of narcissism.

It took a few years of mildly painful self-awareness and more than a few uncomfortable dinners to realize I was missing the point. After realizing how I sounded, I changed my tune so that when someone asked why I celebrated Christmas despite not believing in Jesus, I instead would reply, "Because Christmas is fucking awesome."

One particular December found me back in my pastel-colored room on the Nassim Compound in Saudi Arabia, listening to my overplayed Christmas playlist and scrolling through friends' social media. Lights. Matching pajamas. Dogs in sweaters. Perfect couples kissing under garlands that matched their emotional availability. It was like an ad for seasonal capitalism disguised as emotional intimacy. Black Friday spilled into Cyber Monday like a retail oil spill. Families bankrupted themselves annually to express love through gift receipts. Q4 profits soared as CEOs whispered "Jesus is the reason for the season" into a branded scarf made by children. Good thing Americans have Thanksgiving—a warm, wholesome, totally uncomplicated holiday free from colonialism, disease, land theft, or government-sanctioned betrayal, right?

Still, I missed it. The noise. The lights. The organized chaos. I missed the warmth of shared food and inside jokes and having your mom ask, "Do you really need another beer?" with a mix of concern and judgment only a mother can weaponize. But I never quite knew how to be part of a community without sensing some underlying power struggle.

Even so, I craved the same things as everyone else: safety, familiarity, tradition. That's why, in spite of the commercial machine and the lingering whiff of colonial arrogance that clings to most Western holidays, Christmas still lived inside me. Even when I was alone. Even surrounded by sand instead of snow. Even when the only "Silent Night" I got was if the Wi-Fi dropped.

Music became my holiday passport. The Trans-Siberian Orchestra, with its operatic intensity. The swelling emotion of "O Holy Night." The humble drama of "Little Drummer Boy." The child-like awe of "Silent Night." And yes, the Home Alone soundtrack. Throw in Star Trek: Generations and I positively glowed with Christmas cheer. Somewhere between Captain Picard's existential grief and Kevin McCallister's booby traps, I found something that felt like home.

Of course, the Royal Saudi Air Force had made it clear that we were not, under any circumstance, to wish our students a "Merry Christmas." Not that I was bursting to do it. My students were often lazy, entitled, and allergic to curiosity. Easy for me to judge. Me, the atheist Christmas lover. The Thanksgiving enthusiast who scoffs at sanitized colonial myths but hoarded leftover turkey. Hypocrite much? If there was one holiday tradition I'd truly mastered, it was feeling slightly superior and deeply conflicted—preferably while humming along to "Carol of the Bells" in a country that thought I was a Christian. Merry Christmas ya filthy animals, indeed.

The morning we left Población, Rodolfo and I witnessed the most astonishing sunrise of our lives. I'd seen sunrises before. I'd seen postcard skies and golden-hour Instagram bait. But nothing, nothing, had ever torn open the sky like this. We had barely started walking, our boots crunching lightly on the frost-hardened path, when the horizon lit up like a wound in the fabric of space. A deep, bleeding red—thick and alive—spilled upward into the retreating black of night. The transition wasn't gradual. It was a kind of celestial violence. The colors didn't blend; they collided. Crimson veins cut across the sky like lightning made of fire. It was the kind of red that made you question whether it was beautiful or dangerous. Like the inside of something holy, or the last breath of something divine. For an hour, I just kept looking up, breath fogging in front of my face, my neck craned like a man seeing the ocean for the first time. The stars hadn't even finished disappearing. They clung to the corners of the night, stubbornly twinkling through the encroaching light like they didn't want to leave yet either.

Everything around us had gone quiet—not just Rodolfo and me, but the world. Even the wind held its breath. The earth didn't feel like earth anymore. It felt like we were walking through some myth older than language. I half expected a deity to rise out of the soil, just to acknowledge what the sky was doing.

Up to that point, I'd spent the Camino quietly interrogating my own belief systems. Three weeks before, I had been in a Muslim country where religion saturated everything—calls to prayer echoing from minarets, God invoked in every greeting. Now I was in Catholic Europe where the bones of saints slept beneath the cobblestones and weathered stone churches stood like ancient anchors on every hilltop. Faith seemed to cling to every culture, every language, every rhythm of daily life—but I didn't belong to any of it. I'd always thought of myself as an outsider to religion. A non-believer. A polite skeptic. But as I walked under that bleeding sky, I stopped needing names for what I was feeling. It wasn't doctrine. It wasn't God with a capital G. It was something else—something vast and intimate at the same time. The universe. Or love. Or whatever force keeps stars burning and people healing. Whatever it was, it was inside me too, and I could feel it swelling. I wasn't alone out there. I never had been. The Camino was changing me like a tide carving new shapes out of old rock. Every sunrise peeled back another layer of cynicism. Every quiet mile made room for something new to bloom. Gratitude. Forgiveness. Even, in a way I hadn't dared admit before, belief. Not belief in religion per se, but belief in meaning, in grace, in the idea that I could feel awe and still belong to the world. I had begun the Camino wanting answers. What I was getting instead were moments like this one—unexplainable, undeniable, and absolutely sacred. I realized that transformation didn't have to be loud or dramatic.

I looked over at Rodolfo, and for once, neither of us needed to speak. What could we even say? It didn't feel like it was morning. It didn't feel like any known time of day. It felt like the universe had paused and opened a window just for us to peek into something primordial and sacred. Something not meant to be photographed. Even ten years later, I still don't know how to explain it. All I know is that every sunrise since has felt like a polite imitation. That one? That one was real.

Carrion de los Condes was halfway between Saint Jean Pied-de-Port and Santiago. Although I had expected to make this trip with Francessca, I was glad to have only positive energy around me. I wondered if I should have felt more guilt than I already did for lasting less than half of the Camino with Francessca. With two weeks behind me, I knew I would spend the next two weeks unpacking all my thoughts and feelings.

After lunch, Rodolfo and I pressed forward with energy and enthusiasm along the flattest and most barren stretch of the Camino. Rain blasted against us for seventeen kilometers until we arrived at the albergue at Calzadilla de la Cueza. The tiny hamlet had just a couple of pubs and a few houses, but it was enough for us. Rodolfo and I feasted at a small restaurant near the albergue.

After dinner, I logged on to the albergue Wi-Fi before bed and saw Francessca decided to take a zero day at Carrion de los Condes to see a doctor. He told her she should take it easy for a few days and let her feet heal. Hansoo, SuBin, Sue, and Kay said they would catch a ride to meet up with me in Leon.

Free to see how much ground we could cover; Rodolfo and I hiked thirty-eight kilometers to El Burgo the next day. At the albergue, our hosteler served us the best pilgrim's dinner to date. Rodolfo would have gladly eaten a damp sock drizzled it in olive oil, but instead we started with sopa de ajo—garlic soup that revived us followed by Pollo al ajillo (garlic chicken) with chips (french fries) and veggies on the side. But the true highlight? The vino tinto—a bottomless jug of rough red wine that costs less than bottled water and is as vital to morale as sunscreen and quality shoes. After two glasses, everything became hilarious. By the fourth, Rodolfo and I signed up to walk 38 kilometers the next day because "por qué no (why not)?" Dessert was flan that we passed around the wobbly table, sharing stories and wine like it was the blood of Christ.

"Chris, I want to finish the Camino soon," Rodolfo said between bites.

"What's your rush, Rodolfo?"

"I have decided to fly home to Brazil in time for my son's birthday in a week. I don't have time to slow down and take time in Leon with our friends."

"I admire your motivation. Your son will be happy to see his Dad," I said as we clinked pints of Spanish beer.

The next morning, we woke up early as we were both wont to do. When we arrived in Mansilla, Rodolfo and I bid each other *Buen Camino* and promised to keep in touch. After spending the night alone in the Mansilla albergue, I hiked twenty kilometers to the bustling European metropolis of Leon. Buildings of steel and glass flanked me as I followed yellow shell symbols on the pavement and building corners, letting me know I was still on the Camino.

The San Francisco albergue was more like a hotel. Instead of getting a bed or a cot in an open church, for ten euros I was handed a key to a room with three beds. On top of that, I made use of their laundry room while watching movies from their library of English-language DVDs. The albergue was spacious, warm, and offered solace from the unwelcome city chaos I'd become sensitive to, so I took my first zero day on the Camino in Leon.

Hansoo messaged me to let me know what time they expected to arrive, so I toured a couple museums and the cathedral. I took in the full majesty of each place I visited, even though I couldn't help but consider the unapologetic abuses and social controls I held Mother Church responsible for. I looked at how spiritual power offered widespread peace, contentment, confidence, and hope to others. It seemed like everyone around me connected effortlessly with this limitless loving energy. I was the anomaly for not seeing any evidence of the Divine.

Despite the stormy internal debates, I'd been wrestling with over belief, identity, and belonging, I made the conscious effort to absorb the sheer majesty around me. Spanish artistry didn't demand belief. It simply existed. In the museums and galleries, I found brushstrokes of people long gone, who had once stood where I stood, looking at the same hills, breathing the same air, even doubting themselves in the same damn way I was. Their depictions of Basque and European landscapes were familiar, not just because I'd hiked through them, but because their confusion and yearning leaped out of the artistry. Their stories—of love, of uncertainty, of letting go—echoed mine. My short-lived saga with Francessca didn't need to be a tragedy or a romance. We weren't meant to walk the same road forever—but that didn't mean I had to frame it as failure. We shared laughter, wine, and a few tender moments. Instead of clinging to what we weren't, I could appreciate what we were. Friends? Friendly ex-flirts? International comrades? I'd take any of those.

"Meant to be" . . . meant by who, though? God? Fate? The great Cosmic Screenwriter who loves to throw in a good plot twist for character development? It was just the collective human current I'd been feeling ever since I started walking the Camino—the subtle spiritual dragnet of centuries of pilgrims all putting one foot in front of the other, hoping to find grace, healing, or just decent Wi-Fi.

The more I observed, the more I realized how religion had, for better or worse, been the blueprint for moral cohesion throughout history. Not just in the obvious, fire-and-brimstone way, but in the soft conditioning, the reward-punishment logic wrapped in ritual and incense. And while I still didn't buy into the need for supernatural surveillance to keep people kind, I was starting to understand the allure: it gives structure, comfort, and story. It makes people feel less alone.

I didn't have to convert. I didn't have to rebel, either. I could just accept. Accept that faith gives people something real, even if it's not for me. That it knits society together, even as I sit outside the circle doing my best impression of respectful indifference. I didn't have to beat them or join them—maybe I just had to walk beside them.

And as if on cue, Francessca and our ever-growing gang of Korean pilgrims rolled into León like a scene from a feel-good indie movie. I'd spent the day solo, lost in introspection, and overpriced pastries, but now here we were hugs flying, languages blending, laughter echoing across the old stone city. It was glorious chaos.

Sue was finishing her Camino to return to Seoul and the grown-up world of jobs and schedules. Hansoo, ever the diplomat, suggested we go across town to a Chinese buffet to celebrate her impending soul death—uh, return to work—with proper reverence.

"A Chinese buffet in Spain?" I asked, raising an eyebrow.

Hansoo grinned. "Why not?"

With that, our mismatched menagerie of Camino-weary oddballs from around the world trekked—this time in search of spring rolls and soft-serve ice cream. That was the truest part of the Camino: not the prayers, not the cathedrals, but the friends, food, and the shared knowledge that none of us really knew what came next.

"Are you no longer hiking with Detlef?" I asked Francessca as we walked to the restaurant.

"He started acting like a creep, so I told him to leave me alone."

"That's too bad, y'all woulda made a great couple." I said with a smile.

"I look good with anyone, honey," Francessca said, sashaying across the street as Sue and SuBin cheered and catcalled after her.

The restaurant Francessca picked out was ideal for our evening of revelry. We ate like it had been a month without food as we piled up our used plates before returning to the buffet. Even without our backpacks, we felt like misfits in a world that didn't know what to do with. It was as if we existed outside of reality.

That evening Francessca encouraged me to keep doing big miles. "Here's an idea: we could get to Santiago ahead of schedule, then hike the Camino Portuguese backward and meet in Porto."

"I'm not good at hiking backward," I said.

Francessca rolled her eyes at me. "Let's stay in touch to let each other know where we are."

The next morning we said goodbye to Francessca and Sue before returning to the Camino. Kay, one of the Koreans who joined our circle, and I managed a small conversation as we hiked fourteen kilometers together. Although I was stationed for a year at Kadena Air Base in South Korea, it had been fifteen years, and my ability to navigate Korean had all but disappeared.

By noon, my hunger was impossible to ignore, so Kay and I stopped to eat lunch at The Amstel, a cozy café right on the Camino while waiting for Hansoo and SuBin to catch up.

Traveling like this felt powerful and free, with time only as important as daylight. I savored the opportunity to enjoy my existence without the minutiae of normal life to distract me. I began to sense the spiritual comfort and emotional safety pellegrinos felt around each other. I remembered theft was a real possibility on the Camino Santiago, but I still had to hand it to social cohesion, bringing all of us strangers from various cultures and countries to connect with each other.

In no time at all we'd cultivated an easy sense of belonging that improved our social health and emotional well-being. I felt safer about taking risks and being vulnerable when I was with my Camino friends. It wasn't that I was averse to the lure of safety and calmness, but I preferred the atmosphere of safety and moments of shared joy in-between threatening environments we seemed to trespass into. Whatever stresses I anticipated facing in the normal world were less threatening thanks to the comfort I felt on the Camino. After battling kilometers, weather, and language barriers, we found solace in cooking together in the albergues, playing music, teaching each other card games, and trading jokes. Even in strange and cold places, we found security. I wish my normal life felt a bit more like the life I lived on the Camino. That evening, we made it to St. Martin and one of my favorite albergues on the Camino. Albergue Vieira's hosteler, Sheida, cooked us a vegetable casserole as delicious as it was nourishing. I shared a bottle of red wine I'd gotten earlier.

The next day was my 39th birthday, and I kicked it off with a warm cup of coffee and the modern sacrament of logging onto Wi-Fi to respond to a cascade of birthday messages. I basked (Basque'd?) in the digital affection like a cat in the sun. I scribbled a note for Sheida and my Korean friends wishing them a Buen Camino, then set off on what would be my longest day of Camino hiking: forty-four kilometers to Rabanal del Camino.

My feet moved with the rhythm of someone younger than I was the day before. Not a single ache. No blisters screaming mutiny. Just the quiet pulse of forward motion. Maybe it was adrenaline, or maybe turning thirty-nine just meant I was officially at the age where endurance replaced speed and stubbornness became a superpower.

I stopped only twice. First at Hippie Dave's break spot, where I shared a snack and a drink in the sun with fellow pilgrims and a man who may or may not have been stoned since 1984. The conversation ranged from the Camino to quantum mechanics to Dave's conspiracy theory that socks are interdimensional beings who feed off foot sweat. I was happy for the shade.

Later, I paused again in Astorga for a birthday lunch at the Gaudí Café. I approached the counter with a grin.

"I don't suppose you have a birthday deal for customers, do you?" I asked the barista, weaponizing my charm shamelessly.

"Happy birthday, and have a café latte, on the house," he replied with a chuckle. I left him a generous tip and left Astorga with a happy heart and caffeine-fueled optimism.

That night in Rabanal, I met Yung Hwan and Dong Ho from Korea and Jurgis from Denmark. We pooled our pilgrim resources and threw together a pasta dinner that was more like a minor feast. I opened the bottle of wine I'd bought earlier, and the whole evening settled into this deep, golden kind of contentment. The Danes call it hygge—a word that doesn't translate neatly, but lives somewhere between cozy intimacy and effortless connection—the spiritual opposite of Catholic guilt.

I'd spent thirty-nine years of my life under the influence of institutions that treated pleasure like a sin and comfort like a trap. Catholic school, for example—where even joy had a dress code and laughter needed a permission slip. Where desire was dangerous, doubt was punished, and silence was mistaken for virtue. Hygge? It said something far simpler: "You're worthy of warmth." Light a candle. Pour the wine. Unclench. It didn't just feel good. It felt healing.

For someone who'd spent years being told he was too much—too geeky, too curious, too silly—that little dinner was proof that sometimes it's pasta and wine shared with strangers who, even just for a night, were family. Maybe personal growth wasn't always some dramatic realization.

The next morning was crisp and brisk; the kind of weather that makes you question your life choices but in a poetic way. As I ascended one of the highest points on the Camino, snowcapped mountains came into view and framed the famous Cruz de Ferro. There, at the base of the iron cross, sat a mountain of stones—tokens carried by pilgrims from their home countries, meant to symbolize burdens left behind.

I hadn't brought a stone.

It wasn't that I didn't have burdens, but I hadn't earned that kind of ritual. If I had tossed a rock onto that pile, I would've felt like I was crashing someone else's funeral. For those who believed it was a sacred act. For me, it would have just been performance art. Still, the weight of that collective vulnerability wasn't lost on me. You don't need to believe in magic to be moved by sincerity. That place was powerful not because of dogma, but because of the love of the thousands of people hoping, hurting, and healing. I was glad to be there.

The descent from the Cruz de Ferro was gentler than expected, and I coasted thirty kilometers into Ponferrada with a surprisingly cheerful stride. There, I found a cozy albergue and splurged on a sumptuous dinner at the pub next door. I sunk into a plush chair and journaled like a man in a Jane Austen adaptation, responding to more birthday wishes and savoring the wine of solitude.

Then, a message popped up from Yung Hwan: "Hey Chris. I hope you made it to Ponferrada like you said you wanted to. Did you hear Leonard Nimoy passed away today? RIP Spock."

I stared at the screen as a stillness settled over me. I looked out the window, watching the wind stir the branches like something out of a eulogy. I was grateful to be alone. It felt fitting. Quiet. Sacred, even.

Leonard Nimoy had always been more than Spock to me. He was a lighthouse for those of us navigating our own logic-versus-emotion dilemmas. He made curiosity cool. He made restraint feel powerful. And he made it okay to feel alien sometimes. He reminded me that wisdom wasn't just knowing things—it was choosing compassion when things didn't make sense. I was still fumbling through cultures I didn't fully understand, stumbling over my own assumptions, trying to become someone better than the sum of my habits.

When my expat crew in Saudi Arabia found a sliver of free time (translation: weren't buried in grading papers or writing training manuals), we'd load up the cars and make like a caravan of heathens to the coast. Unlike us sunburn-prone Westerners who apparently thought "midday desert heat" meant "beach day," most Saudis had the good sense to stay indoors with the AC. That left us with a stretch of the Red Sea so empty and pristine it felt like we'd accidentally reserved it on Airbnb.

We'd dive straight into the warm waters, welcomed by shimmering fish who looked confused but politely nonjudgmental. After a few hours swimming around like half-drunk dolphins, we'd crawl back onto shore, covered in salt, sunscreen, and satisfaction, then fire up a beach meal while the scuba divers regaled us with their tales from the depths.

"Did you see that shark?"

"Yeah! I never knew they were so tiny!"

"Good thing it wasn't into what we taste like!"

Snorkeling near the surface, where the sea kissed the sky, was gorgeous, but what lay in the deeper blue? I was no longer content to float—I wanted to descend. I wanted to enter that realm my friends talked about so reverently, where gravity is a memory and fish glide without a worry in the world.

I decided to take the plunge and get scuba certified. Lucky for me, there was a PADI-certified trainer right on Nassim Compound named Achille. As a proud geek, I was already in. I mean, how could I *not* want to train with someone named after one of the most legendary heroes of ancient literature?

Achille took diving seriously. Like, "I've survived things you only dream of and I'm not about to let you flail around underwater" seriously. He wasn't interested in giving out easy certifications or signing off just because I dusted off my high school French when we hung out. This guy was all about the process. He worked one-on-one with me in Nassim Compound's pool, corrected my technique, and taught me how to be safe underwater. I studied the PADI coursebook, watched hours of diving videos, and learned to calculate oxygen and nitrogen levels to pass the written exams.

Then came the real deal—open water tests in the Red Sea. Achille administered my practical test and watched me perform area sweeps and safely manage tasks at depth. I wasn't even nervous. When we surfaced Achille shook my hand.

"Bon." He said as he handed my certification, and just like that, I was certified to roam underwater—anywhere on Earth—up to sixty feet down. A whole new world. A new fantastic point of view, even. Weightless, suspended, surrounded by bubbles, I was in a sacred space. Every inhale echoed like a whispered spell. Every exhale shimmered upward toward sunlight. Beneath me, an endless abyss. It was like outer space, except wetter and with fewer starships. Down there, I was a traveler welcomed silently by creatures who had no interest in my résumé. The ocean itself invited me to discover what things were like beneath the surface. Who was I to say no?

Shining, shimmering, splendid.

"Momma always says there's an awful lot you could tell about a person by their shoes. Where they're going. Where they've been." —Forrest Gump

12

From Ponferrada to Vega del Valcarce, the Camino and I moved in sync through forty picturesque kilometers through towns and fields, along rivers, and past cemeteries. Dong Ho, Jurgis, and Yung Hwan surprised me with hugs at the Vega del Valcarce albergue. The steep decline from Cruz de Ferro gave their legs hell, so they hitchhiked to where the four of us sat planning the rest of our Camino schedules. While they planned to hike small days to recover, I planned to hike big days. We made dinner together and feasted once more, not knowing if we would see each other again. Dong Ho was a trained chef, so he cooked chicken while Jurgis made spaghetti. Yung Hwan and I each contributed a bottle of red wine. After our repast, I looked at the map and realized I would arrive in Santiago in less than a week. I loved meeting people on the Camino from all over the world. I enjoyed sharing meals, exchanging jokes, and having worldly conversations. When we waxed political together after meals we felt like philosopher kings and queens, offering each other glimpses into our homelands, and making us yearn to see even more of the world. I wasn't ready for this Camino experience to end. While I wasn't keen on bringing an end to this routine of daily accomplishment, the reality of accomplishment excited me.

Despite the workplace frustrations, there was something electrifying about trying out a totally unfamiliar way of life and thinking, "Alright, let's figure this out." I worried I'd become a bit addicted to that wide-eyed sense of wonder. Local markets bursting with spice and chatter, ancient landmarks older than my entire home country, even humble neighborhoods with odd street signage and stray cats that looked like tiny judgmental kings—all of it added texture to my life abroad. So, when I was invited to attend one of my student's weddings, I jumped at the chance.

Saleem, the groom-to-be and one of our more charismatic students, had extended the invite with warmth, and two of my fellow American colleagues, Stu and Mark, agreed to join the fun.

"A wedding on a Tuesday?" Mark said, checking the calendar like he'd read it wrong.

"Hey, that's Saudi Arabia," I shrugged. "Weekends are a vibe, but weeknights are a statement."

"Do I need to buy a thobe or something?" Stu asked.

Saleem laughed. "Wear jeans and a t-shirt if you want."

"Good," I said. "I left my entire thobe collection in the States. Tragic oversight."

We set off from Nassim Compound and followed the most chaotic set of directions since Moses wandered the desert. Eventually, we pulled up to the pre-party rendezvous point as Saudis parked their cars chaotically. It was part tailgate, part traffic jam, part magic.

We followed the tide of students, relatives, and total strangers, all there to celebrate Saleem. We were, quite literally, the only foreigners there—which meant we got a lot of attention. Think royal guests, if the royal family was three tired Americans trying not to step on anyone's sandals.

At sunset, we followed the group across a busy street to the venue, our students chanting in Arabic like a jubilant parade:

We are the friends of Saleem!

We come to celebrate and wish him the best in life!

Make way for us or join us as we welcome him!

Into the days Allah wishes for him to enjoy!

Inside, the cultural separation of the sexes was . . . well, not subtle. There was no ceremony we could see, no first dance, and no sign of the bride—just hundreds of men packed into a lavish room full of plush cushions, louder cologne battles than a middle school locker room, and enough gold watches to crash the economy. Ornamental weapons were presented as wedding gifts—curved knives, silver-plated handguns, and enough bling to make a rapper sweat.

"Mr. Chris, do you like my watch?" one student shouted over the din.

"It's elegant," I said, ever the diplomat.

"How much do you think it costs?"

"Um, $500?"

He laughed. "My father paid two thousand."

Stu leaned over. "Yeah, Chris. Don't you recognize a two-grand timepiece when you see one?"

The room erupted in laughter, including mine. What else do you do when you get flexed on by a twenty-year-old?

The Saudis greeted each other like long-lost brothers—even if they had seen each other earlier that day. It was joyful chaos. We met half the room, each introduction sounding like the start of a political alliance: "This is Mr. Chris, from America. He teaches Aircraft electrical systems. He is a good man." Nod, handshake, onto the next. Over and over. I felt like I was at a beauty pageant.

Despite the warm welcome, no one went deeper than names and job titles. I don't know if it was a language thing or just unfamiliarity with how to talk to Westerners who don't show up with ornamental swords. My Arabic was basic at best, but I tried. Combinations of smiling, nodding, saying "mabrouk" a lot, and using polite gesturing worked in most situations.

After a couple of hours, we followed the group into the dining hall. By this point, our stomachs were staging quiet revolts. Everyone sat cross-legged on the carpet around enormous silver trays of rice and roasted goat. We went to the lone Western-style table in the corner, set just for us. It was both thoughtful and awkward, like being offered a fork at a finger-food party, and the three of us appreciated the gesture.

The goat? Shockingly delicious. Tender, juicy, flavorful. I felt like I was betraying my lifelong allegiance to chicken. We remembered the all-important rule: right hand only. No one wants to be the foreigner who uses the unclean hand. When we were full and slightly delirious with meat sweats, the festivities spilled back outside where we congratulated Saleem, bowed politely to his many relatives, and soaked in the surreal magic of it all. It wasn't our tradition, but being included was a gift.

Hikers like me often feel like we belong only to the trail, suspended between places, never quite home. But traditions—even unfamiliar ones—have a way of stitching people together across time and distance. They're vibrant, strange, and wildly specific. And, if you're lucky, you sit in front of a silver platter of goatmeat.

I've always preferred that quiet, misty rain that gently soaks your soul over the loud, drama-queen raindrops that hit like they've got a grudge. But the weather on the Camino de Santiago has its own ego, and it clearly wanted to keep me humble. When I summited Alto de Poyo hoping for a cinematic vista, all I got was fog, fog, and more fog. My glasses fogged up too, so I took them off and hiked blurry.

Despite the gray skies, my head was up among the stars. Not just metaphorically, either; Spock was on my mind. He'd been a quiet, lifelong role model, probably because he always managed to balance logic, loyalty, and deep friendship without ever turning it into a Hallmark moment. He had been, and always shall be, my friend.

As I neared Santiago, the numbers on my dwindling budget started to resemble a magic trick. Somehow, 25 euros a day got me a bocadillo (Spanish for "hoagie," if you're from Philly), a couple beers, a banquet-style dinner complete with wine, and a clean albergue bed.

Lately, I'd been noticing more fresh-faced hikers joining the trail. Many were only walking short distances each day, and while I missed the familiar faces who had journeyed long and far with me, there was something liberating about not having to match pace with anyone. It was just me, my backpack, and my thoughts—which, let's be honest, were mostly about food, fictional Vulcans, and the occasional existential crisis. Did preferring solitude over camaraderie make me a sociable loner? Maybe. But I wasn't about to psychoanalyze myself while trudging 37 kilometers into Triacastela with wet socks.

"So long, Basque Country. Hello Galicia!" I nearly shouted into the rain like a maniac. But I kept it internal. No need to alarm the cows.

That night, warmed up and fed, I felt the thrill again—that irrational, hiker-specific desire to do another long day tomorrow, just to see if I could. With Santiago on the horizon, my mind began drifting toward my next big obsession: the Pacific Crest Trail. The Camino had given me beauty, but it had also handed me a mirror. It's one thing to hike through different landscapes; it's another to realize you're carrying your own cultural biases like an extra thirty pounds in your pack. American culture loves to parade around with the slogan freedom of choice, but I was starting to see how that lens can distort, especially when applied to people walking different paths toward enlightenment—or just toward dinner.

That night, a message from Rodolfo lit up my phone:

"I saw the pictures you posted. Keep up your pace and meet up with me in Santiago before I fly home to Brazil."

Could I really keep this pace? Fifty kilometers a day to see a friend one more time?

"I'll see you in Santiago," I sent back.

Mousa and Fahad were my newest students. Smart, funny, and charming in that we'll-pretend-we're-listening-but-we're-definitely-leaving-class-early way that most Saudi students perfected. Ramadan was coming, and I remembered from the year before how class turned into a zombie flick: students pale, slow, half-awake after fasting all day and feasting all night. I wanted to try something new.

"If we finish this next block before Ramadan starts," I told them, "you won't have to crawl through class like dehydrated ghosts."

"I like it," Mousa said.

"Good idea, Mr. Chris. Especially if you keep bringing penis butter," Fahad chimed in.

"Peanut butter," I corrected, trying not to laugh. "But now I'm bringing extra."

That semester was different. We had a goal: finish the course three months early. It was ridiculous. It was ambitious. And together, we chased it.

Test day came. I remembered Sameer—a student who ghosted my efforts despite months of investment. I didn't expect history would repeat itself, but I looked forward to this day being in my rear-view mirror.

"How did it go?" I asked as they came back from the testing center, trying to keep my voice cool.

Mousa looked grim. "I scored a 55%."

Fahad followed suit. "I got 60%."

My heart sank like a bad soufflé. What had I done? I pushed

them too hard. Again. I should have slowed down, paced them, adjusted—

"Just kidding," Mousa grinned. "I scored 93%."

"95%," said Fahad.

With palpable relief, I joined my students in laughter. "That's badass, guys. Let's go to the discipline office and get you a day off."

We marched in with pride, knocking on Myron's door on the way.

"My guys passed."

"Fuck yeah, man," he said. "You getting them tomorrow off?"

"That's the plan."

But when we reached the sergeants' room, the energy shifted. We let them know how the students did, and the sergeants sipped coffee and continued on with their conversation like we weren't there.

"Excuse me, I have students who passed their tests today," I said again, trying to sound casual and not like I wanted to flip a desk in joy.

The sergeants murmured in Arabic. Then came the question I hoped was rhetorical: "What will they do for the remaining eight months?"

"Continue training. They've got hundreds of aircraft systems to certify on," I said, politely clenching my jaw. "They're examples of what's possible with focus."

"Let them leave at noon," one said.

Nope. Not good enough. "Excuse me," I stepped closer, adrenaline kicking in. "Aren't students who score above 90% promised a full day off?"

"They can leave today at noon," he repeated, turning back to his coffee.

"*Shukran,*" I said before turning to Mousa and Fahad, fuming. "You deserve better," I said as we walked back to my classroom.

"It's okay, Mr. Chris," Mousa said. "Thanks for trying."

I paused. Screw it.

"You know what? Go home. Don't come in tomorrow."

Fahad blinked. "Are you sure? Won't that get you in trouble?"

"Maybe. Probably. Don't worry about me. Just go enjoy the win."

I wanted to strike the balance between honoring others' traditions and questioning my own assumptions, between pushing hard and being kind, between being a lone wolf and a justice warrior. In that dusty Saudi classroom, I realized the goal isn't to be perfect. It's to get a little better, a little more open, a little less reactive. Every test, every misstep, every weirdly translated peanut product—it's all part of the curriculum.

And damn if I'm not trying to pass with at least a 93%.

Even before I opened my eyes, I remembered my mission: *catch Rodolfo in Santiago.* I left Triacastela at 0700 and reached Sarria four hours later, legs humming like tuned guitar strings. I had planned to rest there, sip something warm and gaze into the drizzle like a pensive French film character—but no. I couldn't stop. Not when my friend was waiting. The rain draped itself over everything like a wet wool blanket, and while it didn't slow me down, it also didn't exactly write me any postcards.

It wasn't until Barbadelo—twenty-three kilometers in—when things got biblical. The top of my left foot started whispering: Hey . . . do you feel that? That's gonna suck soon. Nine kilometers later, arriving in Portomarín, that whisper had turned into a banshee scream. When I finally stumbled into an open albergue, I was hobbling like a wounded knight returning from battle. I should've stopped in Sarria. I knew it. I felt like a stubborn child trying to outrun his own shadow.

Normally, I avoid aspirin like I avoid small talk at parties, but when the hospitelera handed me some ibuprofen, I accepted it like holy communion. I went to bed early, humbled, reminded that my body wasn't an unlimited resource. I told myself: If you don't see Rodolfo in Santiago, you'll see him in Brazil. Maybe. Someday.

The Camino hadn't just shown me the bones of old churches and dusty saints; it had shown me the living, breathing faith of its pilgrims. It wasn't about relics or rituals—it was about the resilience of human hearts across time. Cultures rising, falling, reaching for transcendence. The more I traveled, the more I realized that true spirituality wasn't built from certainty but from curiosity, compassion, and the occasional course correction. Every pilgrim who made it to Santiago had one thing in common—they didn't overdo it like I did.

I began to pace myself. I drank water even when I wasn't thirsty. I took breaks even when I felt invincible. From Portomarín to Arzúa— my biggest day on the Camino—I kept a slow, steady rhythm.

The Camino softened. Not just with the rain, but with new pilgrims. They moved like drifting clouds, slower but sure-footed, fresh legs and wide eyes. Every time I asked if they'd seen a happy Brazilian in a red jacket, their faces lit up. "Oh yes! He's ahead!" With every step, I was catching up. Not just to Rodolfo—but to the end. I reached Arzúa, with only 39 kilometers left, and went to bed in a crowded albergue with a full belly and a quiet mind. No pain. No dreams. Just rest.

I woke under a sky so clear it looked scrubbed clean by angels. Winged feet carried me across sun-splashed fields and cobbled lanes. When I finally stepped into Santiago de Compostela at 1500, I had a stupidly huge grin on my face.

At the Pilgrim's Office, I presented my battered credenciale, stamped by dozens of albergues, taverns, and restaurant. The man behind the desk looked it over like it was a sacred manuscript and handed me the certificate with approval.

"Gracias," I said, rolling it up with reverence.

"Buen Camino," he replied.

And just like that . . . it was over. Or maybe it was just beginning.

Outside, I wandered. For the first time in weeks, I didn't have to go anywhere. I could simply be. I soaked in Santiago like sunlight—its Romanesque beauty, its cathedral bells, the laughter of pilgrims turned poets. I was about to find Wi-Fi and message Rodolfo when—

A pair of arms hugged me from behind.

"Help! Police! I'm being kidnapped!" I yelled, laughing.

Of course it was Rodolfo. And Joachim, both dressed like civilians again, transformed from sweaty pilgrims into handsome ghosts of their former selves.

"You need a shower," Joachim said.

"And a beer," Rodolfo chimed in.

I cleaned up. We went out. That night, we partied like underfed rock stars in one of Earth's most spiritual cities. We drank with pellegrinos from across the planet—England, Holland, South Korea, Argentina, Germany. The kind of night that cracks the universe open.

When Rodolfo left early the next morning, late as always, I hugged Joachim goodbye and ran into Dong Ho later that day. Over wine and museums, we talked about who we were before the Camino, and who we might dare to be after.

And then . . . the cathedral.

I announced I'd attend the famed "swinging" mass and everyone from our Camino family came—including Sue, Kay, Yong Hwan, Hansoo, Subin, Jurgis, even Francesca had all caught rides to be altogether that day. All of us sat shoulder to shoulder in the pew as the botafumeiro swayed above us.

I looked around the church and thought back to our first mass in Roncesvalles, all those kilometers ago. I remembered how earnestly I was searching for my own spirituality, and in that moment where countless pilgrims trekked to, not to mention all those who would in the centuries to come made me feel part of something greater than myself. The Camino wasn't a road. It was a living memory.

A heartbeat. A whisper passed from generation to generation. We weren't just following footsteps—we were the footsteps. Every shell, every yellow arrow, every Buen Camino—it all meant something more. I saw myself as a ripple in a much bigger river. The kind that holds knights and farmers, outcasts and prophets, and at least one American who believed in grace, even after all he questioned.

If humanity could leave behind anything worth keeping, let it be this: that when we get lost, we walk. That when we break, we share wine. That when the world weighs heavy, we find each other again on a dusty path with blistered feet and open hearts. The Camino made me more whole. It peeled me raw and stitched me back up with laughter, mud, and kilometers. As the botafumeiro arced over us like a great holy pendulum, I surrendered to the moment.

I wept.

First taste of the Spanish Coast

13

After spending two unanchored, dreamlike days in Santiago that felt like walking through an echo of something ancient and holy, Francessca and I had a plan. We'd continue westward to Muxía, then to Finisterre, that legendary precipice where the land surrenders to ocean and the old world ends. Afterward, we'd bus back to Santiago, then trek the Camino Portugués in reverse toward the city of Porto. I had never been to Portugal, but the name itself tasted like citrus and smoke, and the vision in my mind gleamed with sun-glazed cliffs, grilled sardines, and the kind of relaxed joy that only flourishes where land meets sea.

The shoes that walked me into Santiago were beyond ripped, they were dissolved by pilgrimage. Rodolfo, like a parting saint, gifted me his as he left for Brazil. I laced up his shoes the morning I departed Santiago, aware I was now carrying a piece of his journey forward with mine. I followed the yellow arrows away from the great cathedral and with every step, I felt the ache of leaving people behind. I'd just begun to know my Camino family—and now I was peeling away again. It hit me harder than I expected. These souls had helped stitch me back together after I cracked, and I wasn't ready to let go. My thoughts drifted to the sterile plastic seat at Abha airport the day I left Saudi Arabia and felt he same strange grief for something I was barely brave enough to name.

I cried no tears this time. The day was too full of light. I let the sun warm the sadness right out of my skin as I pushed through twenty kilometers to Negreira, where I found a quiet albergue and shared it with Claire and Celeste, two earthy sisters from Vermont. That night, I made a big batch of ratatouille and they brought a fresh baguette to the table, as well as Galician blue cheese, and a bottle of red wine that tasted like stone and fire. We sat outside and watched the sky bruise into dusk, laughing like old friends who had only just remembered each other.

The next morning, the three of us hiked thirty-five kilometers together, each step a kind of defiance, a refusal to fade. By 1600, we collapsed into chairs outside the next albergue with cold Spanish beers in hand, feeling our bodies buzz from both exhaustion and glory. Then, out of the late afternoon gold, Jurgis was suddenly there like some road-weary guardian angel. He'd heard about our plans to meet in Finisterre and decided he couldn't resist the call either.

I'd forgotten how much younger Jurgis was—he'd been born the year I graduated high school—but hiking with him made me feel like time didn't matter. Age felt like a suggestion, not a rule. His pace made me feel lighter, loose, more alive.

That night, when Claire and Celeste suggested we cowboy camp under the stars, it felt right—like something from a dream I hadn't had yet. We gathered wood while the sky dimmed into dusk. I built a fire that crackled like memory. Ramen and tuna tasted like a feast. The sisters passed around chocolate and cookies to make s'mores, European-style.

We talked about the wildflowers bursting into bloom all around us, like the earth itself was in on our secret. As the last warmth drained from the sunset, we slid into our sleeping bags and stared up at a sky thick with stars—so many they looked like paint flung by a desperate god. It felt like the edge of the world—like we were camping not just beyond civilization, but outside of time. This wasn't just another night. This was the space between stories, the place where epics go to rest.

I looked up at the stars, whispered a plea to the universe not to rain, and let the fire in my chest keep me warm.

Myron could be an insufferable micromanager even on his best, most well-rested, coffee-fueled days. He had decades of experience with the F-15, and he wielded it like a sledgehammer on a thumbtack. He regularly ambushed lessons bursting through the classroom door, demanding to know why my students weren't doing exactly what he'd expected. Never mind my syllabus or any trace of instructional autonomy—I was starting to feel like a marionette in an unscripted Kafkaesque puppet show.

Our flightline training center had taken on the energy of a prison yard—complete with bored inmates (my students) and jaded wardens (us instructors). Things hit a particular low when Royal Saudi Air Force leadership, in their signature passive-aggressive tone, frowned upon Mousa's initiative to work ahead of schedule for Ramadan. Initiative was only praiseworthy if it followed the correct bureaucratic script. Otherwise, it was just suspicious.

By the time my final season in the Kingdom rolled around, our instructor headcount had ballooned to six—despite having whittled our student load down to a mere seven. It was a far cry from the early days when Myron and I were sprinting laps around a full classroom of twenty-four. Now we had so much downtime, we could've held a TED Talk on the history of whiteboards.

That's when Paul showed up with an escape plan I didn't even know I'd been manifesting—my personal parachute out of the Groundhog Day loop I'd been stuck in. I would miss watching Fahad and Mousa stretch themselves to absorb complex material, but the truth was, I was ready to bite into something different. My job satisfaction had started to feel like a half-inflated balloon—technically still airborne, but awkward and doomed.

The next morning, the discipline sergeant wandered into my classroom with the expression of a man who either smelled gas or believed I was secretly harboring anarchists.

"Why are so many students marked 'Late'?" he asked.

"Because they arrived after 0830," I said.

He blinked back, equally unimpressed.

He then took over the class for twenty full minutes, covering the exact same rules I'd already explained every single day—like a boot camp déjà vu—but now in uniform and with the full authority of State-sanctioned monotony. I couldn't tell if this display was meant to bolster my position by showing a united front, or if it was just another reminder that I, the clean-shaven American civilian, could be overridden at any time by a man with epaulettes and an inflated sense of mission. I leaned toward the latter.

After the lecture, I dismissed the students for break and pulled him aside.

"Excuse me," I said carefully, "if you need to speak to the students, I'd appreciate a heads-up, and a touch of politeness next time. Especially in front of them."

He gave me a sheepish smile and clapped my shoulder like we were old war buddies. "You're right. Shouldn't have interrupted. No disrespect."

"None taken," I lied, the way people lie to in-laws, or on work visa application forms. Before walking off, he offered some closing instructions: "Just teach the course, keep the students here until 1600, and send them to me if they get out of line."

Ah yes—nothing says empowered education like turning your classroom into a holding cell with PowerPoint slides.

From that point on, I began to notice just how much ambient noise was eroding my sense of purpose. The bureaucratic static, the cultural undercurrents, the looming reminder that no one ever retires happy from this kind of post. All of it chipped away at the core of what I liked about teaching here in the first place.

So I started bribing my own brain. Tiny carrots. A pint of beer at The Camel after a tough day. A diving weekend at the Red Sea. Loud music on the ride home. I lowered my expectations just enough to keep them from snapping in half. Somehow, through this janky cocktail of lowered standards and stubborn pride, I held the line. Even if the job wasn't going to last, I would.

Sleeping under the stars was thrilling right up until the moment I woke up under a sheet of ice, shivering uncontrollably. I got to my feet and started moving on the Camino to warm up. Jurgis, Claire, and Celeste were still sleeping soundly, so I wriggled out of my sleeping bag and rolled it up as quietly as I could before moving away from the happy dreamers.

With Muxia in my life, I was free to focus on the trek to Finisterre and reuniting with my friends. I savored a frittata, which the menu called an omelet, while I drank my first beer to the beauty of the Spanish coast. When a field of lush grass beckoned to me, I didn't resist it. I was alone and vulnerable, and although I heard animal sounds in the distance, I felt comfortable surrendering to the universe.

I left my albergue at 0700 and caught the sunrise over the Atlantic Ocean at the Nosa Señora da Barca (Our Lady of the Boat) Sanctuary. The crashing waves and cool morning air made me feel like I was a younger man. It reminded me of my first glimpse of the Pacific for the first time from Monterey, California at eighteen years old, newly enlisted in the Air Force. Muxia was where Martin Sheen's character finished his journey in *The Way*, the movie I watched about his hike on the Camino Santiago. Unlike his, my journey continued on to a place called Lira, halfway between Muxia and

Finisterre. Claire, Celeste, and Jurgis arrived there a couple hours after I did, and we all settled into an albergue that only charged us six euros to spend the night there.

Celeste and Claire liked to sing Paul Simon songs, and I chimed in when they played "Me and Julio Down by the Schoolyard" as they cooked up garbanzo beans, tomatoes, cauliflower, peppers, garlic, and curry in a yummy casserole. I made wild rice and creamed garlic spinach, and Jurgis sprung for a bottle of red wine to enjoy before heading the following day to the end of the earth.

Me and moo-cows down by the schoolyard.

"El mar lo cura todo." (The sea cures all.)

14

very step along the coastline felt like a love letter from
Spain. The sun drenched the cliffs and sea in honeyed
light, glinting off the Atlantic like it was alive and winking
at me. With each footfall, I wasn't just walking—I was arriving
into something wide, golden, ancient. It was as if all of Spain, the
ocean, my soul, and the sky itself had collapsed into one radiant
afternoon. When I reached Finisterre just after lunch, I did the
most pilgrim-y thing I could think of: I sat down and ordered a
beer. That drink tasted like reward, like time itself had poured into
my glass. Sitting there, I realized I was in the same chair thousands of pilgrims had landed in—dusty, sunburned, fulfilled. I felt
small, but gloriously so. Small the way stars are small—pinpricks
in the infinite, yet burning just the same.

Then I heard it: Kay's unmistakable Korean shriek of joy. We ran
into each other's arms like movie characters at an airport reunion.
Behind her came Hansoo and SuBin—tired, hungry, smiling in that
Camino way that says, We made it. This would be our last meeting,
our final knot in the thread that had tied us together across hundreds of kilometers. They were flying back to South Korea soon, and
this sunset city at the edge of the earth would be our shared goodbye.

Hansoo's guidebook—his sacred Camino compass—pointed us toward a perfect albergue that only cost fifteen euros each. "You're the real MVP," I told him, thanking him for always knowing where the hell we were going. As a traveler guided more by impulse than itinerary, I knew I either had to start reading guidebooks . . . or keep embracing the magic of winging it.

When Francessca joined us, our little tribe of five hiked together to the lighthouse at Finisterre—the place where the world used to end. We watched the sun melt into the Atlantic like a clementine dropped in ink. For a second, I flashed back to my first taste of the Pacific in Monterey, years ago. That same cocktail of awe, solitude, and limitless potential bloomed in my chest. We stayed until the sky turned bruise-purple and the wind hinted that it was time to head home.

Dinner that night was nothing short of legendary: steak, pork ribs, creamy spinach, trail-fresh mushrooms fried up with eggs, garlic, and onions. Francessca had bought a silky chocolate mousse, and I uncorked two bottles of Galician red. We feasted like kings who had bled their way to the throne. We laughed until our cheeks hurt and our stomachs were sated.

The next morning, we made coffee and breakfast together like a little Camino commune, then wandered down to a stretch of white-sand beach that looked like something out of a dream. The water was impossibly blue and the sun was warm without being overbearing. We sat together and talked about the strange beauty of the journey—how people from all over the world felt some inexplicable pull to walk toward Santiago, how every footstep carried its own reason, secret, or prayer. The shell may have been our shared symbol, but we all knew the truth: the Camino is different for everyone. It's not a path—it's a mirror.

"You know," Francessca said, eyes glinting with mischief, "It's Camino tradition to run naked into the Atlantic after reaching Finisterre."

I had no clue if that was true, but I was already unbuttoning my shirt. Kay squealed. Hansoo got up and stripped next to me. And just like that, an American and a South Korean sprinted into the frigid bite of the Atlantic. Maybe it was tradition. Maybe it was something brand new. Either way, it was glorious. And cold. So fucking cold.

Later that afternoon, Hansoo, SuBin, and I caught a bus back to Santiago. Francessca and Kay stayed behind to soak up one more evening in that coastal hush. That night, I had my last dinner with Hansoo and SuBin in the Pilgrim's Capital. One final bottle of Santiago red. One final toast. One final shared silence. We promised to stay in touch, and tears welled up when we hugged goodbye. Not because we doubted our bond, but because we knew: no Camino friendship is ever quite the same when it leaves the trail.

The next morning, I set out alone for Porto, heading north against the tide of pilgrims walking south toward Santiago. I didn't expect to make many friends this time around. This next stretch felt like epilogue—bonus footage after the credits have rolled. The greatest part of my Camino was behind me. I'd survived frozen Pyrenees, navigated heartbreak, arrived in Santiago, hugged old friends in Finisterre, and tasted the salt of the Atlantic on my lips. Now I was walking forward with no one but Francessca somewhere ahead, and a strange peace in my chest.

Working in Saudi Arabia came with the usual challenges: language barriers, cultural friction, and the humbling realization that "miscellaneous" was just as elusive to explain in Arabic as it was to define in English. Still, I tried. I learned to say *muktahlif*, even if I was mangling the pronunciation. Students laughed—not unkindly—and I laughed with them, always hoping that the exchange meant we were connecting, building some kind of bridge across the gap.

Even the best days had cracks. Cheating was rampant, and no one seemed to care—not the students, not the administrators. Students who showed up late were punished by their Discipline officers by doing formation drills in the sun, but those who whispered answers during tests were simply ignored. A system that punished tardiness more than dishonesty was one I could never wrap my head around. I kept thinking I could beat the apathy with engaging lessons, humor, and encouragement. I clung to the delusion that hard work mattered in this place.

It didn't.

Students with wasta—that insidious blend of privilege and connections—acted like princes, dozing off mid-lecture and smirking through feedback. Effort was for the unfortunate. Self-improvement was a foreign concept. What passed for ambition here often came down to who your uncle was, not what you knew or what you could do. A few bright souls tried—they studied, respected the class, respected me—but they were in the minority. Most others coasted, joked, and sabotaged the motivation.

Still, I taught. Out of duty? Stubbornness? Hope? I'm not sure.

The job improved, briefly, when I transitioned to teaching an officer and advanced enlisted course. These students were older, closer to my age, and refreshingly professional. Some of them were even fascinating—talking to me about music, hobbies, and the outside world. When Abdul shyly confessed his love for Beethoven, I almost hugged him. It was the first time a Saudi student had ever opened up to me about art. We chatted about symphonies and smartphones. It was, for a brief moment, fun.

Until the drive home.

There is no way to prepare for Saudi traffic. No textbook, no training video, no cultural orientation can teach you what it feels like to share the road with people who treat it like a warzone. Lanes are optional. Drivers ignore turning signals. Aggression is currency. What should have been a 20-minute commute became Russian roulette.

One Thursday afternoon—weekend eve, when testosterone and urgency saturated the air—I was halfway from the air base to the compound, white-knuckling the steering wheel, already bracing for the usual onslaught of tailgaters and reckless merges. Then it happened. A Toyota Cressida launched itself across three lanes like it was fleeing a demon. A GMC Yukon, plowing down the road at 120 kilometers per hour, slammed into the rear quarter panel of the Cressida.

The impact happened just twenty feet ahead of me. The Cressida pirouetted like a cursed ballet dancer, glass shattering in slow motion. The Yukon rolled. A body flew sailed through the windshield like a ragdoll and bounced on the road until it rolled to a stop. Screams. Honks. The chaos of men in thobes sprinting toward the wreckage. Some tried to resuscitate the dead man. Others took out their phones and filmed. The dead man's bloodied robe fluttered as the wind caught it. I couldn't move. A police officer banged on my window and barked something in Arabic I barely registered. I understood only this: Get out of here. I put the car in gear with shaking hands and navigated around the carnage—splintered bumpers, broken glass, and body parts I didn't want to identify.

Once I was clear, I pulled over and just sat, staring into the rearview mirror. My mouth was dry. My body was buzzing with leftover adrenaline and horror. I drove the rest of the way to Nassim Compound in a kind of stunned autopilot. I couldn't cry. I couldn't even think. Just . . . go. I had never seen a man die before—certainly not like that. The image burned into me. The sound of metal snapping, the thud of a lifeless body hitting asphalt. For days, I relived that moment every time I closed my eyes. That motionless, crumpled man haunted my dreams, his blood like ink spilled across a desert page.

In Khamis Mushayt, near-misses were a daily occurrence. Death danced constantly just beyond the windshield. Every time I arrived at my destination I was exhausted. The trauma wore me down. The constant edge of fear dulled every other sensation. I had to keep my head on a swivel. There was no margin for error. Expat work isn't just tax-free salaries, big compounds, and the mystique of working overseas.

I wandered through Santiago's historic city center with the hollow feeling you get after a long, vivid dream. I had a flaky croissant, a coffee strong enough to shock a confession out of a stone. I kept an eye out in vain for something familiar—a face, a laugh, a nudge from the universe, but everyone I saw was strange and new. My friends were scatted on the Camino, and though the sun was shining and the birds were singing like they'd been paid to perform, I felt a quiet ache. The Camino I knew had given me a kind of communion with people, with place, with purpose—and now it was evaporating into memory.

That feeling—that whispering emptiness—made me restless, so I started walking. Fifty-five kilometers in two days, straight to Pontevedra, chasing a rhythm my soul danced to.

I'd walked across a country, I'd watched the stars breathe, I'd wept, laughed, blistered, and healed, but there was something missing. Not in a dramatic, existential spiral kind of way—more like a quiet hum in the background of my thoughts, like a word on the tip of my tongue that I couldn't name. I realized I wasn't searching for the end of the trail; I was searching for meaning. The Camino had cracked something open in me, but it hadn't handed me a life plan. Instead, it gave me space to ask better questions—and to let go of needing all the answers.

In Pontevedra, I met Sara and Daryl, a Canadian couple who knew the American trails well. Sara and I swapped Appalachian Trail memories like war stories from another lifetime, and when I told her the PCT was waiting for me, she grinned like someone passing a torch. Suddenly, my life felt split between two beautiful directions. The Camino under my feet, and the next horizon calling me forward. I felt torn but by abundance. I owed the present my full attention, so I watched my thoughts and held space for my fears without letting them drive the bus.

I feared becoming lonely. I feared I was walking in circles. I feared I was running away from the "real world." I also knew fear was just the mind's way of asking for reassurance. If I could smile at my fears—even make fun of them—they'd shrink. If I was hiding from civilization, I was doing a damn decent job of it: eating tuna straight from the can like a feral poet, cracking jokes with strangers in Spanish, and airing my socks on Spanish church lawns like hikertrash. Humor, it turned out, was my best spiritual weapon. It kept me light when I started taking myself too seriously, and reminded me that seeking truth doesn't mean being somber.

I extended my lunch in Redondela into an overnight stay, sprawling in the sun like a cat in the final act of a romance novel. My book—A History of English by Clive Owen—rested on my chest as I watched clouds shape-shift overhead. I let my socks dry and my heart settle. I'd walk thirty kilometers to Tui on my last full day in Spain. This country had fed me in countless ways. Its mountains and meals and unpredictable graces had nourished something I didn't even know was starving.

By the time I crossed into Portugal, I didn't need to pretend I had everything figured out. I had hope. I had movement. I had stories. I had an appetite. I had the suspicion that spiritual fulfillment wasn't about getting anywhere at all.

"Wet or fine, the air of Portugal has a natural happiness in it, and the people of the country should be as happy and prosperous as any people in the world." —H.G. Wells

15

It had been days since I'd seen the same person twice—long enough to start wondering if I was the last character left in a film whose plot had wandered off. I hadn't needed my jacket since leaving Santiago. I moved alone through space and time for thirty kilometers until arriving at Tui on an empty stomach, as I forgot it was Sunday. Living without a schedule has its perks—sunrises, mystery meals, an inflated sense of freedom—but it also meant Sundays snuck up on me like a ninja. In Spain, Sundays mean everything shuts down, so I trudged up and down the rollercoaster streets of Tui, and eventually found the one open pub—my promised land of beer and tapas.

After eating, I explored Tui Cathedral. Even as a proud heathen, I felt the weight of reverence hit me like incense. Despite having seen dozens of glorious churches along the Camino, this one still took my breath and a bit of my atheism away. Something in the soaring architecture, the hush of ancient stones, and the dusty echoes of prayers long gone stirred a feeling I couldn't name. The Camino wrapped me in a spiritual atmosphere that didn't ask for belief, just attention.

I couldn't ignore how many people around me seemed to exude

divine confidence. They walked like they had God on speed dial. Meanwhile, I was still trying to decide if the yogurt drink had expired. It amused me to think of the Camino as a holy road to Heaven—because I was walking the wrong way. What does it say about my spiritual trajectory that I passed dozens of people headed toward salvation while I was moonwalking back into the world?

That night at the albergue, I connected to the Wi-Fi—our modern altar—and booked my flight back to the U.S. after two years away. The thought of being airborne in eight days gave me a flutter in my chest, equal parts anticipation, and fear. I raised a pint to the future and then lumbered through Tui's uneven streets like a drunk pilgrim-goblin until I found my bunk.

The next morning, I sipped my final Spanish Camino coffee with as much ceremony as a coronation, then crossed the border into Portugal with a song in my heart. I walked twenty more kilometers to a sunny albergue in Rubies, where I washed my clothes and swung in a hammock like a philosopher between two nap-worthy trees, contemplating the subtle differences between Portuguese and Spanish sunlight.

Two hours later, a couple pellegrinos arrived from the opposite direction: Yao from South Korea and Hugo from Argentina, both of them bright-eyed and buzzing with questions. I told them what the Camino had offered me—how the Pyrenees froze my bones, how the bocadillos saved my soul, how overexertion humbled me, how the Atlantic wind slapped me around, and how the laughter of friends warmed me in ways no sleeping bag ever could.

"God be with you," Yao and Hugo said before we turned in for the night.

"Buen Camino," I replied, meaning it more than they could know.

People often told me—lovingly, persistently—that if I would just give myself to God, the signs would reveal themselves. I tended to think if God exists, He (or She or Whatever-They-Are) lives in time, space, physics, music, longing, and the weird coincidence of two strangers on opposite continents dreaming the same dream. I might never believe in the God of scripture, but I believed in the magic of trail friendships, in the sacred joy of shared wine and stories, in laughing about religion without disrespecting it, and in honest questions asked under starry skies. I didn't know if I found God on the Camino, but I found something—or I had become okay not knowing. It felt like a kind of blessing to me.

After working in Saudi Arabia for a while, some of my students would ask why I wasn't married, so I'd give them reasons they hadn't considered before:

"I don't want to have any children."

"I am not worried about not leaving a legacy behind."

"No, I don't have any problems with my genitals, but thanks for asking."

"Why, do you think I'm handsome?"

"No, I'm not bothered by the idea of not having anyone to look after me when I get older. Is that why you decided to have kids?"

The students silently processed how people around the world live differently from them. I even suspected more than a few of them thought less of me because I chose not to have children. I heard "hike your own hike" for the first time on the Appalachian Trail, and I have found the adage applies off-trail just as powerfully.

To have that authentic level of communication and access to each other's personalities allowed us to better defy stereotypes purported by the media and television tourists. Discovering similarities across the globe has to be one of the most satisfying achievements I've always valued as a traveler. To discover unity across the expanse of countless obstacles is as healthy and satisfying as homemade ratatouille.

"Are you a Christian?" one of my colleagues asked me when we were alone.

I considered deflecting the question or telling a lie to avoid his disapproval or anger, but I felt compelled in that moment to tell the truth.

"Waleed, I am an atheist." I exhaled nervously.

"It's okay. You don't have to watch what you say."

That day, we went against the advice our superiors had staunchly given us about having such controversial conversations. I told Waleed how I felt religions didn't make sense to me and could often be toxic. I talked about how I'd been an atheist for most of my life without ever wanting to be one. It was the first of several honest conversations, and we always made sure no one could overhear us.

After each conversation I would ask Waleed, "Please don't tell anyone what I told you about my beliefs."

"I won't, Chris."

The following Camino day was overcast in a kind, gentle way. I could not take my eyes off the clouds as they floated dramatically against the pure blue sky. I saw the flowers in larger numbers under the warmth of Portugal's sun. I hiked forty-three rock-filled kilometers from Rubies to Portales alongside stray dogs, and I was excited about being just two days away from the city of Porto, the end of my Camino.

I rewarded myself at the end of the day with a well-deserved dinner before resting for the night at a Portales albergue. That I was about to complete the Camino walk without loss of limb, sanity, or wallet was cause for celebration. I accepted I was a lucky individual. Blessed, even.

When Face Jacket, a friend I made on the Appalachian Trail in 2011, messaged he wanted to hike the PCT with me, I felt even more blessed. With the next adventure upon me, I gave myself permission to begin thinking properly about my next adventure.

The next morning, for once in my hyper-scheduled, forward-marching life, I let myself not hit the ground running. I lounged. I lollygagged. I dilly-dallied like a man who had just remembered the concept of brunch. It felt weird—almost illegal—but delicious. My twenty-seven-kilometer day got off to a fashionably late start, and I practically swam through the Portuguese sunshine like it was warm honey. Ten kilometers in, I stopped in Barcelos for breakfast and unlocked a version of myself I now call "Espresso Bohemian."

I sat by a baroque fountain that looked like it had opinions about art history and chain smoking, and ordered my third espresso and the second of two of the most absurdly sensual eclairs I've ever encountered. I'm talking fluffy pastry flirting with collapse, ganache that whispered come hither in five languages, and cream so silky I blushed. I lingered, pretending to be a person who uses phrases like "notes of almond" when describing wine, until a friendly fellow breakfaster recommended the Barcelos Tower Museum.

Naturally, I climbed it. From the top, I surveyed the city and convinced myself I could see all the way to Porto—thirty-eight kilometers away. It was either a divine moment or caffeine psychosis, but either way, I loved it.

That afternoon, the sky got dramatic. Three kilometers from my evening stop in Rates, the heavens cracked open like a biblical metaphor. I arrived at the albergue soaked to the soul, looking like a wet sock with a dream. After a hot shower, dry clothes, a five-euro pilgrim dinner, and a two-euro bottle of wine that tasted like cherry cola and poor decisions, I was reborn.

And then a long-held dream slid from the "someday" shelf into the "hell yes I did that" category. Porto, the golden goal at the end of this particular road, slowly revealed itself to me. A sea breeze carried scents of salt and mystery as I strolled in. Azulejo-tiled buildings winked in the light, Baroque churches stood around like heavily ornamented bouncers, and the alleys wound down toward the Douro River like veins leading straight into the city's beating, beautiful heart.

The Camino was over. I was over—over the hills, over the limits I once had, and nearly overwhelmed by joy. I paused any planning for the Pacific Crest Trail, even though it was practically vibrating on my mental dashboard. I still had time. This wasn't the moment to plot and strategize. This was the moment to bask. I would savor this city like a last bite of cake before beginning a brand-new buffet. I might not be a pilgrim anymore, but I could be a damn good tourist.

Porto gave me everything: historic tours, wine tastings, sumptuous restaurants, and art museums with paintings that might've judged me for wearing trail shoes. Like Rohan answering Gondor, I showed up. I shaved. I put on city clothes. I stopped looking like hikertrash long enough for my reflection to consider inviting me back in. I got word that Francessca would arrive in a day or two, so I soaked up all the modern joys: fresh water on demand, toilet paper in every stall, and food menus that didn't just say "menu del pellegrino."

It took about a day for me to stop smiling at strangers like we'd all just come back from a war together. The city folk nodded politely and resumed their inner monologues about taxes, renovations, and what their barista actually meant by "medium roast." I didn't blame them. Why did some of us choose to suffer on purpose? Why did I hike across a country to chase blisters and sunsets?

Porto spoke to me—not with words, but with its pulse. With its soul. I had earned this arrival, and in the marrow of my bones I knew: the journey had been worth it. The pain had washed me clean, and now the PCT was calling.

Josie, a fellow ex-pellegrino from my hostel, invited me to explore the city with her. We toured wine caves like tipsy archaeologists and found the francesinha sandwich the city is absurdly proud of—and rightfully so. It was a meaty tower of culinary audacity: bread stuffed with sausage, ham, cold cuts, and a beef patty, slathered in melted cheese, drenched in a tomato-beer-chili sauce, then crowned with a fried egg and flanked by fries like eager courtiers. I earned that run-on sentence and I ate every glorious bite.

When Francessca arrived, we reunited with Josie and a handful of new hostel friends, then wandered the cobbled streets like mythological creatures who had survived something sacred. We found a cozy pub, raised glasses, swapped stories, and toasted the end of the Camino.

The knowledge that I was about to trade the stone cathedrals of Europe for the soaring peaks of the PCT thrilled me. My legs were ready. My spirit was crackling. The fire that got me to Santiago still burned.

When Ramadan approached, I asked my students if it would be disrespectful for me to fast with them for a week. I didn't want to be the cringey foreigner who thinks he's being respectful but is actually stomping through someone else's sacred tradition like a clumsy oaf in hiking boots. "Be honest," I told them. "If this feels like a mockery, I'll bail. But I'm genuinely curious, and I want to understand what this experience feels like."

Sameer smiled like he'd been waiting for this. "Do you know the benefits of fasting?"

"Umm . . . losing weight?" I replied, shamelessly optimistic.

He laughed, but kindly. "It's not about that. It's about everyone being equal—rich and poor, everyone feels hunger. Everyone feels thirst. It reminds us of those who feel this all the time."

Right. So, not a diet. Got it. I wasn't exactly thrilled about giving up food—or worse, water—for most of the day, but I figured the best way to answer my own questions was to walk a few sandy kilometers in their sandals. Even without complaining.

That night, I went to the Camel Club and promptly lost five games of pool to Leo, a fellow expat with the soul of a Vegas pit boss and the grace of a hungover giraffe. "It's kind of like their Christmas," he explained, cue stick in hand. "But without the Santa, the booze, or the tinsel. Just the food. Lots of food. After sunset, the whole country pauses to celebrate—quietly, but with gusto."

"So that's why everyone's half-asleep during the day?" I asked.

"Yep. Fasting all day, feasting all night. Technically, you're not supposed to overeat either, but you know how people are when they've been thinking about biryani since sunrise."

My alarm tore me from sleep, and I stumbled to the kitchen for my pre-dawn breakfast: strawberries, yogurt, and an entire pitcher of water. I chugged like I was about to cross a desert. No food, no water until sunset. It was only the first day and my throat already felt like someone had scrubbed it with fine-grit sandpaper.

I remained professional. I smiled through meetings. I taught my lessons. I tried not to stare at my students' water bottles like a starving dog watching a steak commercial.

Two weeks earlier, I'd read a book called Never Wipe Your Ass with a Squirrel by Jason Robillard—because of course I had. He suggested training while fasting to build mental grit. So naturally, I decided to hit the gym.

Normally, I'd run ten miles, burn a thousand calories, then flex in the mirror like an idiot. But not this time. Eight sluggish miles later, I looked like a cartoon cactus and smelled like something left in a hot car. Still, I was proud. I earned every drop of that post-run water—the most delicious liquid to ever grace my dehydrated existence.

The second day was harder. The third day was spiritual warfare. By the fifth, the smell of someone's coffee made me consider morally justifying a crime. At one point, Leo casually offered me gummy bears, and I nearly tackled him.

I started questioning everything: Would one sip of water ruin the whole experience? Was this even worth it? Was I turning into an actual psychopath?

The cravings were physical, sure, but also strangely emotional. I began noticing how I tied food and drink to my sense of routine, control, and joy. Every minor annoyance was amplified. People humming? Rage. Coworkers talking about soccer? Get out of my face. When I got too cranky, I assigned myself solo tasks so I wouldn't accidentally declare holy war on my office mates.

On my last night, Turki invited me to iftar. I felt like I was being knighted into some sacred society—except instead of swords, there were samosas.

We sat cross-legged on cushions around a massive plastic sheet covered in glorious Saudi comfort food. There was cheese pasta, flaky meat pies, rich chicken stews, and an outrageous potato curry. I brought homemade ratatouille, which I introduced in my best Arabic. They said it "wasn't awful," which felt like a Michelin star under the circumstances. Nobody had seconds, but I chose to see that as a gesture of restraint rather than polite rejection.

After the feast, we retired to a TV room where Turki introduced me as "the American who speaks Arabic and didn't die fasting." The group of students treated me like an honorary member of the team. It was beautiful.

During one slow afternoon, one of my students asked me what happens to bad people who get away with their crimes.

"Well," I said, "some people are just sociopaths. They don't feel guilt. They might get away with it forever."

He looked concerned. "But surely they mut answer to someone?"

I asked him who created Allah.

"No one," he said. "Allah always was."

"So maybe," I said gently, "the universe just always was too."

He didn't fully buy it. That was okay. We respected each other's beliefs. These weren't debates—we were two curious minds on different continents of the same map, comparing notes.

I wanted to go out strong. I ran another hour at the gym. It was hot. I was dry. I was delirious. But I did it. At 1900, I raised a glass of water to my lips and swore I could hear a choir of angels sing as it slid down my throat.

I didn't feel normal for a couple days afterward, but I also didn't regret a thing. I'd earned a front-row seat to a cultural and spiritual tradition few outsiders get to witness firsthand. Even more importantly, I'd earned a mutual sense of trust and affection from my students.

Later that week, Leo and I celebrated my survival with fried chicken and French fries at Happy Chicken, which had never tasted better. I had fasted, feasted, struggled, and learned. I didn't become a better man overnight—but a little more empathetic, a little more connected, and aware of what we can learn when we lean in with humility, curiosity, and an empty stomach.

On the Camino—and in the wide, untamed reaches of life beyond it—I met pilgrims of every kind, draped in the flags of every continent and the quiet conviction of a thousand worldviews. Some people walked quietly beside me for miles without a single word exchanged, a gesture of mutual presence rather than absence. Others felt called to share their faiths with the urgency of a missionary breathless at a cliff's edge. Through it all, I learned to let people be. Blessedly, many let me be too.

People told me in many languages—whispered with compassion, preached with fire, pleaded in wide-eyed desperation—that I risked everything if I did not accept their particular rendering of the Divine. That without formal allegiance to their Book, their prophet, their rituals, I was a wanderer in the dark. That all my efforts—my kindness, my health, my clarity, my love—amounted to nothing without a specific prayer whispered in a specific tongue to a specific God.

I worked to cultivate habits to ground me—curiosity, gratitude, kindness, sweat. These are the disciplines I chose. The fruits of these habits: resilience, awe, a deep and quiet joy didn't need me to shout them out. I guess I' preferred to write about them in a book, instead.

There were those who insisted that I couldn't live my best life until I followed the God of the Bible. Or the Quran. Or the Talmud.

And to that, I could only smile.

I no longer wanted to argue. I didn't need to. The path I walked was not one of rebellion, but reverence. I thanked them sincerely for caring enough to share their truth—and then I carried on, attending the service of the nature around me. The rustle of wind in eucalyptus trees. The curve of a distant mountain that mirrors the arc of an open palm. The silence of a sunrise. Those were my temples. My altars. My scripture.

I've always pondered faith—every flavor, every thread of it. The Quran's poetry. The Torah's stubborn wrestling. The Bible's thunder and light. The way Buddhist monks smile like they know something you forgot. The way Hindus celebrate divinity in color, and the way animists see God's fingerprints in stones, feathers, and bones. It's all beautiful. I no longer tended to think enlightenment and grace passed through only one gate. I learned to trust the long path, the open horizon, and the questions that didn't demand immediate answers. I came to believe that sincere seekers of truth, love, and humility walked parallel roads—even if our destinations went by different names. A full life wasn't confined to a pew or a prayer rug. Enlightenment was in letting others believe as they must—and still loving them deeply. It makes sense to me that if God ever wanted anything from us, that would be it.

"Vienna is a handsome, lively city, and pleases me exceedingly." —Frederic Chopin

16

I went once more to the Red Sea before leaving Saudi Arabia. A handful of us, including Leo, arrived at Frenchman's Beach, near the hamlet of Al Birk, and it hit me how so much warmer sea level was. King Khalid Air Base and Nassim Compound had us working and living at 7,000 feet. Despite the sweat-inducing heat, the breeze was refreshing. I ran into the crashing waves of the very sea Catholic school once had me believe that Moses had once parted. Even though I'd seen the showcase of vividly colored fish of all shapes and sizes, I still swam with them as a part of their underwater flight as though it was the first time. Not everyone had such enthusiasm for sensations they've already experienced, but when it came to moments and environments like being under-water, that was my experience. Maybe I'm brain damaged. Maybe it's Maybelline. I simply could never get enough of the sunlight shimmering against the coral. Bathed in wonder, I looked in every direction and befriended fish as they passed by coral formations without a second glance.

"Look at your home, all the shades of blue and red, don't you like it?" I said to a large flat fish with yellow highlights hovering near my scuba mask.

I suddenly felt silly. *"Ahelen wa sahellen!"* I said, realizing my mistake and hoping Arabic would make me better understood to these local fish.

The fish ignored me still, as if I was just another unthreatening part of the background. Laughter bubbles tickled my face while I swam away from my conversational goals with my fish friends. Being underwater was nothing less than traveling to an alien world. Here, I gently flew above and around fish that sometimes ignored me, sometimes swam circles around me as I stared back; two species, curious and free. I never forgot I was like a stranger. I conducted myself the same way underwater as I did in a foreign country, with respect, grace, and dignity. I was careful not to touch anything, but I couldn't resist exploring while keeping an eye out for sharks and the like. I splashed my way back and looked from the water onto the beach. I traipsed up the beach to where my friends were, careful to step around piles of sun-bleached water bottles, burger wrappers, unpaired shoes, and a car tire. The obscene mass of litter didn't stop with the land. Flotillas of garbage undulated in clumps of plants in the sea. Even after spending years in Saudi Arabia, I still wasn't used to the neverending trashscape.

We started a campfire and dined on grilled chicken, steak flanks, potato salad, pancit, and cookies for dessert. Since the Saudi locals hardly ever spent time at the beach on hot days like this, the girls in our group ignored the requirement for women to wear their body-covering *abayas*. After we cleaned up from dinner we brought out a couple tall plastic water bottles filled with homemade vodka we had carefully packed away from Saudi eyes. The evening painted an image of beach frivolity that belonged anywhere but Saudi Arabia right up until distant headlights shined on our campfire. The girls went into the vehicles while we turned off the music, hid all the red Solo cups of disobedience and played it cool as the Saudi Coast Guardsman pulled in and rolled his window down.

"Massah al khrehr!" I greeted him. *Good evening.*

Even though I didn't understand everything he replied, I understood this was a routine beach patrol.

"*Assif, la arrif,*" I confessed. *I'm sorry, I don't understand.*

"Passports," the officer said clearly, gesturing to each of us.

We handed him our passports. After a half hour holding onto our documents and verifying our information, the patrol officer smiled and handed our passports back to us.

"*Ma'a salaam,*" I said to him. *Peace be with you.* He replied in kind and slowly drove off to keep the kingdom's shores safe. We were close to the Yemen border, so we weren't surprised authorities maintained a vigilant watch for undocumented immigrants. After the patrol car lights vanished in the distance we turned on the music, sang around the campfire, and admired the shooting stars above us as we passed around bottles of vodka. I couldn't decide if I wanted to stare at the campfire or the constellations. We laughed at stupid jokes, wondered about the universe, then went for a swim as one of my friends drunkenly mused, "the ocean is full of stars."

The realization that I'd been so focused on my obstacles at work, flaws within myself, and even the litter that imprisoned my attention span, I'd ignored the infinite majesty of the cosmos. I'd been thinking of myself as an optimist, a child of the world. What a fool I'd been, neglecting the inconceivable beauty around me to spend so much of what precious little time I had focusing on temporary disappointments.

I dared to do better.

"I'm glad we did the Camino Santiago," I said to Francessca as we hugged goodbye at Brixen's train station. "I hope you love teaching English in China."

"Take lots of PCT pictures. Be safe."

"I will."

I envied the future she was heading for even as the train spirited me to Vienna. I had a day to explore Vienna before catching my flight to the United States, so I found a quaint restaurant and ordered garlic soup and a cordon bleu. I spent an hour touring the Belvedere Museum, then wandered around St. Stephen's Cathedral while a choir sang with exalted voices.

Airports are the best kind of nowhere. They're like a spa where you're stripped of all obligations except showing up at the right gate in clean pants. No one expects anything from you in an airport, except to remove your shoes and pretend your toothpaste isn't a threat to national security. Honestly, it's the closest thing to purgatory I've ever experienced—except with overpriced hummus wraps and questionable massage chairs.

In this fleeting, in-between space, I nestled into a plastic seat that vibrated every time someone walked past and popped in my headphones. With my Camino-weary body and mind somewhere between Santiago and Seattle, I started tuning into the internal hum of "What now?" voices that always get louder at departure gates. You know the ones: Did I forget something important? Did I savor enough of this place?

I glanced around. Most people seemed like they had life figured out—the kind of folks with tidy pensions, regular dentist appointments, and meal-prepped quinoa in their fridge. Their faces carried the serene smugness of routine. Mine, on the other hand, said, This guy packed six books, two passport pouches, and absolutely zero chill.

I scanned my collection again: Why the World Around You Isn't as it Appears by Albert Linderman, Kama Sutra (for academic purposes, of course), The Ultimate Hong Kong Travel Guide, History in English Words, What I Was Doing While You Were Breeding (relatable), and halfway through America Unchained—because who doesn't want to read about road-tripping through the U.S. while boarding a flight to, well, road-trip through the U.S.? If your luggage reflects your fears, mine screamed, Dear God, please don't let me be bored for five minutes.

I'd spent much of my adult life dodging the gravitational pull of routine like it was an asteroid hell-bent on killing my imagination. Still, I couldn't help but feel a soft envy for the people who found peace in predictable rhythms. The ones who had weekly grocery lists and went jogging with people they actually knew. I'd romanticized spontaneity a bit too much—maybe having a real address and a stocked fridge could be its own kind of rebellion.

As my flight time crept closer, the idea of creating a home no longer sounded like a trap but a new frontier. A place where I could host wild, wine-fueled reunions, collapse after big hikes, cook ratatouille without translating it, and maybe—just maybe—build a little patch of something that didn't vanish the second I zipped up my backpack.

Leaving Europe felt sudden—like I'd only just arrived and the continent was still untangling itself from my shoelaces. Beneath the parting ache was the bubbling joy of going home to people who knew my stories and my laugh, to meals I didn't have to explain, to a bed that remembered the shape of me. Two years was too long to be away, and my heart beat louder with every tick of the departure board.

The wilderness still had my name carved in it somewhere, and the trail never stopped calling. But right then, I didn't have to define myself. Was I a secular spiritualist with a passport addiction? A barefoot atheist with a reverence for sacred silence? A Camino pilgrim-turned-suburbanite? All of the above?

Maybe identity was less of a fixed point and more of a playlist. Chantal Kreviazuk's voice drifted through my headphones. I sat with the courage to face the unknown and the faith to believe something beautiful was waiting.

Returning to my home country and reuniting with my brother felt like exhaling for the first time in months. The pressure to plan, to figure out the next big thing, melted under the easy rhythm of our banter. We were two melodies from the same composer—distinct but harmonizing effortlessly, syncing across years and distance without a hiccup. With him, I didn't have to be anything except exactly who I was, and for a traveler living mostly between goodbyes and new hellos, that kind of grounding was rare, almost holy.

When I passed through Albuquerque, a stillness settled over me. Not heavy or dull—different. After the noise of foreign cities, crowded dorms, and the ever-churning questions of What's Next?, the quiet felt like an invitation. I'd always seen the world as my home, a patchwork of sunrises and station stops, but now—sitting in that desert light—I realized how aware I was of my own transience. Albuquerque had never claimed to be my forever, and I had never promised it anything in return. But still, something in the silence held me.

I played my music loud—rebelliously loud—like it could hold back time, or at least mute the background static of uncertainty. Music has always been my lifeline, my translator when I didn't know what I felt, my refuge when everything else crumbled. After every heartbreak, every death, every "I'm sorry" said too late, music stitched me back together. It didn't ask for words. It just asked that I feel.

Then, as if summoned by the beat of my restlessness, adventure called again.

I coordinated with Face Jacket, my next hiking partner, to meet in California for our northbound assault on the Pacific Crest Trail. We plotted mileage between trail towns, downloaded the latest PCT app—our sleek, digital, mapless future. I took inventory of my gear: a new ultralight shelter, tougher trail runners, fewer comforts, more faith. I folded away the shoes Rodolfo had given me in Santiago like they were relics, symbols of a chapter honored but complete.

Messages trickled in—Francesca was moving to China, Rodolfo to Brazil. Their returns to "normal" life were blooming beautifully. I was happy for them, even as I packed for more beautiful chaos. There wasn't a single day I didn't wonder where I'd land after the PCT. Hong Kong whispered promises. Graduate school in the U.S. tempted with stability. A quiet, pulsing part of me longed to finally sink roots into a place I could call mine.

But I couldn't commit. Not yet. Maybe not ever. Maybe the trail would answer what nothing else had.

Before the hike began, I flew to Las Vegas to see friends who had become like family. Susan—my sister-in-arms since Air Force Basic Training—met me at McCarran Airport with her husband Chad and their kids. They'd just retired from service. Their next chapter was opening gently, filled with home-cooked meals, new hobbies, and Sunday mornings not ruled by alarms.

"After you finish the trail, before you leave Washington, I want you to visit Whidbey Island," Susan said, eyes sparkling. "I'll tell my niece Janis to bake something sinful, and you can meet her and Jeff."

"Deal," I grinned, sealing the promise like a sacred waypoint in my mind.

"What are you going to do after the PCT?" Chad asked, his tone light but the question weighted.

"Hopefully, I'll have a better answer when I swing back through. Want me to bring anything from the Pacific Northwest?"

"Just your safety," he said, that old line of his softening into something more than a catchphrase.

The Camino had helped me leave behind ghosts I'd been dragging for years. It didn't give me all the answers, but it reminded me that moving forward sometimes meant letting go, not solving. The PCT loomed ahead now—wild, demanding, seductive. I was nervous. Exhilarated. Humbled by the unknown, but hungry for it. The Appalachian Trail had tested me once before, and this time, I'd be pushing through it in one go. My knees had arthritis and my fears had teeth, but I was going anyway.

I'd feasted on connection, family, and belonging. I'd touched stillness and tasted movement. Now, with no fixed address and no tidy plan, I boarded the flight toward the start of the PCT. I didn't know where I'd end up. But the trail was calling—and I was ready to listen.

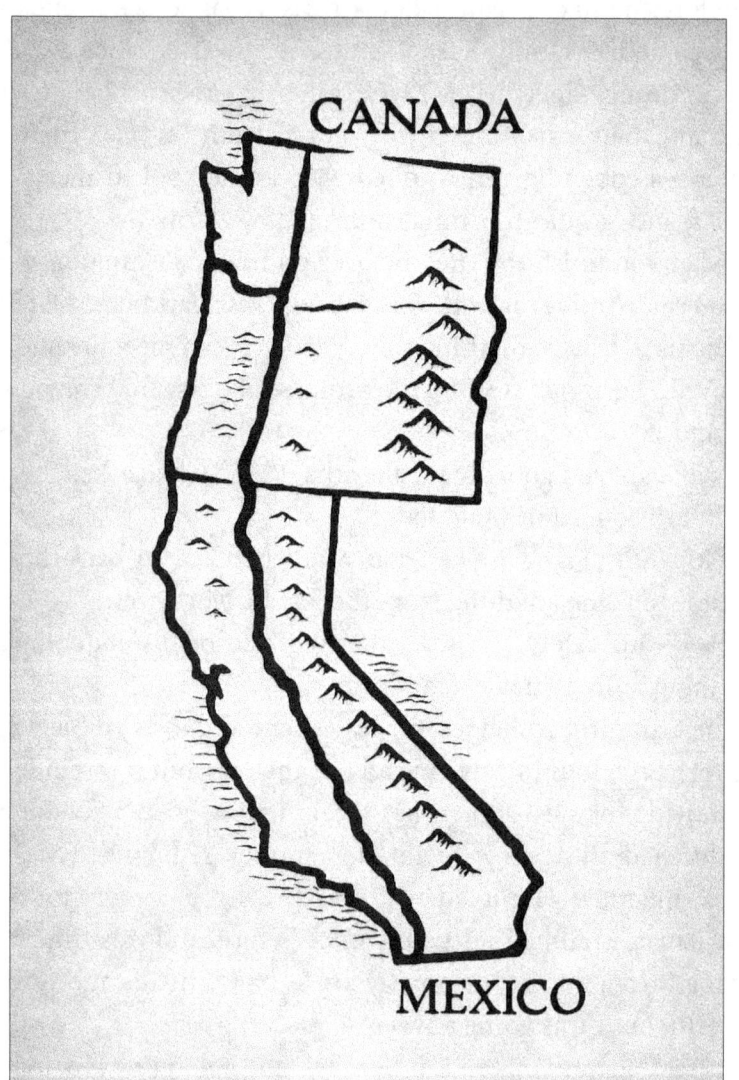

PART 3

Campo, California to British Columbia, Canada

"There is a pleasure in the pathless woods; there is a rapture in the lonely shore; there is society, where none intrudes, by the deep sea, and music in its roar: I love not man the less, but Nature more."

—Lord Byron

Windscreen & Face Jacket—Mission ready

17

After three weeks back in the States, I landed in San Diego, burning with anticipation, poised to hike. The Camino's dust still clung to my soul, but the pull of a new trail was stronger than jet lag or second thoughts.

First stop was a reunion with Joe, a battle-tested buddy from my years in Iraq. He came down from Los Angeles just to hang with me before I disappeared into the wild. We met up in the Gaslamp District, the clinking of silverware and the occasional mariachi riff providing the soundtrack for our table-side life check-in.

"Any idea what you'll do after the hike?" Joe asked as we dug into our food.

"I'm not sure, man," I said, half-laughing at myself. "Nothing's speaking to me yet. I'm hoping the trail knocks some clarity into me."

"Well," he shrugged, "there's always the Middle East."

"Ah yes," I smirked. "The land of sand, stress, and subtle existential dread. What's not to love about combat zones?"

He grinned. "Seriously though, if Albuquerque starts to feel too small, I'll put in a word for you out here. I think it'd be cool to be coworkers again."

"It would be," I said, struck by how generous that offer felt. "Let me wander a bit and figure things out. I appreciate you, man."

Then, like some kind of sentimental sniper, Joe pulled a Superman doll from his backpack.

My mouth dropped open. "No way."

"Oh, yes," he said, with the satisfied grin of someone who knew they were about to emotionally wreck you.

The colors on Superman's cape had faded into a soft wine red, his body a little saggy from wear, but his face still beamed that unshakable look of hope that made him iconic. I held him in my hands, and a lump took up residence in my throat.

"I can't believe you kept this," I said.

I'd first tied that doll to my pack back in Iraq. It was a joke at first—somewhere between comic relief and warding charm—but the longer he stayed, the more he meant. That little guy crossed provinces with me, hung on through the sound of mortars, escorted me on helicopter flights from Balad to Tikrit, and reminded me that even though I wasn't indestructible, I didn't have to feel alone. I gave him to Joe when I left Baghdad, not really expecting to see either of them again.

"I figured you could use him for this crazy hike," Joe said as we hugged goodbye.

"Well," I smiled, "if you can't hike with me, I guess Superman will do."

The next morning, I packed methodically. Headlamp, trekking poles, food bag, Kindle, journal. A week's worth of dehydrated dreams and oatmeal. Then I tied Superman to the outside of my pack using a spare shoelace, giving it a few extra knots to make damn sure he wouldn't fly off.

Face Jacket was already waiting when I arrived for lunch. His real name was Zach, but names from the "real world" didn't apply out here. He was Face Jacket. I was Windscreen. We had earned these ridiculous monikers on the Appalachian Trail, and they meant something to us that civilian names never could. He introduced me to his friend Beth, who had volunteered to drive us to Campo—the PCT's southern terminus, the line between our ordinary lives and whatever came next.

We wolfed down our final pre-hiker meal, our conversation ping-ponging between gear setups and mileage goals.

"Maybe we can squeeze in ten miles today," I said optimistically.

"Why stop at ten?" Beth smirked. "Do twenty."

"You sure you won't join us?" Face Jacket teased.

"I would," Beth said without missing a beat, "but I'm summiting Everest tonight. Gotta conserve my energy."

The city faded behind us. Asphalt gave way to chaparral, sagebrush, and cacti—like the Earth was shedding its armor and showing us its bones. The hot wind smelled like dust and nervousness. It reminded me of Saudi Arabia: sharp, brutal, unflinching. A place that doesn't care how ready you think you are.

That's when the nerves hit me—not butterflies, but something more primal. A quiet dread coiled deep in my gut. What the hell was I doing here again?

This wasn't naïve optimism like my first steps on the Appalachian Trail. This wasn't the spiritual breeziness of the Camino, where croissants and cathedrals softened every challenge. This was the Pacific Crest Trail: vast, wild, and unapologetically indifferent to my comfort.

The PCT wasn't going to hand me trail angels or albergues or well-meaning tourists saying Buen Camino. It was going to throw me into a desert without water for twenty miles, then shove me through snowfields in the Sierra, then dare me to survive the thin air of high alpine ridgelines. It was solitude in a harsher key.

I was—older, slower, with knees that creaked louder than a haunted barn. I knew too much now. I knew how blisters could sabotage momentum. I knew how injuries could slide in on silence. I knew how a single storm could make you question everything you believe about your strength.

So why was I back here?

Because somewhere inside, I still believed in the sanctity of struggle. I believed that even in the uncertainty, there was sacredness. That the trail wouldn't save me, but it would teach me—if I let it. That's what spiritual integrity really is: not certainty, but surrender. Not dogma, but daring.

I gripped my trekking poles, shouldered my gear, and stepped into the wild. Superman flopped gently against my pack, a faded reminder that courage doesn't mean the absence of fear. It means carrying that fear and hiking anyway.

For a lot of thru-hikers of American trails, the PCT has its own mystique. It's sleek, cinematic. It's Cheryl Strayed. It's John Muir's playground. It's the "cool" trail—the one with the Sierra glamour and crestline views. That kind of cultural weight can put pressure on even the most accomplished hikers. Shouldn't I be fearless by now? Not really, because the PCT has its own rules, and I had yet to immerse myself in them. The expectation alone made my guts twist. By now I realized that I wasn't not the same person I was on the AT, or even the person I was on the Camino. I'd grown, yes—but I carried new vulnerabilities and even new aches. Was I stronger, or more cautious? I wanted the PCT to save me from me and my life the way other trails had, and I was more than a little scared that it wouldn't.

It seemed that with so many things, no matter how far I'd walked before, that first day on trail always felt like stepping off the edge of a familiar world and into a raw unknown. That would always be the sensation of transitioning from Chris into Windscreen. I looked through the eyes of Chris at the desert and braced for months of feeling the heavy pack with essentials biting nonstop into my hips. And still, the trail pulled me forward. But it didn't pull me as Chris, it pulled me as Windcsreen. The trail still had power over me. What I felt was unbridled reverence. I liked to think my nervousness meant there was a modicum of wisdom within me, and I was because I was brave enough to be better. I didn't know what I was going to face over the next few months, but I would show up open-hearted, if imperfect. That was part of the pilgrimage.

"You guys want a picture together at the monument before you start?" Beth offered as she rolled the car to a stop at the weathered wood pillar that marked the southern terminus of the Pacific Crest Trail.

"Yes, please," Face Jacket and I said in unison. We slung on our gear like armor, both silently aware this moment was the edge of something. Beth was already on it, phone in hand, snapping photos like a proud mom dropping her two dirtbag sons off at war.

"It was a pleasure meeting you, and thanks for the lift," I told her, giving her a sincere hug—the kind you give to someone you've known for an hour but already owe something cosmic.

After Face Jacket hugged Beth, the car pulled away. Just like that, we were on the trail.

We hiked fifteen and a half miles that first day, which is either idiotic or brave depending on your hydration level. But it felt right—like we were burning off the last layers of the front country. That evening, as the sun spilled molten gold across the desert, we set up camp and stared into a wild new silence. There were no buildings, no headlights, no refrigerator hum—just a cool breeze, the long breath of twilight, and the kind of stillness that only comes when you've left the known world behind. I curled into my sleeping bag with Superman tied to my pack, the naked desert sky above me, and fell asleep trying to remember if I'd ever felt this far away from everything and yet this close to something true.

The next morning, we rose with the light, full of optimism. We'd barely hiked five miles, when we stumbled into Kickoff.

It was like a mirage that had taken shrooms. A huge clearing, buzzing with energy: cars parked in chaotic rows, music bumping from speakers, hikers darting around like caffeinated ants. A hundred or more thru-hikers clustered together in this temporary village of tents, vendors, trail angels, gear reps, and people in short shorts. It was like Burning Man for dirtbags, minus the EDM and glowsticks. Kickoff, also known as ADZPCTKO (Annual Day Zero Pacific Crest Trail Kick-Off), was part trail festival, part wilderness safety seminar, and part social jungle.

Face Jacket and I wandered into the fray with the wide-eyed daze of pilgrims at their first rave. We met Vince and Andy from Phoenix, Brandon from Flagstaff, and a woman named Susan who had sewn her own pack and claimed it weighed under two pounds. Every conversation ricocheted between the absurd and the practical: poop trowels, snowpack conditions, bear bag strategies, blisters, base weight, water caches, and how to tape a pinky toe without crying.

We were Windscreen and Face Jacket again—trail names, earned identities, self-assignments that meant more than birth certificates. Our friendship didn't require backstory. It had been forged in Appalachian rain, bonded over the dumbest jokes imaginable, and strengthened with the kind of deep trust that grows when you suffer gloriously with another person day after day.

Eventually, when our brains were overloaded with gear talk and unsolicited advice, we peeled ourselves away from Kickoff. We hiked a total of twenty-one miles that day, earning our first real trail fatigue. I was too tired to cook, so I gnawed through two Clif Bars like a desperate squirrel, unrolled my sleeping bag, and passed out before the sun even said goodnight.

Eight hours later I woke up before dawn, refreshed and buzzing with childlike glee. I'd forgotten that kind of rest existed. I paused at a trail store and bought a cheap sun hat with a little neck cape—instantly going from "rugged adventurer" to "lost Civil War reenactor." I didn't care. The sun was ruthless and the hat was a godsend.

At every break, hikers huddled in little shade patches, asking each other the most trail-nerdy questions imaginable. "How many liters are you carrying to Cibbets Flat?" "Did you hear if the cache at Rodriguez Tank is dry?" "Is your Sawyer Mini clogged already?"

We were like children pretending to be astronauts, trading tips for surviving an alien landscape. And honestly? That wasn't far from the truth.

My insoles ached like they'd been personally insulted by the desert floor. I gritted through it. The Camino had been a lovely, soulful walk. But the PCT didn't have cafés. No towns on the horizon. No gentle safety nets of European civilization. This was the terrain of thirst, lizards, rattlesnakes, and volcanic stone. This was the Earth in its feral form. And us? We were the awkward primates crawling back into it, hoping it would still recognize us as its children.

Out here, you didn't hike for status. You hiked for survival. You hiked to remember what the hell you were made of. Even though I was hobbling and sore, I liked who I was becoming with every blister, every dusty mile, every cracked laugh shared with Face Jacket about our aching feet and our bad oatmeal. The world had shrunk to two people, one pack each, and the long, winding spine of a continent that we had somehow convinced ourselves we could walk.

The next day was a burst of twenty-five miles, the biggest PCT day so far. I'd never hiked so intensely in a desert terrain before, but following the water report was a solid way to measure water consumption and manage expectations. Face Jacket and I decided to take our first detour off trail into the town of Julian after we heard rumors of beer, sandwiches, and pie. We stayed overnight in a hotel on Julian's Main Street and had our first showers in four days.

Smelling of lilac soap and herbal shampoo, we met in the lobby in our clean clothes and looked in town for the tastiest way to fill our bellies. Julian looked to me exactly like what I should envision anytime I hear about "Smalltown, USA" and reminded me of those cozy and welcoming towns I loved passing through along the Appalachian Trail four years prior. Towns like Julian are much more peaceful than cities like Dallas and Albuquerque where I seemed to spend so much of my life. I could get used to the cozy, friendly, simple feel of the neighborhood, where everything is in walking distance and the traffic was all but nonexistent. Face Jacket and I found the shop offering free slices of pie to thru-hikers, so we asked for a couple fresh slices topped with scoops of French vanilla ice cream. I picked the finest pie of them all: strawberry rhubarb.

After a great night's sleep in plush beds and clean sheets, Face Jacket and I ate a huge breakfast with bottomless cups of coffee. We were eager to get back out on the sun-drenched trail and hike fourteen miles before taking a *siesta* in a shady grove. While my strength and stamina were unabated, the heat made me yearn for even just a few clouds to block the oppressive sun. Flies spent the day landing on my arms and legs to dine the crusted sweat and dirt that coated my body, but the shade where we were taking our *siesta* was so comfortable, I remained there for two barefoot hours as Face Jacket took a cat nap. I knew there would be a full moon, so I gave myself permission to relax in the hot part of the day and cover distance under the cloudless cover of night. We would soon hit up Warner Springs, a place we heard would offer a respite for weary thru-hikers as well as a place to replenish food.

I acquired a taste for sleeping under the stars, on the desert floor, with the eye of the universe upon me. As I hiked under the moonlight (the *serious* moonlight), I felt the pleasure of being awake in liminal time and space. I wondered about the triviality of humankind, like how cultures perpetuated all kinds of racism, warfare, and exploitation of the weak and less fortunate. Such aggressive behavior negatively affected human health, but attempting to learn about traditions and histories in a neutral and objective way made critical thinking an act of enlightenment. More than a few people have claimed the collapse of civilization is already in progress and may speed exponentially quicker over the next few hundred years before exhausting crucial resources that sustain civilization. While I had no idea how many centuries we had until our civilizations collapsed, I knew I'd better figure out how best to spend the rest of my time in this life.

We had been averaging twenty miles a day, which I thought was excellent for the first couple of weeks. As if in a dream, the trail kept getting better. Under full moons and wide-open skies, Face Jacket and I found out how much we loved night hiking. The moon was so bright, and the desert landscape shone so completely, we didn't even need our headlamps.

Warner Springs didn't offer much of an actual spring, but there were trees around for shade and comfort as well as a recreation center that welcomed hikers to relax, organize their gear, and nap the heat of the day away if they wanted to. After a few hours at Warner Springs, I saw Vince and Andy, the friends I met at Kickoff, sharing a single Jetboil stove between them.

"How about that sunshine?"

"Hey, Windscreen." Andy and Vince greeted me with big smiles. "We're just making lunch."

"For a football team?" I asked as they sat down to eat a huge pan of tuna noodles. "You know something, I don't use my mini stove. I think you would get more use out of it." I said, holding it out for one of them to take.

"Seriously? What will you use to cook your food?" Vince asked, confused.

"I like to cold cook," I replied.

"Cold cook?" Andy asked.

"Yep. I soak my rice for an hour or two before I eat it. I'm always so hungry, I don't care that my food isn't warm."

"Man, it *would* be nice to have another stove . . ." Andy considered as I handed it to him.

"It's yours," I said, glad it found a happy home.

"Thanks, Windscreen."

"Do you guys have trail names yet?" I asked.

"Not yet." Vince said with a mouth full of tuna noodles.

"I guess that means you gotta keep hiking." I chuckled, savoring the shade for a few more seconds.

"Only 2,700 miles left," Face Jacket said as he sidled up. "You ready, Windscreen?"

"These miles aren't gonna hike themselves." I said, heaving my backpack on.

On the PCT, everyone was easy to befriend. The next couple days Face Jacket and I met new faces who answered to names like Second Lunch, Baggins, Catwhacker, and Pine Stick. We discussed our favorite movies, books, songs, and the food we missed to make the sun-baked miles less taxing.

The trail brought us to Mike's Place, a Trail Angel's Ranch for sore feet and hungry stomachs. Mike and his family invited thru-hikers to help themselves to burgers, grilled chicken, ice cream, beer, pancakes, potatoes, and water. Once again Vince and Andy showed up and joined our group as well as Brandon from Flagstaff, Arizona. After a few hours of refreshments and relaxation, we were all energized and upbeat enough to hike a total of twenty-five miles for the day.

The next morning, we climbed in altitude, bringing us cooler weather. I enjoyed a perfect view of the sunset from the mountain ridge. Although the desert was prickly and the wind was sometimes fierce, the landscape made me feel like I was still home in New Mexico. It was my home, wasn't it? I'd seen so little of Albuquerque these last three years I didn't know anymore.

Face Jacket, Catwhacker, Pine Stick, and I woke up on the ridge of the San Jacintos where we made camp after watching a double feature of sunset and moonrise, the graceful dance of an indifferent cosmos. I hiked like a machine as the sun rose, savoring the desert isolation even as I was obsessed by a restaurant I'd never been to. The first thing I did after adding my name to the Paradise Valley Café waiting list was turn on my phone to let the world know I was alive and well. Susan wanted to know how far along the trail I was, as she and Chad were planning to visit her Mom in Barstow and wanted to see if I could meet up with them nearby Big Bear.

I did some trail math and messaged Susan. "I'll see you in Big Bear on Friday." I became excited by the promise of seeing Susan and Chad even if it was just for a day. Nothing put a skip in my step quite like the thought of crossing paths with friends. Nothing except tasty food.

The Paradise Valley Café had a line out the door filled with hungry people, and, after polishing off a Genovese Omelet, I understood why. Brandon, Face Jacket, Catwhacker, and Pine Stick were still waiting in the crowded line, so I finished my plate, surrendered my table, and squeezed my way out the door.

"This place is worth the wait," I said to my friends as I put on my pack.

"Wanna meet up in Idyllwild?" asked Face Jacket.

"Sounds good!" I said, happy to get back on trail. Getting to spend time in nature like this, I remembered how much healthier my body and my disposition became just from breathing pure air and taking in the sight of land uncolonized by civilization. Surrounded by so much stark beauty of the surrounding unblemished desert, I couldn't help but speculate about the unsustainability of how I viewed normal living, and it inspired me to take stock of my place in society, not to mention the universe. As I considered the flaws of civilization, I wondered what lasting changes I could make in my life so I might someday stop feeling guilty about being a part of society.

"The trick . . . is not minding that it hurts." —T.E. Lawrence (played by Peter O'Toole)

18

I rose early with the kind of energy that would make a teenager jealous, then hiked ten miles with sublime vistas in every conceivable direction. Face Jacket liked taking long breaks,. Neither of us wanted to get in the way of the others' hiking enjoyment, and we liked it better when we didn't have a deadline or specific destination over our heads. The ridge was easy to traverse, and the trail descended gently into the small town of Idyllwild, a picturesque village I could envision Henry David Thoreau having coffee and buffalo burgers with John Muir. Catwhacker and I grabbed our own coffee and breakfast at the Red Kettle Restaurant, then I made plans to explore what the town offered.

One of the ways Windscreen and Chris Homan overlapped was a deep love for books and reading, so I satisfied both halves of me by visiting the charming town library. I shared photos of the PCT journey so far with friends and family around the world. Most of my friends and relatives enjoyed following my adventurous months of me posting nonstop pictures of gorgeous vistas, but there were a few people who responded with jealousy and annoyance.

"Don't you have a job?" one of my friends captioned under a picture I posted of me and Face Jacket taking a siesta under a sagebrush.

"I'm between jobs," I replied.

"Must be nice," she said.

"Sorry I picked different life priorities than you," I typed then immediately deleted it. I had a heavy enough load without taking on the additional weight of others' passive aggression and resentment.

"It is." I replied.

Resupplying at grocery stores was a fun part of stopping through towns. Perusing through the air-conditioned corridors of food and beverages while calculating what I should bring that I liked most and offered the most calories while weighing and costing as little as possible. Food options I never tired of included Clif bars, crunchy peanut butter, prepackaged rice meals, chewy granola bars, and peanut butter M&Ms. Finding a couple water bottles able to stand the rigors of the trail was something I'd look out for as well. The soles and sides of my socks had disintegrated to almost nothing, so I visited the local outfitter to gawk at shelves full of gear I coveted but didn't actually need. I settled for a couple pairs of Darn Tough socks. In my experience, there was no better sock for the contemporary thru-hiker.

I returned to the cabin where a half-dozen of us thru-hikers were splitting for the stay and feasted on spinach salad and vegetables, the kind of nourishing food I didn't get on trail. Hiking long distances meant vegetables were too heavy and cumbersome to carry for the few calories provided, so when I visited towns I indulged in fruits and vegetables I constantly craved.

Despite my love of Idyllwild, I had an early breakfast, then caught a lift to the PCT trailhead. After ten miles I felt like I deserved a break, so I paused by a rushing stream to rinse my sweaty head, replenish my water supply, and munch on snacks. I met Adam from Fort Lauderdale, who was hiking the PCT as a way to figure his life out after having been in rehab for a year. Adam and I took time to savor the beauty of the untamed landscape around us and agreed we were privileged being able to attempt this insane walk from Mexico to Canada.

Adam was happy to hike shorter days than me, so we said goodbye before I consumed afternoon mileage with the energy of a younger man. I found a spot at the top of a peak for my second break where I could admire the desert landscape. The weather picked up just as the sun started to set and the wind blew desert sand against my face, making it hard to see, so I packed up and started descending. The switchbacks were so acute, I was tempted to break trail and carve a direct path of my own down the mountain. Only my desire to not disturb the surrounding ecosystem kept me on trail as I kept my lips pursed tight so sand wouldn't blow into my mouth.

As the evening bore down on me, I picked up my pace so I could get to *some* kind of shelter. Rainclouds overtook me despite my ambitious pace, and I started feeling raindrops on my face. Not long after I crossed the 200-mile marker I found a spot to camp in the shelter of some large rocks, but I gave it to a couple of women who showed up after me who were even more desperate for relief from the weather than I was. So, I hiked another five miles until I found a camping spot just big enough for me to crawl into my sleeping bag. Rain clouds passed over as I celebrated my first thirty-mile day on the PCT by falling into a deep sleep without bothering to eat dinner.

Rays of bright sunshine hit my face as I shimmied out of my sleeping bag the following morning. Wind picked up as I hiked six miles to the famous trail angel destination hosted by "Ziggy and The Bear." The married couple welcomed me, and they told me I could relax there as long as I wanted. I was content to rest for a few hours sheltered from the fierce wind while I watched familiar and unfamiliar hikers pour in. I hadn't seen Face Jacket or Catwhacker in a few days, but they messaged they were only a few miles behind me. Even though meeting new friends on trail was fun and interesting, I still looked forward to seeing friends from normal life. I messaged Face Jacket to let him know I would be stopping off in Big Bear for a day or two and would catch up afterward. My trekking app showed I had thirty-eight miles until Big Bear, so I rehydrated myself, showered the crusty layer of sand off my body, and took a nap.

In the late afternoon I split a pizza with Brandon then returned to the hike. I like resting, but it never took long for me to answer the beckoning trail. I was addicted to the flow state I found myself in when hiking. It was more than progress, more than exercise; it was surrendering completely into the universe like a Zen parable. With energy on my side, I delved into the desert wilderness of the PCT to hike more miles. I made camp in an area crisscrossed by little streams and welcomed sweet sleep.

As I hiked deeper into the unscarred realm of California's Sierras, I felt myself blending in with my surroundings. Now I was more sand than flesh, reality took on a new perspective. Maybe it was due to me spreading too few calories over so many miles. The more I considered what normalcy was, the more my beliefs made me laugh out loud among the cacti. Without the stressors of normal life, the idea of being independent from what existed around me made no sense to me at all. The more time I spent in the natural world, far away from the noises of humankind, I couldn't help but seek enlightenment.

As a boy I read as much as I could about foreign and ancient beliefs. By my teenage years I became aware I no longer subscribed to the same faith as my parents. At first I felt like I was walking on a tightrope without a net under me. For many years, I wondered what was wrong with me until I accepted the self and the religion surrounding it are merely social constructs. Feeling these were arbitrary boundaries, I began to better see the world as a hopeful place. In the decades since my teenage fear, I found comfort by dismantling ideological and denominational borders religions have built all over the world (or at least the parts of the world I've seen). The faces I met on trail hail from all parts, but as hikertrash we moved together, united by a shared destination. I liked trying to understand what shared consciousness there might be.

I explored spiritual questions and cosmic ideas for days as I journeyed toward Canada and hoped I was similarly getting closer to the truth I yearned for before returning to normal life. Without socioeconomic distractions, I was able to consider how spirituality was goodness toward oneself and to others. I wanted to do good with my viable skillset, healthy body, active mind, and earnest heart. Just as the miles passed under my shoes, I was mindful there might soon be fewer years ahead of me than behind, even though I felt like I had only just begun to live. My soul embraced the solace of infinite possibilities of the unknown as I traversed the miles. I contemplated the known and unknown wonders of consciousness and what my place in the universe was. My awe and excitement grew as I considered fresh insights and perspectives, unveiling the interconnectedness of all things and the profound beauty of existence. It was an indescribably beautiful revelation to explore how my life might be one instance of the universe experiencing itself. I left my footprints over mountain ridges and under the shade of countless pines and incense cedars as my mind danced among the stars.

I camped overnight with Brandon, Face Jacket, Catwhacker, Pine Stick, and about a dozen others in a mountaintop cabin at mile marker 246. We bundled ourselves up against the cold, warming our bellies with food as best as we could. Jam-packed on the floor, we rested in our sleeping bags and spent the evening telling funny stories as the freezing wind screamed outside.

Hours later, I quietly slid out of my sleeping bag thermal layer, packed up my warm sleeping bag while braving the arctic drafts. Yearning to get warm, I walked over sleeping bodies through the cabin and almost made it without waking anyone up.

"See ya, Windscreen!" Brandon whispered as I softly pushed the cabin door open.

"Later, Brandon!" I replied before turning outside to put footsteps in the virgin snow. I felt like I was the only human being on Earth for a while at least. Hiking alone reminded me of thresholds between senses of being. If you've been in an empty high school, airport, or stadium, you know what feeling I mean. The trail first thing in the morning made me feel the same kind of temporary energy and mystique that captivated my imagination. I felt like I was in a doorway between worlds, an in-between place, where ordinary rules of existence seemed to dissolve into a sensation of pure potential. In these realms I felt a sense of both anticipation and trepidation, as if anything could happen, and reality could shift in unexpected ways.

I felt like I knew myself better as I night-hiked past snowy desert shrubs. I experienced a sense of being neither here nor there, breathing between the familiarity of the known world and the enigmatic allure of the unknown. I felt like I was momentarily attuned to the music of the wind swaying the trees as the earth continued to sleep beneath my feet. The wind caressed my skin affectionately and hungrily as if I was the only creature it could find.

Time approached gradually with the sunrise, and I saw my first sign for Big Bear. I left trail, and a friendly driver gave me a lift into town.

I waited until 1000 until I felt comfortable enough to dial the number for Susan's childhood friend, Robbie, who lived in Big Bear.

"Hello?"

"Hi. Robbie?"

"Chris?"

"I heard through the grapevine I might stay in your guest room for a couple days."

"Correct. Where are you right now?"

"I just had breakfast at Thelma's Restaurant. It looks like the restaurant that Sarah Connor worked as a server in *The Terminator*."

"I know where Thelma's Restaurant is. I can pick you up in a couple of hours. Sound good?"

"Perfect."

"Don't let the Terminator get you," Robbie said before hanging up.

I used my free time to upload pictures and sort through email. Roger, an Air Force buddy I was stationed with in Iraq, asked if he could hike a section of the PCT with me in the next few weeks. I consulted my map and calendar, then proposed we meet in Wrightwood. Once again, I had an appointment to keep with a friend.

Robbie offered to let me do laundry at his house while we watched *Star Trek*. The recliner I relaxed in was so heavenly, I kept winking in and out of sleep. When I couldn't stay awake any longer, Robbie showed me the guest room. The previous night's mountain cabin slumber party seemed like it was a universe away from the big, billowy bed I cozied up in.

Susan and Chad made the two-hour drive from Barstow to Robbie's house the following morning. As we hugged, Susan couldn't help but sniff the down jacket I was wearing. "You need to do laundry, Hun."

"I washed everything yesterday. Twice." I chuckled.

"You're so hikertrash." Chad laughed. "Do you at least have a hug for me?" Chad smiled back.

"Aren't you worried you'll get my smell on you?"

"All boys smell bad," Susan chimed in, making all of us laugh.

"Even *me*?" Robbie asked, pretending to be hurt.

"You're not as bad as Chris."

"You mean *Windscreen*," Robbie added.

After looking for a place to eat breakfast, we saw a sign that had "Chad's Place" on it and unanimously decided to eat there.

We caught each other up on our lives over refills of coffee. "Have you figured out what you'll do after trail?" Chad asked as we polished off our plates.

"I haven't given it a single thought all hike," I replied with a wink.

"Working is overrated. Wanna see a movie?"

"What's playing in theaters these days?"

"*Avengers: Age of Ultron*, what do you think?"

"I watched X-*Men: First Class* when I was on the Appalachian Trail. This'll be my treat."

After the movie, the four of us toured downtown Big Bear, then stopped at a supermarket where I took my time going up and down every aisle, savoring the enormous variety of everything to the point I almost had decision fatigue.

"Don't you carry vegetables?" Susan asked as she watched me put tuna packets, rice meals, candy, and granola snacks into my basket.

"Vegetables are fragile, heavy, and they don't have calories for energy. I miss them being a part of my daily life, but this is just how I eat during the hike. It's not permanent."

"Yikes."

"I know. You have no idea how much I crave spinach salads when I'm on trail."

As we hugged goodbye, Susan gave me a hand-knit beanie.

"I'm just happy it fits your huge melon," Chad said with mock relief.

"This is going to be perfect for snowy peaks. I love it," I told them.

Robbie and I waved as Susan and Chad drove away, ordered a pizza, and watched episodes of *Star Trek*.

I slept in on my final morning in Big Bear and journalled until Robbie came out of his room. We were still full of pizza, so Robbie gave me a ride to the PCT Trailhead where I thanked him once again for his kindness and hospitality.

It didn't take long to smell like sweat again as I hiked from the trailhead at Big Bear to the Splinter Cabin at mile marker 298. The tiredness I felt was nothing compared to the feeling of accomplishment that coursed through me. My sleeping bag kept me toasty warm as the temperature plummeted overnight. I woke up before daybreak and hiked thirty miles to the campground at Silverwood Lake. A friendly couple that I said hello to at the Rainbow Bridge arrived after me and offered me a couple tangerines, which I relished with grateful tastebuds. "I'm eating fruit, Susan." I chuckled to myself.

I took my second break of the day in a clearing alongside a small group of hikers, when all of a sudden I recognized one of their faces.

"Dave! You're here!"

"I wondered if we would run into each other in this section!" Dave said, beaming.

I befriended Dave at the Albuquerque REI when I was preparing for my Appalachian Trail hike five years ago. He had been hiking the PCT in sections year by year, and I had been keeping an eye out hoping to see him.

"I guess I should call you 6'2" since we're on trail."

"Well, then I'd better call you Windscreen."

6'2", his friends, and I hiked together for the rest of the evening until we found a spot to rest for the evening.

I ate dinner around a campfire with 6'2", Ironclad, Hendrix, Armstrong, and Honey Badger. They told me about a McDonald's that was just up the trail. Although I hadn't eaten fast food for over a decade, I wondered if I couldn't make use of the calories. Even if they were McDonald's calories. I checked my hiking app and saw that Wrightwood was just forty miles ahead, so I messaged Roger to let him know I'd see him in just a couple days. Ironclad, Hendrix, Armstrong, Honey Badger, and I spent that evening telling jokes and exchanging stories into until we were ready for sleep.

I left the campground the following morning at 0615 and said goodbye to 6'2". I hiked for thirteen miles when through the trees I could see the golden arches. I went off trail and ordered a dozen chicken nuggets, two cheeseburgers, and a large soda. The food didn't taste that great, and lacked any usable nutrition. After eating the mere illusion of food, I surrendered myself to reality of desert solitude. I found a quiet little spot just big enough for my sleeping bag only seventeen miles away from Wrightwood. I was sure that I would have to hike smaller days, and I decided to look at it like a good change of pace. I mean, if I was willing to eat at McDonald's again, even once, was hiking smaller mile-days so unthinkable?

I liked how the trail offered me a chance to develop my spirituality, and I thought that if I kept hiking the PCT at a breakneck pace I might not get all that I could from this once-in-a-lifetime experience. The trail was free of philosophical assumptions, premises, and myths, and I appreciated the world around me better and better. Getting to experience the greatness of the universe in this way helped me to pay attention to what was important.

Surrender to desert solitude.

In a snowstorm that couldn't wait; atop Mt. Baden-Powell

19

As I hiked the seventeen miles leading me to the trailhead at Wrightwood, people passed along the news that a storm was on its way. I kept my eye on the swirling clouds, and it was with great relief when I hitched a ride into Wrightwood. I spirited myself to the Grassy Hollow Visitor Center, where I saw a familiar face.

"I thought you were a mirage," I said as we opened up for a hug.

"And I thought you'd be fatter. Look at you."

"You still smell like diesel and regret, Rog."

"How long's it been?"

"Since we were in Iraq? Ten damn years."

"Here we are in another desert. We gotta stop meeting like this."

"This time we get views. And granola," I said holding up my snack bag as proof. "Plus, no one shoots at us, here."

"Speak for yourself, Chris. My knees are firing off warning shots every mile. Still carrying the squadron coin?"

"Nah. But look what I do have," I said as I turned to show the Superman stuffed doll secured to the outside of my pack."

"Oh my God, that is SO Chris!" Roger said smiling.

"You mean it's so Windscreen."

"Oh yeah, Windscreen. Do I get a trail name?"

"Hell yeah. But not now. You don't pick your trail name—it picks you. It usually comes from something funny, stupid, or just plain weird that happens on trail. You spill your entire dinner on yourself one night, and boom, now you're 'Spaghetti.' Or you take a wrong turn and, and suddenly everyone calls you 'Detour.' Sometimes it's about a habit—like if you always carry extra snacks, you might end up as 'Scooby.' And if you try to give yourself a name? Forget it. The trail gods won't allow it."

Roger nodded, taking it all in. "So, I humiliate myself, then get a trail name?"

"Pretty much." I said. "It'll probably happen when you least expect it."

"What if I already humiliated myself?" Roger said with a smirk.

"Nah. It's gotta be on trail. Air Force mistakes don't count out here, I'm afraid. For either of us."

"Bummer. Hey, look at what I found," Roger said, gesturing at the bottles of wine that adorned his picnic table.

"Napa Valley Cabernet Sauvignon. Just what every growing thru-hiker needs."

"I couldn't find any Rip-Its." Roger confessed.

"If you had, we could be at the Canadian border by Tuesday."

"Who cares if they tasted like battery acid." Roger said, feigning disgust.

"Not me. They still tasted better than MREs."

"Can you believe that we are about to hike this section of the PCT together?" Roger said, holding a glass up to toast the occasion.

"You never know where you'll be when you drink wine with a friend."

"Cheers to that, Chris."

"Call me Windscreen."

We finished the wine, then checked our weather apps. There had been reports of a snowstorm, but it wouldn't arrive until late afternoon the next day. It was already sunset, so Roger and I decided to camp overnight at the visitor center rather than be on trail exposed at night without campsite or shelter. Since I was primed for sustained hiking, Roger would hike slower than me and demand more breaks, we agreed to get up and summit Mount Baden-Powell by morning. That way, we would be safely below tree line before the snowstorm hit.

True to our ambitions, Roger and I started early like we planned. Although Mount Baden-Powel was a formidable climb for poor Roger and even a challenge for me to take in stride, we made it to the summit by 0900 Unfortunately, the weather was just as ambitious. Before getting to the summit, the wind and snow were already blustering around us to the point that our fingers and toes were freezing. By the time Roger and I made it to the Baden-Powell memorial plaque, the trail was already underneath a solid blanket of snow. As the trail disappeared into a white void in front of my eyes, I was gripped by the fear of losing the trail completely. I was desperate for us to get below tree line where we might stay oriented and avoid the possibility of getting stuck on the mountain peak where we might be walled in by snow for days.

I kept following odd trails, what I thought was the PCT, and kept backtracking as the pressing wind stung my cheeks and eyelids. I sensed panic nearby as I tried desperately to think my way out of our dilemma. Roger spent the last of his energy staying close to me as I looked for a way of the mountain.

"Chris, let's take a break."

"We can't. We must get off this mountain."

"I gotta rest. I mean it." There was no humor in Roger's face.

I stopped walking and faced Roger. "Follow me for two more minutes. Let's get to the tree line, and then we'll figure out what to do."

It only took us a minute to get inside the tree line, but the snow was falling even heavier. The grey clouds above looked like they were here to stay, so I took off my right glove so I could pin our current location on my phone. Just in those few seconds, my fingers had already began to lose feeling.

It wasn't the cinematic, screaming kind of fear of death—it was quieter and meaner. It crept in cold through the seams of my jacket and stung the back of your throat and down my spine. I felt the kind of fear that sharpens every sound: the sudden silence of the wind dropping, the attack of ice pellets on my cheeks, and Roger's ragged breathing loud beside me with the rhythm of a ticking clock.

The trees had thinned out long ago leaving us no cover. The sky, bruised and ominous all morning informed me all the weather forecasts had been optimistic. I had counted on a window, and now I felt the edge of something ancient and indifferent closing in.

I realized Roger was further behind me than I thought.

"I just need a minute," Roger whispers, and I saw his legs were trembling like jelly.

"There are no minutes left." I said matter-of-factly. "The snow's already erasing our tracks, and the trail is vanishing, man."

The fear isn't just I might die. I might have to watch Roger die. What if I can't get him down in time? What if this is where it ends for both of us?

I keep my voice calm, for him, not for myself. Inside, I'm flipping through scenarios like flashcards on fire: backtrack to the saddle, glissade if we can, find the tree line, move, just move. I realized that my muscles had been trembling with adrenaline and exposure and only the mountain knew we were atop it.

"This is what we will do. You stay here. Right here. Set up your tent now, and don't move. I'm going to hike until I find some shelter or building where we wait out the weather together. I'll message you as soon as I can from wherever that will be."

Roger nodded.

"Are you good with that?" I asked, needing confirmation that he understood our situation before I separated us.

"I am. Go find us a place to camp. I'll stay here."

I had no idea if I was doing the right thing as I pushed myself through the increasing snowstorm. A sign pointed toward Little Jimmy Saddle which was where I would have camped in decent weather. Out of the corner of my eye I saw a sign for Crystal Lake Campground. A small part of me thought of the Friday the 13th movies, but the idea that there was an actual campground with water and power was more promising than anything else I could envision in that moment. I deviated from the PCT at mile 383.5, having no idea if I was fucking things up worse than they already were. The possibility that I was wasting my ever-diminishing energy hiking in the wrong direction only caused me to hike faster. I lost all sense of time; the accumulating snow was the only thing I cared about. With feral energy I hiked on as my brain fed me one horrific scenario after another. I wiped sweat from my frozen face and took off my steamed-up glasses so I could see the woods better. I stayed on trail, even though I didn't know which trail it was. I raced with blurry vision through the whiteness and put more distance between me and my friend. My mouth filled with sour panic. Because I committed the sin of taking risks, the threat of danger Francessca and I avoided in the Pyrenees was gnashing at my heels. I could almost hear fate laughing at me as I ran.

I wanted to fast-forward to the end of this crushing anxiety. Would the campground even be open this time of year, on a day like today? The more thoughts that came to me, the worse my prospects looked. But it was too late to backtrack and hike uphill to where I left Roger; I kept heading in the same direction with certainty that it was the dumbest and most irresponsible decision I ever made. With only speed at my control, I moved my legs with the single-minded obsession of someone who was about to lose everything.

I don't know if I'd been hiking for one hour or three when I caught that first glimpse of a parking lot in the distance. I almost didn't believe my eyes when, across a sea of snow-covered cars, I saw a neon-lighted OPEN sign glowing over the entrance to Crystal Lake Resort. Although I felt like I wandered into a dream, I tested the door to see if it would, in fact, open. When it gave way to the force of my gloved hand, I became weak with relief. I walked into the warm supply store of a resort, past aisles of canned beans, potato chips, frozen pizzas, beer, and wine to where the aroma of hamburgers and bacon almost distracted me from seeing a park ranger refilling her coffee. She was suddenly aware of a frozen man's wild eyes searching for her attention.

"Well, look at you. Where did you come in from? Is there anyone with you?"

I liked how she immediately asked the right questions.

"My friend Roger is on the PCT right now. He needs help getting here. What can we do?"

The marshal keyed her radio at once and began saying words with confidence and authority. I pulled my frozen gloves off and dropped them as my trembling fingers struggled to get my phone out so that I could give the ranger the coordinates where I left Roger.

"He is right on the Pacific Crest Trail, the north side of Mount Baden-Powell's peak, at the start of the tree line. He's in his early forties, a bit taller than me, black hair, blue coat. He has about three days of food with him, so he's not hungry or thirsty. I told him to stay put, so he should still be there." I paused, letting her pass the information along by radio.

". . . early forties, black hair, about 5'10", blue coat, equipped with food and hiking gear," she relayed to the listening party, and my brain buzzed with unrivalled gratitude.

Copy, a man responded back through her radio.

"The snowstorm rolled in quicker than all forecasts reported, and it's gonna stick around for the next several hours, making the ridge dangerous impossible to him to hike through by himself. You have no idea how helpful these coordinates are to the search and rescue team. Have you tried to message him?

"I just texted him to see if he's in the same spot . . . no reply yet."

"Keep me posted. Reception isn't great, but even slow communication is better than none." She rested her hand on my arm. "Relax; you're safe."

"Why don't you sit by the fire and get some coffee?" offered the man behind the counter. "Take your pack off. Let me know if you want a menu."

"Oh man, thank you," I said, discovering even more layers of relief. I realized I'd been subconsciously expecting him to ask me to remove my snow-covered form from the hallowed corridors of commerce.

The sound of my phone getting a text hit my ears like the sweetest music.

I set up my tent right near you last saw me, by a signpost to Windy Gap Trail Junction, and the snow is piling up," Roger reported.

"Don't move," I texted back. "I'm at Crystal Lake Resort. Search and Rescue is coming to get you."

"Keep an eye out for Jason Vorhees."

It felt good to chuckle.

"I think I'm ready for a menu. I don't suppose you have a room for rent with two beds, do you?" I asked the man behind the counter.

"I think we can arrange that," the man replied, piling on me even greater sensations of relief. I saw that it was 1400 and realized I could stop worrying. I ordered two cheeseburgers, onion rings and a large soda.

"I have one cabin available."

"Two beds?"

"Two beds, and a shared bathroom. Want it?"

"Yes, please," I replied as I tried my best to act like I hadn't just escaped certain death.

Even though I was safe, I couldn't stop playing out scenarios in my mind where the team found Roger dead in the snow-covered wilderness. It helped that Roger replied to my texts, but my guilt for leaving my friend wasn't going anywhere. Considering the myriad of possibilities, I wouldn't have blamed Roger if he had wanted to end his hike right then and there. Six hours later, the search and rescue team radioed to the ranger they located Roger. The team then spent six hours making its way down the mountain with Roger through the still-ongoing snowstorm. I was wide awake when Roger finally arrived at the cabin at 0200.

Roger and I were content to stay at the resort for two whole days with warm hands and dry feet as the weather stormed outside. We preferred hot meals, snacks, and beverages instead of snow and wind. There was even a library of movies on DVD, so we weren't even bored.

While we were happy to be out of harm's way, Roger was as eager as me to get back out on trail once the weather was safe. Reception and Wi-Fi were both weak, but there were weather updates in the resort. Neither of us wanted to risk our lives in the snow again, but we were beginning to go stir crazy. I was envious of people who could shrug off such an encounter and chalk it up to adventuring outdoors and turn their thoughts toward other things. My overanalyzing brain liked to savor the complex computations that such an obstacle invites. I considered every option I had on that mountain peak and played them out in my head like calculus. As we put on one movie after another for two days I second-guessed my ability to act in a life-threatening situation, my trust in Roger to know his own limits, my ability to move the way I did without stranding myself off-trail in the snow, and the way I dealt with the unpredictability of weather. I didn't feel like I solved anything; I felt like I'd been rescued by dumb luck.

My mindset had been shattered and sharpened at once—like glass struck clean with a hammer. Warm, alive, and nursing hot drinks far below the mountain's wrath, my brain was still coming down from the summit. It kept replaying moments of fear and making me carry the weight of my decisions. I still heard Roger's breath stuttering. The white swallowed everything when I tried to sleep, only managing to rest when my brain obsessed over the brutal clarity that I almost killed someone. For what . . . a summit photo? A plan I couldn't let go of?

At least now all the mental clutter that filled my mind before— the looping stress about deciding what work I would do next and wondering if I was ever going to fulfill my potential, was . . . not gone, but gutted of its old power. Things in my head were recalibrated. I was glad for that moment when my gut took over and it worked. I didn't have a neat philosophical epiphany, but I did possess a hard, earned reverence for instinct and the unbearable weight of leadership when I tied someone else's life to mine. Beneath it all, a quiet question hummed: If I almost died for nothing, what would be worth living for? I didn't have the answer yet—but I felt like I was finally asking the right kind of question.

Thanks for the water cache, Trail Angels

20

We had two days spent playing cards, telling stories, and watching Wes Anderson movies. I'd become used to my hiking community, and I didn't like not knowing where or how Face Jacket and the others were. There were 2,500 intimidating miles of PCT for me left to hike, and waiting out the weather in that cabin forced me to relax and appreciate the fate had we had narrowly missed.

Roger had considered staying a couple more days, but I gently reminded him that the weather was, by all reports, sunny and bright. I could see he was intimidated and even a tad scared; it was up to me to help him get back on that horse. Roger graciously let me plan the next few days of hiking, and he surprised me by being the one to check out of the cabin after we settled the bill.

Once we were actually on trail, we felt energized enough to hike thirty miles. We came across chests of trail magic in the form of fresh fruit, water bottles, and candy provided by friendly locals who encouraged hikers like us to stay strong. We crossed paths with Honey Badger and IronHusk who I hadn't seen since the day before McDonald's. I was overjoyed to stumble upon Andy and Vince taking their break by a cool stream. They told me their story of hiking through the snow, and I told them about our near-death experience on Mount Baden-Powell. The weather on the ridge where a few of us tented for the night was chilly, but the night sky was full of stars, making us feel snug and safe.

The next day was a chilly one, but I took comfort in how there wasn't any precipitation. I hiked a little with Roger in the morning until he took an early break and told me it was okay for me to hike on.

"I have something for you," I said.

"You do?" Roger asked, a little surprised.

"Yeah. Your trail name."

"Oooh . . . tell me!" Roger said with interest all over his face.

"Snowstorm," I said, knowing he'd love it.

"I love it." Roger said with a hearty laugh. "I love it a lot."

I moved across miles like a gazelle through Vazquez Rocks, which I geeked over as a Star Trek enthusiast. More than a few episodes had been filmed there, and seeing with my own eyes how alien the desert landscape looked added a surreal layer to the hike.

A handful of us took a break in Agua Dulce and set phasers to pizzas and beer. By now our appetites had no limit, so all calories were good calories. Roger hitchhiked to Agua Dulce, and we examined our plans for the section he was hiking. He confessed that he preferred to hike fifteen-to-twenty miles a day, which made my preferred thirty-mile-a-day pace a problem. I confessed to him that I missed hiking big-mile days, and I asked if he'd mind us hiking our own hikes.

We enjoyed each other's company, but it wasn't worth one or both of us to feel imprisoned. We had ventured onto the PCT to find a rare kind of freedom, not a new kind of resentment.

With that, Roger and I parted PCT ways feeling refreshed, refilled, and relieved.

I called my brother Andrew the next morning to wish him a happy birthday. He was happy to hear from me, and I spared him the story of snow-filled terror on the mountaintop.

"It's super easy, you should fly out here and hike with me," I said.

"Ha! I would, but I'd hike so fast, it hardly seems worth it." Andrew said dryly.

"I guess I'll keep trudging along. See you in a few months."

Going places meant life taking me away from my friends and family, and it might always be that way. It was upon me to accept that, and trust that we would continue to be there for each other. My loved ones, hopefully, never doubted they were important to me.

I was a day behind Face and Catwhacker, according to the hikers who I met that told me about them. Catching up to them was possible if the miles kept flying the way they had been. With Roger and I free to hike at our preferred speeds, I embraced freedom without any of the pressure or trouble that came from compromise.

The next day Vince, Andy and I hiked at the same ambitious pace, and our conversations flew from religion to movies, to books, to the meaning of life. We hiked about twenty miles together and came up on one of the PCT's most famous trail angel houses: Casa de Luna. The hosts greeted us and showed us around their massive property, where there was plenty of room for hikers to camp out and congregate. It was a place made for hikertrash like me to gather and party without society judging. Familiar faces popped up around the sprawling campground and took advantage of the offers for laundry and clean showers. Beer flowed freely and songs sprang into existence. There was great energy around the campfire as if the hiking community exhaled in the same breath and celebrated life on the trail, even with weather scares like what we had all just experienced. I hoped Roger would make it while I was there, but I didn't see him. My mind flashed back to that wild speedhike from Mount Baden-Powell's peak, driven instinctively as if on cruise control on a long, boring stretch of highway without music through stormy weather, clutching the steering wheel, keeping eyes peeled for signs of hope. That yearning to stay alive had brought me to this moment where I was among music, warmth, food, and friends.

When I was in this mental autopilot, my logical thoughts operated unobtrusively in the background, barely noticeable to my conscious mind. However, when I needed to activate that slower, deeper-thinking processes, it could be uncomfortable and time-consuming. Hiking long treks like this allowed for remuneration, reflection, problem-solving, and long-term analyses across the miles. So much of my life was determined by instinct, so I savored the times when I had the peace and freedom to enter into the kind of thinking that enriched my life. The deeper I delved into my mind, the less conscious I would be of my footspeed, which made hiking with others a problem if they wanted to stay together. My body and my mind operated in a kind of flow that sometimes transported me to another plane of existence, far removed from reality. It was like traveling *within* traveling. Envisioning the Canadian border after flirting with failure and death in a snowstorm made the PCT seem not only possible, but certain.

About thirty of us hikers partied hard at the Casa de Luna that night, and I woke up for a hearty breakfast the following morning of pancakes and coffee before getting a ride out to the trailhead. Next was a long road-walk along speeding cars and trucks that reminded me of the Camino Portuguese. I'd become acclimated to the peacefulness of nature, so the traffic noise was something new for me. The road was level, and the sky smiled warmly as I walked the easy day to another campground called Hikertown and considered how all this hiking affected my identity. Windscreen was almost an entirely separate entity from Chris Homan. Windscreen never worked for anyone, never drove a car, rarely saw the same people twice, and ate like a teenager without supervision. Chris Homan had to follow orders, drove everywhere, got haircuts, spent time with family and lifelong friends, and had to watch his caloric intake. I noticed that I identified more with my logical mindset than my instinctive thought process. The reasoning body of thought that cultivated my beliefs, performed cost benefit analyses, and planned ahead was the hero of my identity, while my instinctive and nature-seeking side was the trusty sidekick. As I deconstructed myself I rolled over in my sleeping bag to get more comfortable and felt something crack loudly under my butt cheek. I lifted myself up to see what was under me and saw my shattered Kindle screen. Feeling momentary panic followed by despair, I settled into a feeling of acceptance, knowing I couldn't do anything about it. Without anything to read, I peered inside the chambers filled with uncertainty that filled my mind.

I had already hiked 517 miles, about twenty percent of the PCT. Canada was not an inconceivable distance away anymore. One of the hikers, Stringer, talked about how he was thinking about driving the Pacific Coast Highway after finishing the trail and had me thinking what exactly I would do after reaching the Canadian border. I thought increasingly about getting another college degree using the last credits on my G. I. Bill. All I had to figure out was what I would get a degree in. Languages? Helicopter flying? Creative writing? Underwater basket weaving? I had no clue which academic discipline would lead me to become my best self. Fortunately, there was still a long way to go.

Flying home sounded boring after the idea of a road trip started taking root (or taking *route*, ha) in my head. I could buy a cheap motorcycle on Craigslist and ride from Washington to New Mexico, especially if I finished hiking by the end of September. Gearing up for my post-hike life, thinking that I would spend a few more years living in Albuquerque and pursue higher learning, I decided to peruse university options when I had internet signal in the weeks ahead. Noticing that I had phone reception, I told my renters that I would be moving back to Albuquerque in six months. I'd already let my renters stay a couple months beyond their contracts, so they had the benefit of time to look for their next places. It felt good to move that first chess piece, and now it was my faceless opponent's turn.

I left Hikertown at 0615, before the warmth of the sun hit the earth. There wasn't a single drop of rain, and even though the first half of the day was as flat as a pancake, it wasn't easygoing. The miles of flat terrain brought with them a boredom I'd not encountered before. The level, unbroken vista that met my eyes in every direction I looked had become more difficult to bear with each hour, making me yearn for the maddening climbs and sharp descents of mountains.

Before succumbing completely to the sameness of the landscape, I put music in my ears. Far from water sources, I was beyond thankful to see a reliable water cache that trail angels kept well-stocked. I quenched my desperate thirst and replenished my resolve, pressing on toward Tehachapi with a skip in my step into the windiest section of trail I'd ever encountered. There were wind turbines spinning for miles and miles. The dust blasted me with indifference to my comfort and well-being, and I removed my glasses so they would not become scratched. I hiked for hours feeling like a crowd of invisible elephants was pushing me. I took a couple breaks that helped me to keep up my energy until I finally made it to the peak where I would camp for the night. Without a Kindle to read, I fell asleep watching the sunset, snug in my sleeping bag with the night wind swirling above me. I had hiked a satisfying thirty-two miles, and sleep was my reward.

I started beating feet by 0645 the following morning, and I stumbled across Andy and Vince in their sleeping bags as they were just waking up. We were all eager to get to Tehachapi and take shelter from the sweltering sun with a cold beer or two. We were already sweltering and caked in sand when we sidled up to the road and stuck our thumbs to get a quick lift into town from the trailhead. As usual, getting a hot breakfast was our first priority, so we found a café where we encountered the familiar face of Gazelle, a Canadian hiker who overtook me earlier in the week. I was in awe of how she moved as gracefully as she did swiftly, no matter what the terrain.

Gazelle offered to share her hotel room with us. Never wanting to miss a chance to enjoy cheap shelter, we accepted her offer, took turns showering, and left our backpacks in her room as we resupplied our food for the next big section of trail.

We relaxed in Tehachapi, each in our own ways. Andy and Vince made phone calls to their families while I uploaded pictures and answered messages online. By evening, we had agreed we would have dinner at the nearby barbecue restaurant, and when we walked back to Gazelle's motel we noticed the movie theater across the street was playing *Mad Max: Fury Road*. We found comfy seats and let the movie capture our full attention.

All except mine, as I suddenly had to keep making visits to the bathroom starting halfway through the show. Used to an ironclad constitution I didn't like what three trips to the toilet bode for my immediate future. Too bad for me, the movie looked like I would've enjoyed it.

On our way back to Gazelle's motel, I picked up a copy of Stephen King's *Revival* at a little library and left my copy of Neil Gaiman's *Good Omens*. I enjoyed reading physical books again, but I missed having the conveniences of backlit pages and not having to hold the book open while I was reading.

Andy, Vince, and I were thrilled we didn't have to brace against the sandy wind that gusted outside. I was additionally grateful throughout the night that I had the luxury of a bathroom for my body to expel whatever evil had violated it.

"Face it, Windscreen. You've been spoiled," I whispered to myself.

In between frequent trips to the motel bathroom, I consulted the trail map to see where I could have a new Kindle delivered. Jimmy, an Air Force buddy I was stationed with in Germany, was planning to meet me at Lake Tahoe. I asked him if he minded having a Kindle delivered to his place so he could bring it with him. An hour later my phone lit up with Jimmy's affirmation, so I placed an order for my Kindle without delay. What a time to be alive!

The evil inside me persisted, turning my overnight in Tehachapi into a couple of zero days in Tehachapi. I ended up getting my own motel room and was unable to keep food down. I spent more time in the bathroom than ever and used up more toilet paper than I care to describe. Although I kept the door and window open to let in the hot weather from outside, I shivered with cold in my hotel bed even with my down jacket on. I don't know if my stomach bug was from bad water or from something I ate at the barbecue restaurant; I was grateful to have access to clean water, medicine, and food. I watched episode after episode of *The Golden Girls* in a state of weakness, empty and tired of spending so many hours indoors. On each trip to the store, I saw more unfamiliar faces of hikers coming in from the trail. I could feel my hiking bubble slipping farther and farther beyond the point where I would see them again. All I could do was relax, sip Gatorade, try to eat food that my body would agree with, and wait it out.

I hoped my strength would return soon. Not only wasn't I being Windscreen, but I wasn't being Chris, either. On that bed as I watched network television punctuated by commercials for things and services I neither wanted nor needed, I wasn't being much of *anyone*. I was docile but straining to find inner peace as I examined my experiences. It could be discouraging when I looked at what I was doing with my life without emotional context. Like, why would I, in a world where cars and airplanes exist, feel any kind of impulse to walk across some of the most difficult miles within the United States? There was no answer resembling truth without incorporating emotion. By examining and surrendering to these impulses, I was able to keep my eye on distant goals even when I couldn't control the world around me. Giving myself over to positivity, happiness, and health kept me energized and inspired, even as I mopped my brow and waited for my health to return.

I used to be interested in comparing myself to others who were wealthier, further up the organizational ladder, fitter, younger, and more handsome. Learning to surrender the impulse to compare myself to others helped me to wish others well more genuinely. Conforming to the dictation of strangers could be like trying to dance to a song I couldn't stand, so I stopped trying to be a successful person and focused on being a fulfilled person instead. With that new mindset, I was more successful at being a healthier person in mind, body, and soul. Since then, self-doubt didn't weigh down on me as heavily or as often as it used to, even stranded in the desert with a stomach bug.

As Windscreen, I could free myself from my culture that focused on control, multitasking, getting ahead, competing, and growing profits. Trying to capture the environment and the outcome of our lives is a human impulse, but not necessarily always a healthy one. There have been chapters in my life when I thought nothing was more important than my job, where I would volunteer to work overtime to the point of rabid exhaustion, maniacal stress levels, and ever-depleting depression, all to get ahead and be "successful." Although I never regretted that kind of ambition and I never besmirched those who championed that energy, my life became noticeably healthier the more I surrendered to uncertainty and abandoned my pursuit of control. The more I invited spontaneity, the more I was able to trust that important and significant things would happen than when I micromanaged every detail of my life. I found that I was better able to embrace creativity, serendipity, joy, balance, and health when I succumbed to the flow.

God damn, my mind takes me on crazy walks when I'm bedridden. It was time to take the power back and let my feet do the walking! After two zero days in Tehachapi, I laced up my shoes again, feeling well enough to hit the trail. I was a little scared to face the harsh desert trail again, but nevertheless, I checked out of my hotel and had a big breakfast. Once I was underway, I felt nothing but contentment and certainty that the worst of my last few days was behind me. I still felt queasy, weak, and reluctant, and although I was frustrated by not knowing what caused my toilet torture, I was relieved (pun intended) when it became certain that it had run its course.

I hiked thirty-five miles on my first day after being sick in Tehachapi, so I felt as grateful as I felt powerful. The energy that coursed through me made me think that if I was careful, ambitious, and lucky, It felt nourishing to finally be on the move again and rest my head somewhere new. There were long stretches between desert water sources, so I was extra lucky to be at peak health again. I carried four liters of water with me, so I could hike about five miles on one liter if I needed to. There were pockets of trail magic along the way which helped my water budget stretch and calm my fears of dehydration and death. I hoped that trail angels knew how much they deserved to have constellations named after them.

I took a break after twenty-five miles, with five more planned before I would call the day complete. I was astonished by how gorgeous this desert was, but I would certainly welcome a little more greenery. I'd seen only six hikers all day which added to the undercurrent of desolation that characterized this part of the trail. I settled in at a suitable campsite before sunset, which put me less than a hundred miles away from Kennedy Meadows, the end of the PCT's desert section. I hiked in faith, hoping that my feet would take me to where I not only might find nourishment, but peace, too. Faith is a word I want to reclaim, not content for it to be owned purely by god-fearing types. I had faith that I would once again feel quenched, even without proof in a prime mover or their sacred texts. It occurred to me that if everyone let go of their tendencies to control the beliefs and lives of others, we all might actually experience peace on Earth. I never found a sense of purpose by going blindly into harm's way without weighing the consequences, and I savored my ongoing responsibility to recognize the beauty and joy of living. By releasing my urge to control and focus instead on cultivating empathy, I felt better able to see value in the lives of other people as much as I saw value in my own. I wished people could better pursue their shared ethics instead of imposing dogma upon each other. Was it possible to find a path toward a continued existence on which we could all learn walk? My hope was only as useful as my understanding of the world.

The following day was thirty-two miles of dreadful thirst, so I carefully sipped water across the miles without ever feeling quenched. I dug my heels in and hiked all the way to Walker Pass where rumors spoke of trail angels, food, water, and an end to all suffering. Music and the smell of grilled meat filled the sky as I neared the junction where filthy hikers drank, smiled, and sang. I joined the revelry and met the host, an old PCT hiker called Chief. Chief knew all about the deep thirst that we brought to his camp, so he provided a banquet of water, sodas, and beer. He handed me a couple of hot dogs, and pointed out where the mustard was. After dinner, as if I wasn't swimming in enough luxury, Sally, Chief's wife, brought out strawberry shortcakes.

I was in the middle of washing the shortcake crumbs off my hands and the caked sand off my feet when Vince appeared next to me.

"You look all better, Windscreen!"

"That shortcake was amazing, right?" I replied as I hugged him.

Seeing Vince, my first familiar face in days, might have been the best surprise of all. My fierce pace as I trundled carrying nonstop thirst rewarded me by catching me up to my crowd.

Catching up to my hiking bubble after those sick, sluggish days in Tehachapi felt like slipping back into my skin after floating outside of it. I'd been a ghost for a minute—knowing my trail family was inching farther up the map while I went through rolls of toilet paper, sweaty and pissed off that I wasn't able to hike. When my body came back online, I pushed. Hard.

Vince yelled "Windscreen lives!" like he never doubted me, but he kind of did. All that time I spent feeling behind, feeling sick, feeling like I wasn't strong enough—gone. The trail didn't mind I took a couple of zero days, and neither did Vince, now called Snipe. A hiker named Mowgli had given Andy and Vince trail names, so Andy was Handwalker, now.

"Y'all grow up so fast!" I said as I patted Vince, I mean Snipe's, arm. In that moment, I remembered that it wasn't about miles. It was about people who make this whole damn journey feel less like a grind and more like a miracle.

Finally, I felt hydrated and well-fed, and I hiked with Snipe a couple of miles past Chief's camp to an overlook where we could cowboy camp. Although the wind ripped through the sky all around us, I sank into the kind of slumber only a full belly could know.

Snipe and I covered thirty-one-and-a-half miles of dry, up-and-down hiking. My hunger never knew satisfaction, and I was consuming my food quickly. With thirty miles left until Kennedy Meadows, dreams of ice cream, pizzas, burgers, beer, and internet danced in our heads. We passed a sign that marked us having completed a full quarter of the PCT, which made me want to celebrate even more at idyllic Kennedy Meadows. I also needed a new pair of quality socks, as the best ones I had on me were too holey to be useful. Snipe and I cowboy camped by the Fox Mill Spring that night and admired the starry universe overhead.

It was easier to connect with people who shared my worldview than to try and understand those whose philosophies differed from mine. I still carried selfish ambitions and more than a few temptations toward hedonistic pleasures, but the more I surrendered to a holistic view of the world and the cosmos, the more I noticed that the lines dividing me from everything else began to disappear.

When I remembered to open myself up—to really be present with the world around me—I could feel myself becoming part of a deeper current, a greater flow, something vast and ancient that I could never fully define. The notion that we are all separate islands, created by some distant or foreign sentience, made less sense to me than the idea that we are all facets of the universe contemplating itself.

I often believed the universe was indifferent to my existence—but that didn't stop me from feeling profoundly grateful for the chance to be here, to experience all I could during this brief flash of consciousness. My unbearable thirst in a single moment might mean nothing to any other living thing, but to me, it was every-thing. It consumed my thoughts, my will, and my focus.

And if that singular, personal need didn't require comparison to anyone else's, then why should my beliefs, passions, goals, or choices be any different? What was the point of measuring my jour-ney against another's when we were each walking entirely different paths through the same unknowable universe?

In the morning, Snipe and I awoke early and hiked with child-like enthusiasm all the way to Kennedy Meadows. There, we found a store and a kiosk to order food, but nary a meadow. I was relieved to see that I could replenish my food supply for the long stretch ahead into Yosemite National Park. I didn't want to take long detours off trail if I could help it, so I bought what had to be enough food to power me for the next 192 miles. It was an ambitious goal, but I remained hopeful. Vince and I reunited with Andy, who was glad to see I put on miles. With each familiar face I grew more grateful that I could make up the zero days I spent recovering in Tehachapi. The three of us drank a couple of beers each to celebrate having now hiked a quarter of the PCT. The place filled up with section hikers and thru-hikers alike, making it difficult to even find a place to sit, let alone have a conversation or take a nap. We welcomed Dustin from Flagstaff into our hiker bubble, and after relaxing for a few hours at Kennedy Meadows, our group of four hiked on a bit to the next campsite. We cowboy camped away from the boisterous crowd and dreamed of what was waiting for us in the Sierra Nevada mountain range.

Mount Whitney—14,505 feet above sea level—the highest point in the contiguous United States. It's kind of a big deal.

21

Hiking a marathon each day made a noticeable difference to my body. When I left Saudi Arabia I weighed 180 lbs. Three months later at the Kennedy Meadows Resort I weighed 155 pounds. My thoughts weren't "Damn, I'm fit as hell!" They were much more "I hope I starve for the next 128 miles." Taking into consideration the additional seventeen-mile Mount Whitney climb, I had no idea what I would do if I ran out of food. All I knew was worrying about it didn't do any good. I could barely process the triumph, relief, and energy I was feeling having finally arrived in the Sierras, finally out of the fucking desert. Dustin and I hiked at a similar pace, even though I was certain he would outpace me eventually, so I enjoyed his company while I had it. I noticed that the upcoming trail skirted Mount Whitney, the highest mountain in the continental United States. It isn't technically on the PCT, but there was a bypass trail for those of us who wanted to climb it. I woke up at 0600 and left my friends sleep soundly in their bags. It was delightful to have trees along the trail after spending the last several weeks in uncovered desert, and since the Kern River intersected the trail thirst never became a distraction.

We took a two-hour break by the river at lunchtime and rinsed off, refreshed for the 2,000-foot trail climb ahead. My legs were powerful, and my energy had no limit. The shade-giving trees made the greatest difference, allowing me to see the beauty all around instead of suffering through the desert and trying to ignore the searing heat and dreadful thirst. It was a kind reality to be able to pay attention to the arboreal surroundings that became gradually greener the farther north the trail went. Crossing the miles seemed less like a chore and more like a privilege. We decided to camp out at the yummy-sounding Chicken Spring Lake. Just saying the name made me think of a delicious destination that my appetite loved even though it didn't make a lick of sense. It proved to be a welcome site with plenty of water where we could relax in the shade with lots of space and sunshine to air out our sleeping bags, socks, and shirts. There was even some trail magic at the campsite. At that moment, a Sprite was exactly what I didn't know I wanted, and I wordlessly thanked the trail angel who bequeathed it to me. Trail angels helped to stave off the trail demons. Trail demons are, I had decided, things that no one wants to happen. Death was one, and so was Destitution. The trail demon I felt nearest was Starvation. I had lots of food and a pair of legs that liked to eat up miles, so I didn't worry about trail demons no matter how close they appeared to be. There was quite a bit of wind with no trees around, so I set up my tent for the second time on the PCT. I had fallen in love with cowboy camping under the stars, but I misjudged the water sources that were supposed to be on trail. I ended up hiking twenty miles on just one liter of water. Hiking with a dry tongue was an odd sensation, and I examined my thirst with a kind of detached fascination. As thirsty as I was, it would have been even worse if I had been in the desert. I still underestimated how much I needed to eat and drink.

Despite my food and water concerns, I couldn't help admiring the blooming nature around me. Even though I had left Saudi

Arabia behind over four months ago, my eyes were still getting accustomed to colors other than beige, and the frequent tree groves made for great reading spots where I gave rest to my feet, back, and legs. Dustin hiked quicker than I did, but he took frequent breaks so our progress on the trail equaled out. Dustin was equally concerned about his food consumption, but we didn't discuss our lightened food sacks. Instead, we chatted about books and looked forward to the vistas we envisioned taking in from the top of Mount Whitney. Handwalker and Snipe still hadn't caught up to us, and I wondered if they just decided to hike slower, smaller days.

Dustin and I woke up early and left our friends a note that we would hike 16 miles, hoping that we would meet our friends at Crabtree Campground where we hoped that the campground at the foot of Mount Whitney had a general store with a selection of snacks. I had a feeling that Handwalker or Snipe might have had a stomach bug like the one I suffered in Tehachapi. It was impossible to know in this area without phone reception or Wi-Fi. At the campground, Dustin and I were disappointed to find there was no store, not even a single run-down vending machine. We encountered a couple of day hikers who offered us leftover snacks they no longer wanted, and that small bounty amounted to an extra day of food for each of us. We thanked them profusely and offered to give them money, but they politely refused. We simply couldn't believe our luck, and we felt more confident than ever that we would make it to Vermillion Valley Resort even with our enormous appetites.

Newly reinvigorated, Dustin and I calculated that it would take four hours to hike up to Whitney Peak, so we decided to wake up at 0400 The sun-filled grassy camp field was dotted with tents of hikers that were on Mount Whitney, so we found spots for our tents and stretched out in preparation for the big climb the next morning, letting sleep take us immediately. The stars, mountains, pristine bodies of water, and forests allowed me to bare my soul and face life more directly and fearlessly than I ever did when I was monitored by managers. Being so close to nature not only made me feel more emotionally honest, but it made me feel younger than I was even when I was younger.

Even with back pain, foot aches, hunger, and thirst, I carried less of the worst kinds of pain whenever I was in the company of nature and removed from the cognitive dissonances that populated the world. This hike reintroduced me to consistent psychological wellbeing, meaningfulness, and vitality. Nature honed my ability to pay attention and allowed me to take in so much of the land without obstruction. There was something about the essential simplicity of being away from the synthetic world that revealed a healthier version of myself. Experiences like this made me think that, as a society, we ought to pay more serious attention to how we preserve the wilderness, even how city slickers can benefit from more urban parks. As a workaholic-turned-adventurer, going for a hike or camping trip may be one of the most spectacular ways to achieve a greater level of mental and physical health.

Dustin saw my headlamp on in my tent at 0330 as I shuffled to get ready for our hike up Mount Whitney. Like me, Dustin was always ready to hike first thing in the morning. We chugged some water, had breakfast, then zipped our unneeded belongings in our tents. Carrying only water and food, our packs were much lighter than usual when we flew up the trail. Moonlight gave way to joyful sunshine, and we made it to the peak in under three and a half hours. The weather was windy but clear, giving us a view from Mount Whitney's summit of all creation. At an elevation of 14,500 feet, the wind was cold and brisk, being so close to space. I had to pause many times to suck air in, but I was beyond exhilaration. After resting on the peak for an hour, Dustin and I agreed to head back down. Although I climbed uphill faster than Dustin, he outpaced me easily on the downhills. I watched him dance effortlessly as I carefully sought my foot holes on the snow packed trail that was slushier than it had been going uphill. I took it slowly on the narrow parts of the trail and navigated around uphill climbers when I recognized a face and did a doubletake.

"Mowgli!" I greeted the hiker I'd taken a break with twice a few weeks ago.

"Windscreen!" Mowgli replied when he recognized me. "What a great day!"

"It's been a perfect day; the views on the top are rewarding," I reported. "Have you seen Snipe and Handwalker?"

"Yeah. I passed them a couple days ago. They were resting off trail due to sickness, and I haven't seen them since."

I sighed with relief; being sick was better than being dead.

"They mentioned how they wanted to catch up with you and Dustin when they could," Mowgli continued. "I guess they'd better put in some big-mile days!"

"Thanks, Mowgli . . . and good luck!" I wished him before we resumed our hikes, both of us feeling uplifted by the encounter. I wondered how Handwalker and Snipe would catch up, but then I remembered my predicament in Tehachapi. With heart and luck, the trail would eventually provide.

The following morning began with a hell of a workout up to and through Forester Pass, the highest point on the PCT, not counting Mount Whitney. Dustin and I ascended up the trail like nimble mountaineers. At the top of the pass, we could see the trail trace north for days. I felt like I was straddling my past and my future. In a way, I was. I was still trying to figure out the finer details of what I wanted to do after the PCT, and I wasn't sure how much I needed to draw from my past. More specifically, was there enough time in my life at the age of thirty-nine to start something new, or was it wiser of me to find a way to keep building upon what I'd done thus far? Putting it that way helped me to simplify all the ambition I felt and all the uncertainty I was facing. The clairvoyance was intense and *welcome*.

The sky was pregnant with snow all day, and it finally opened up as we descended from Forester Pass, making it difficult to keep our footing as we navigated the slushy trail. We feasted our eyes on the incredible scenery, even as the slush slowed us down and demanded more effort from us. The trail went down, then up, pass after pass after pass. Dustin and I dipped into our food bags more than we had planned as the trail took us through forests and crossed us over what seemed like twenty rivers, hardly resting for a break. After twenty-five miles of solemn effort, Dustin and I made camp by a raging river where we quenched our thirsts and rinsed off our salt-encrusted bodies.

There were about eighty miles between us and the resort, so we carefully rationed our snacks and meals. Eighty miles was manageable, but my stomach growled so loudly I took care not to take anything for granted. We could both devour everything in our food bags, and we would still be hungry. Those mountain passes were no joke. Our hunger was persistent, but so was our resolve. Dustin and I were off the following morning by 0535 because we wanted to get through the mountain passes early in the day and avoid the melting afternoon slush, if possible. I liked that Dustin was as inclined as I was to get difficult things accomplished as early in the day as we could. Maybe it was because we're both morning people. Maybe it's Maybelline.

I came upon a campsite for an afternoon break and recognized the friendly faces of Face Jacket and Catwhacker. I had not seen them since before the surprise snowstorm on Mount Baden-Powell, and we enthusiastically caught up on our trail experiences. By now Face Jacket and I were comfortable hiking our own hikes, but I missed his humor and outlook. Dustin and I yearned to get to the resort, and before I left Face Jacket and I promised we'd cross paths again. Then, Dustin and I hit the trail. Sadly, that was the last time I ever saw Face Jacket.

Figuring that our options were to either hike big days and be hungry or hike small days and be hungry, we decided to hike thirty miles. Not only was I starving and worried about making it to the next food source, but I also kept chastising myself silently. I felt like an idiot. Worse, I felt like an imposter. No outdoorsperson would ever let themselves wander into a stretch of wilderness without sufficient food. I thought about how disappointed my friends back home would be if they knew how dire my situation was. I thought about Verty, my buddy who hiked Alaska's wilderness regularly and made Bear Grylls look like a prima donna. I kept envisioning Verty shaking his head, seeing me for the fraud I really was. *Quit thinking like that,* I told myself. *Get through this. Learn from this.*

Dustin and I didn't see sunshine all day until evening, and the cold made for solid snow to help us navigate the mountain passes. Dustin and I ate our dinners as the sun set, glad to have lived through our ever-increasing hunger for another day. Snow hiking is exciting, especially after spending so much time in the desert, but it required Olympian tolerance of hiking in wet shoes and socks for days. It was a chilly night, but having a warm sleeping bag meant that we could cowboy camp under the frozen starlight. I dropped off to sleep craving just one more morsel of food. Always, just one more morsel.

Even with my hunger and discomfort, I was glad to be on the trail. I felt like I was living life on my own terms, making my own bad decisions instead of following the bad decisions of someone else. It was a kind of freedom that I never tired of. I wish more people could experience it, discomforts, and all. In a world plagued by ongoing wars, death, disease, economic uncertainties, so many of us succumbed to viewing the world as an uncertain, dangerous, and scary place. Following the nonstop coverage of global, domestic, and personal tensions, trauma, and anger so often discourages us from doing anything deemed to be dangerous or risky. Risky, like embarking on a long hike without a gun, a clear idea of the landscape, or confidence. Encountering strangers on a daily basis may seem like an unacceptable risk to most people, yet trail culture has been one of the healthiest, kindest, most upbeat I've ever encountered. Traveling and spending hungry time outdoors was good for my mind and creative development about how to live my own life. The natural beauty of our planet and the universe continued to be undeniable, and I still felt awe at the top of every mountain as well as the positivity of being part of something bigger than myself. I can personally vouch for the uplifting effects of getting closer to nature, as it brings out the absolute best of me, even today. I never regretted taking up with nature, not even once.

In a world perceived often to be unfriendly, dangerous, and uncertain, the trail allowed me to get a different impression. I took time to listen to the PCT, be it the casual warning of a distant thunderstorm, the happy-go-luck of the wind through a forest's leaves, the silence of the roots as they drank water alongside me. The gentle way the sun held me in its warmth took me to a new place in my identity. I could almost hear the world invite me to visit with it repeatedly, as there was so much to experience and learn outside of the artificial box I so often inhabited.

Cowboy camping was a great idea, right up until the moment I felt raindrops falling on my sky-turned face. I reached, half asleep, into my pack to drag out my tarp tent and pulled it over my sleeping bag, but I still got soaked. I wanted desperately to get back to sleep, but instead, I packed up my wet sleeping bag and tarp and I climbed the slushy endless approach with Dustin all the way to Muir Pass. Under my feet I heard the sound of rushing water beneath the snow shelf that bore our weight. Each step crushed through weak snow up to our waists, the white field crumbling under us like pieces of toast as we made our exhaustive way past the hut on Muir Pass at 0900.

Hikers filled the hut like sardines. All I wanted was to squeeze inside the hut with them, to join their cozy slumber sleeping bag party, but Dustin and I pressed on, and I'm glad we did. After descending from the pass, we eventually found *terra firma*, and hiking became less of a chore. We came across a pond and agreed to rest for a couple of hours. There was so much space and lots of boulders, so we spread our sleeping bags, tents, and socks out to dry. It was beyond delightful to see the clouds give way to warm sunlight just as we needed it the most. When we regained our strength and put our newly dried socks back on, we hit the trail with vigor.

At this point, the resort represented to both me and Dustin everything that was right in the world—a beacon of caloric redemption, beer-battered salvation, and warm, greasy absolution. It wasn't just a place. It was a mirage manifested. Where thirst gave way to waterfalls of beer, and gourmet hamburgers and pizzas sprouted like wild dandelions from the sacred soil of gluttony. Civilization, yes—but in its highest form: food trucks for the soul.

We camped twenty miles from the bypass trail to the resort, making it a twenty-seven-mile day. Dustin was eager to press on, motivated by his appetite and sheer willpower. It was one of the few times I opted not to keep up—but I didn't feel bad in the slightest. Hunger had given me tunnel vision, but exhaustion reminded me to sleep while I could. I found a cozy enclave of trees just off trail and slid into my sun-dried sleeping bag under the cheerful evening sky, like a tortilla slipping into its foil wrapper. I sent up a quiet prayer of thanks to the PCT itself—not for being gentle, but for being honest. It was unwise, even idiotic, to cross those last few mountain passes with so little food. My body gave itself over to the earth with the kind of peace only desperation and surrender can produce.

The next morning, I woke up starving, the kind of hunger that gnaws not just at your stomach but at your very sense of identity. I mixed all four of my remaining packets of instant oatmeal with fresh river water and devoured it with confidence, knowing more food was in my near future. With that minimal but magical infusion of calories, I bounced onto the trail at 0530, hiking like a man possessed, or at least caffeinated by sheer will.

When I reached Bear Ridge Peak and got cell signal for the first time in two weeks, I lit up. I messaged my brother Andrew, and posted a photo to social media as proof of life to the washed masses. The signal felt like a lifeline, as if the trail itself was giving me a fist bump. When I saw the sign for the Rear Ridge Trail, I nearly wept with joy. I imagined Dustin already at the resort, haloed by firelight, holding flagons of beer beside a spit-roasted hog. I practically jogged those last miles on fumes and fantasy, one small granola bar in reserve, just in case hope wasn't enough.

I almost didn't believe my eyes when I finally saw the Vermillion Valley Resort. It wasn't a myth, not a trick of the light, but gloriously real. Part of me still feared it was closed, or worse, understocked, but I had no strength for doubt. I burst in and ordered the largest hamburger they had, fries, a huckleberry milkshake, and—because the first one was free—a beer. I didn't sit down so much as collapse with purpose.

No other hikers were around at first, which made the food feel all the more sacred. But just as I was knee-deep in french fries, Dustin appeared, clean and glowing like a well-fed apparition. We laughed in unison, a high-pitched, delirious cackle that only those who have gone without can summon. It was the laugh of the starving suddenly full. Of fools who had tangoed with deprivation and lived to tell the tale in between bites of taco.

After lunch, I found the bathroom. The sink mirror was grimy and the fluorescent light above it buzzed and stuttered like a dying insect. I leaned in to wash my hands, and that's when I caught it. A flash. A movement that shouldn't have been. I looked up.

A figure in the mirror was already staring at me, bone-thin, hollow-cheeked, with skin drawn tight across cheekbones like a death mask. His jaw jutted out like a weapon, and his eyes were black pits rimmed with something feral. Windburn, sun-scorched skin, the color of parchment left too long in the sun. He looked like something that had clawed its way out of the woods, like something that used to be human.

My breath caught. My instinct was to turn around, to check if someone else was standing behind me, but I continued to stare at the reflection like a man spotting a ghost in his childhood bedroom. A trespasser. A doppelgänger. A warning. My heart was pounding now, not from exertion—but dread. I had become the horror you find alone in a gas station bathroom at night. The kind of thing that should not exist, but it does. I reached up slowly and touched my face to be sure it was real. The reflection mimicked me perfectly. Weeks of deprivation and isolation had made me forget what softness felt like. It was like seeing a crime scene and realizing you were both the victim and the perpetrator.

That haunted face had earned its shadows. It had crossed snowfields. It had laughed while slipping on shale. It had whispered thank you to mountaintops. The horror wasn't in the ruin—it was in what it had endured. I hadn't dressed this body up in months. I'd just used it, slept in it, bled in it, and walked it across national park boundaries. The creature in the mirror was terrifying, but he was also real and honest. Never again, I thought. I would never treat food as optional again. Never again gamble calories against pride. This nightmare was my masterpiece. From now on, I'd feed the artist.

That afternoon, Dustin and I lay in the sunshine like lazy cats. We drank beer, devoured tacos, washed our clothes, and didn't just feel relief, but grace. We restocked our food bags generously, this time with wisdom enough to carry, enough to share, and enough to fight off the shadow of desperation for the next stretch. We weren't just eating. We were refortifying.

I accepted Dustin's offer to share a joint. High on weed, food, and safety, I floated in a hammock under the trees, letting the sunlight and breeze remind me of everything good about being alive. Hunger had stripped me bare; satisfaction wrapped me up like a blanket I forgot I owned. The laughter came easy. The air tasted sweet. In that hammock, I felt like a billionaire at heart.

There's something about shared suffering that forges bonds

deeper than words. I used to believe no social bond could surpass the camaraderie I knew in the military, but the trail offers a different kind of intimacy. It's not built on uniform or command, it's built on the silent exchange of glances at a summit and the shared recognition of having climbed the same unforgiving miles. The trail flattens ego and leaves only the essence. Travel had taught me to stay open to discomfort, to challenges, and to people wildly unlike myself. That openness was still shaping me. While basking in the hammock warm in my post-hunger haze, I thought about how too much safety starves us of confidence. How only through choosing risk—physical, emotional, spiritual—do we earn access to resilience, perspective, and joy.

Dustin and I camped that night at the resort, slept full, and woke fuller. We breakfasted like kings, clinked coffee mugs like chalices, and caught the boat to the PCT across Lake Edison. Seventeen miles later, we reached Duck Lake Trail. Compared to the hunger-haunted days before, I felt like a superhero—part human, part hummingbird, all engine. That's what food does. It doesn't just fuel the body. It revives the soul. I still had a little trail-litter inside: unhealthy habits, old self-judgments, the reckless pride that made me skip resupplies. I carried more granola bars, more compassion for my body, and gratitude for trail salvation.

Momentary comfort of having plenty.

"Yosemite Valley, to me, is always a sunrise, a glitter of green and golden wonder in a vast edifice of stone and space." —Ansel Adams

22

Dustin and I practically danced the ten sunny miles into Mammoth Lakes—well, okay, we limped with flair. It hadn't been all that long since we'd gorged ourselves at the Vermillion Valley Resort, but having a townful of options made us giddy. Real, non-dehydrated food. Indoor plumbing. Shelves full of goods that weren't freeze-dried or vacuum-sealed like space snacks. Mammoth felt like more than a town; it was a glittering oasis, and we were the two scruffy mirage-chasers who'd finally made it to the buffet.

Hitting Mammoth meant we were a third of the way through the PCT, and that deserved a proper celebration. We didn't go crazy—just a night in a hotel room where we could explode our packs like confetti all over the floor, do laundry like civilized beasts, and walk around town with a kind of reverence normally reserved for national monuments.

I took the longest, hottest, most transcendent shower known to humankind. I think I might have blacked out halfway through, not from exhaustion but from sheer ecstasy. When I emerged, my body had returned to something almost presentable—good enough to walk among the townsfolk without inspiring concerned whispers or impromptu donations.

We stumbled into a café, nostrils flaring at the smell of eggs, grease, and heaven. We melted into booth cushions like over-cooked lasagna and ordered massive breakfasts that might've made our ancestors proud—or alarmed. I could feel my body soaking up calories like a sponge in a gas leak. My muscles sighed. My soul clapped.

After breakfast, we hit the outfitter circuit. My shoes had fully surrendered their will to live, the soles flapping like they were try-ing to speak. I picked out a pair of fresh Merrells that were so clean they looked like they'd never even heard of suffering. My feet practically held a ribbon-cutting ceremony when I slid them in. I whispered a solemn thank-you to my old pair before throwing them out—those crusty warriors had carried me through hunger, hope, snow, sweat, and questionable life choices. I was starting to believe hikers should get to keep their worn-out shoes in a trophy case. Like antlers.

I'd just finished Revival by Stephen King the day before and was ready for a new kind of existential dread, so I picked up Life of Pi at the local bookstore. By evening, Dustin and I found a brewery that sold slices of pizza the size of snowshoes and cold beer that was religion. We stuffed ourselves, stopped by a grocery store for resupply, and exited with so many bags we looked like mobile pan-tries. By the time we reached the hotel, we had serious doubts about whether our packs would hold all the glorious food. By the grace of high-quality zippers, they did.

We mapped out the next leg of our journey over Jurassic Park movies, sprawled out on clean sheets like kings in exile. If raptors had come for us, we'd have offered them pizza and begged for a nap first. The next morning, we filled up again on breakfast and headed back out to the trail. Gray clouds threatened us with drama, but we were too well-fed to care. Eight miles in, a kind soul pulled over and offered us a ride to Red's Meadow. In the backseat were Courage and Mechanic, fellow PCT hikers we'd been leapfrogging since before the resort. We lit up like golden retrievers seeing an old friend at the dog park.

As the skies opened up like biblical revenge, our driver delivered us safely to Red's Meadow. We offered money, but she waved us off with a smile that could cure frostbite. "Just happy to help hikers," she said. Honestly, she felt like a mythic trail angel with a Honda.

Rain battered the world, so we all ducked into the campground café. Patty melts and pie happened. We watched the storm through fogged windows, each gust of wind making us more grateful for roofs, hot food, and company. Eventually we pooled cash and grabbed a cabin, and as the rain drummed on the roof like it was trying to get in, we lay there—safe, full, dry. If it had been a scene in a book, it would've ended in poetry. I passed out instead, because sometimes peace is better than poetry.

My feet loved the light mileage. My stomach loved being spoiled. I weighed myself at the campsite—still 150 pounds. Message received, body: Eat more.

The next morning, with heroic resistance, we snuck out before the café could lure us back in with sizzling bacon sorcery. We took the side trail to Devil's Postpile and geeked out over the tall hexagonal rock formations like a couple of geology fanboys. Later, we descended from Donahue Pass in a cascade of wild beauty and nimbly crossed the Lyell River.

Twenty-five miles later, we set up camp under a watercolor sky, tired and happy. We weren't just hiking anymore—we were living it. Between the slices of pie, the beer, the miracle of warm beds, and the company of fellow weirdos on the same insane path, it all felt like one long, unpredictable, unforgettable celebration of life stripped down to its best parts. We were rich in the things that mattered. The trail—despite the blisters, the storms, and the literal flirtations with starvation—kept on giving. For once, I saw what true freedom could be like. This carefree, almost bohemian life didn't care much about socially acceptable behavior. We called each other new names that gave us permission to try being someone else without besmirching our normal reputations. I liked how we all gave up on being afraid and just went after whatever it was that we wanted. We waxed socioeconomical about the normalcy we were taking a break from on the trail. On the PCT our only prejudices were against prejudiced people. While the laws of civilization were a distant memory without power, I never saw anyone cause harm to any person, plant, or creature. As an upbeat guy, the optimism, positivity, and joyousness I felt being in nature gave me unimaginably mind-blowing trips, in the best way.

While so much of my life centered around the acquisition of means, wealth, and status, I loved dipping into the bohemian life of Windscreen. As Chris, my frontcountry life would always end up becoming—too padded and dull, even as an expat. The fluorescent flicker of routine work by office light would eventually feel like a slow kind of death. I tended to think, on some level, parts of me needed to be ruined to be rebuilt. My preferred kind of repair work meant sun, blisters, wind, and elevation until there was nothing left but truth. I was hiking the PCT because I benefitted from the pain, not in a masochistic way, but because I was sick of numbness. Pain told me I was pushing against the edge of what I thought I could do. Every searing calf cramp, every half-frozen morning, every waterless ten-mile stretch under the nuclear sun was proof I wasn't merely passing through time. There was no waste where danger lived. This trail reintroduced stakes. It didn't care about my *résumé or* my social media posts. The PCT showed me who I was when you're starving, freezing, soaked, scared, and 40+ miles away from precious cell service. The trail wasn't fake. It wasn't anything I could get from a retreat, or a podcast, or this memoir I would take five years to write. It's blood, guts, and mental grit.

I met thru-hikers trying to outwalk some grief or a heartbreak that left a hollow inside them. I connected their gnawing sense that life was meant to be a bit more than the safe path. I met thru-hikers who wanted to feel their body become something new and feral. After my brush with starvation, I shared in their feeling of earning every view and every single goddamn calorie. Some people wanted to see how far and how fast they could complete the trail, which my competitive spirit certainly understood. Some were interested in seeing as many flowers, trees, and birds as they could and stopped whenever they saw something of interest, mileage and weather be damned, which appealed to the hedonist in me. There were many who tackled the PCT just to see if they could, and others were like me, who reveled in the throes of traveling in new environments. Whatever incentivized thru-hikers, I would hike it for the same reason because pain was a necessary part of the transformation.

Other than hike, eat, drink, meet people, journal about my thoughts, and sleep, I didn't do anything that would register as useful to the modern world. Connecting with the trail was as useful to society as chatting idly with a friend. A hiker's only job is to hike their own hike.

Quite possibly the most heavenly slice of the United States, and, dare I say, this particular spiral arm of the galaxy, Yosemite struck me like a thunderbolt the first time I glimpsed its raw, towering majesty. Not in person, but on screen, beaming through a television into the eyes of a wide-eyed thirteen-year-old kid. Star Trek V: The Final Frontier, for all its camp and controversy, opened with a love letter to Yosemite so sweeping, so transcendent, that I found myself stunned by two questions: "Where is that place?" and the more famous one: "What does God need with a starship?" That cinematic moment lit a long fuse in me. And decades later, hiking beside Dustin, I watched that fuse finally reach its payload.

As we passed the elegant art deco sign ushering us into the fabled heart of Yosemite National Park, I felt the fanfare of Jerry Goldsmith's Star Trek score swell in my chest. His music didn't just fill the air—it cracked it open. The notes painted El Capitan and Half Dome not as mere rock but as planetary icons, as ancient sentinels standing guard over something more sacred than national pride: cosmic reverence. Clouds lingered above like sleepy gods, casting a soft gray dome over the earthbound cathedral we walked through. No rain. No harsh sun. Perfect hiking weather—the kind of temperature and texture that made me believe the universe actually liked us.

We trekked in a stunned silence, as if speaking too loudly might shatter the spell. Yosemite wasn't just "beautiful." It was impossibly, intimidatingly, divine. The waterfalls roared like holy throat-singers. The granite cliffs looked carved by beings who dream in light-years. The air was so pure and charged with energy, it felt less like breathing and more like being powered by an ancient, interstellar power source.

Of course, Nature wasn't going to let us get too lofty in our musings. Yosemite's bug population was thrilled by the chance to taste new visitors. Flies buzzed around us in joyful droves, so at night we zipped ourselves into our tents and let the outside world fade. Inside our thin shelters, cocooned from the endless wilderness, Dustin and I each drifted into our own galaxies—paperback voyages in the worlds of fiction. I read myself to sleep by headlamp, the sounds of the forest whispering like static from deep space, my heart still echoing with the strings and horns of Goldsmith's theme. The line between real and imagined had, in my mind, blurred entirely.

Yosemite wasn't just a place—it was a portal, a wormhole that collapsed time and memory, where boyhood wonder and adult gratitude could exist at once. It was where a national park could carry the spiritual weight of a holy site and the cinematic gravitas of a sci-fi epic. Where the divine wasn't above us or beyond us—but all around us. Towering. Flowing. Breathing. Nestled in the cradle of a sacred valley that had enchanted visionaries, rebels, astronauts, poets, and kids who grew up watching VHS tapes, a lifelong dream was finally real.

I was sound asleep halfway between the stars and the soil when a clap of thunder startled me awake. I curled tighter in my warm sleeping bag feeling safe in the universe even as a fierce rainstorm beat upon my tent. Dustin and I were up and off by 0645 and enjoyed a pleasant steady downhill next to waterfalls that escorted us into Tuolumne Meadows, one of the most touristy junctions on the trail.

We took an hour-long break, just long enough for our tents and socks could dry in the sunshine. We breakfasted and topped up our food supplies for the next 50 Yosemite miles. The section following Tuolumne Meadows was my favorite section on the PCT to date; the rushing streams, spectacular waterfall lookouts, views of distant mountains, and weather couldn't have been more uplifting.

That night, the four of us—Dustin, Mechanic, Courage, and me—pitched our tents in a meadow so perfect it could've been hand-painted by a romantic god high on moonlight and nostalgia. The brook beside us murmured like an enchanted stream in a fantasy novel, its waters so clear they reflected the stars like polished glass. This was no ordinary campsite; this was a moment suspended outside time. A hush fell over our little camp, not from exhaustion, but from reverence. Even the mosquitoes gave us a short reprieve, as if recognizing they were in the presence of something sacred.

Mechanic and Courage spoke excitedly about a trail angel who'd invited Asian thru-hikers into their home—a beacon of hospitality shining through the vast wilderness. It wasn't just a hot meal they anticipated, but a cultural recognition, a shared story, a chance to feel truly seen out there in the great anonymous wild. Dustin, ever practical and cheerful, mentioned his stop at Kennedy Meadows North to pick up mail.

Me? I had Tahoe on my mind. Jimmy, Air Force pal and dealer of high-quality beer and conversation, had promised to meet me there with the new Kindle I mailed to him. In this strange and beautiful life, a good friend bearing lager and books felt more divine than any angel with wings.

Dawn greeted us with thick, ethereal dew. No rain, just a gentle baptism from the earth's breath. The fabric of our tents clung to us like the memories of dreams we couldn't fully remember. We packed up in silence, our minds still somewhere between the galaxies above and the wet earth below. As we walked, the sun slowly burned off the mist, revealing a trail laced with the shimmer of new beginnings.

The day's hike was a winding, poetic thing—ten miles of undulating terrain, rivers leaping across our path like playful gods daring us to fall in love with every step. Water was everywhere: spilling, trickling, singing. I still carried my two liters, though I hardly needed them. There's security in self-reliance, even when surrounded by abundance. The mosquitoes, sensing our joy, returned vigorously. Bug spray proved worthless. My salty skin was a buffet, and I was the reluctant host. Still, I preferred their persistence to the indifference of sterile suburbia. This was real. This was wild love.

Dustin broke one of his trekking poles between two boulders—a sacrificial offering to the trail gods—but he remained calm, already planning his replacement run at Kennedy Meadows North. We took our last break of the day, and the mood was bittersweet. It was our final full day in Yosemite, and it felt like trying to say goodbye to a cathedral mid-prayer. Dustin and I exchanged a look—part grief, part gratitude. We both knew this place had left fingerprints on our souls. I promised myself I'd return. You don't walk through heaven and just keep going without vowing to find your way back.

On trail, we may look like destitute wanderers to outsiders—sunburnt, scruffy, gear-laden misfits—but the truth? We were royalty. Demigods in dirt-caked shorts. Trail angels and strangers bowed to us with kind words, meals, rides, and stories. We, the chosen few, had shed society's shackles and reclaimed something primal. Something sacred. Hikers came from every background, belief system, and tax bracket, but out here, we were equals. Liberated animals on pilgrimage. It wasn't rebellion—it was revelation. Somewhere in the middle of it all, a man named Windscreen took over. Windscreen hiked barefoot across snowfields, scaled ridgelines with no destination but onward, sang to the trees, howled at the moon, and fell asleep with dirt in his beard and gratitude in his bones. Chris Homan still lived inside Windscreen like an echo, wondering what the professors and professionals back home would think of this wild-eyed soul sleeping in the dirt, whispering thanks to the stars. Would they see madness—or liberation? Out here, I wasn't more human than plant, wave, or stone—I was equal to them all.

The next morning, under skies painted with serenity, we left Yosemite behind. Twenty-seven miles later, with legs humming and hearts full, we finished the day laughing and buzzing from our thousandth PCT mile. A thousand miles! We weren't walking anymore—we were gliding, like solar-powered spirits on some divine assignment. Kennedy Meadows North whispered to us with its cold beer, warm meals, and clean porcelain thrones. The stars above looked close enough to kiss, but I didn't need to wish on them. I already had everything I'd once thought impossible.

With my new face net from Tuolumne Meadows, I cowboy camped two nights in a row, protected from the mosquito blitzkrieg like a knight in gossamer armor. I slept out under the open sky, my body cradled by the earth, my mind drifting like a balloon across constellations. We ascended Emigrant Pass, swept along by wind that sang through the trees like a hymn only the old gods remember. The climb was gentle and grand, with panoramas so expansive they made my chest ache. The descent was steep and treacherous—loose rocks threatening to rearrange our skeletons—but we made it down unscathed, fueled by grit and a pinch of divine luck. We caught a hitch from a kind stranger and landed at Kennedy Meadows North, where we ate with gusto, resupplied with glee, and I shaved in the bathroom mirror like a man caught between myth and hygiene.

There, among strangers turned comrades, Dustin and I realized we might just be ahead of our hiking bubble. We had become our own wave. We were trail-seasoned, trail-hardened, trail-alive. And as I told Dustin about Jimmy and our Tahoe rendezvous, I felt a rare joy—the merging of lives. The collision of two worlds: Windscreen's untamed spirit and Chris Homan's beating heart.

Some people live one life. I, somehow, had stumbled into two—and was learning how to live them both, fiercely and fully.

Dustin and I hiked twenty-nine miles the following day—taking only one break, not out of duty, but because the trail had cast its spell on us, and we were entranced. The terrain, once a cruel trickster, now opened itself up like a friend waving us onward. Each mile fell away like old skin, and in its place, a lighter version of me emerged—stripped of worry, dressed in wind, sweat and that fierce, quiet freedom that comes only from knowing you're exactly where you belong.

The weather was nothing short of sublime. A cerulean sky stretched endlessly above, punctuated by playful clouds drifting like daydreams. Trees towered with the silent strength of cathedral spires, branches whispering secrets to the breeze. They didn't just grow—they proclaimed. The forest wasn't background noise. It was alive, attentive, as if it had been waiting for us to arrive so it could reveal itself. The trail was merciful, the streams shallow and clear, and I danced across them without so much as a splash. My dry feet kissed the dirt like lovers reunited, and I swear the earth kissed back. When I passed Short Sherrod Lake, its surface shimmered like a silver mirror, and I thanked the trail gods for keeping the mosquitoes at bay. For once, beauty didn't come with a price.

During our break, I lay against a warm rock and turned the final page of Life of Pi. The story lingered in my chest like a prayer I didn't know I was saying. Then, I felt exposed. Not in a fragile way, but in that old, sacred sense: naked before the universe. You see, I've always packed like a man preparing for psychological famine.

Some people hoard food or first-aid kits—I hoard books. Because a life without reading? It's like hiking without water. Dry, desperate, and unmoored.

Dustin, finishing The Alchemist, handed it to me. I gave him Life of Pi in return. A fair trade, a spiritual communion. It felt right. Paulo Coelho wrote his masterwork after walking the Camino de Santiago, and now here we were, swapping stories between saints of the footpath. Coelho was a fellow soul-caster—one of us. He wandered, listened, wrote. I felt less alone knowing that others had chased meaning through miles, not meetings. He saw his journey as worthy of literature, and I believed mine was, too.

That evening, I didn't read—I wrote. I let the pen be my trail. I journaled as wind brushed against me, as if the elements themselves had stopped to listen. We cowboy camped after a thirty-mile day as the stars above watched over us like proud ancestors. My body ached, but my spirit hummed.

At Carson Pass, I checked for cell service and sent a message to Jimmy, letting him know our ETA in Lake Tahoe. I hadn't seen him since Vacaville a couple years back, and the thought of reconnecting filled me with that rare warmth you only get when someone truly knows your laugh. I hoped he could make it. I wanted him to see this version of me. Not the office-casual, deadline-chasing Chris. But Windscreen, wild and alive.

Only twelve miles to go, and we were eager. Not just for Tahoe, but to feel the strange collision between civilization and this raw, elemental world we'd been inhabiting. I loved questioning author-ity—always had. Long-distance hiking didn't just challenge con-vention; it obliterated it. Out here, no one could tell you what to do, what to wear, how to act. The media, Hollywood, politicians, influencers—they all screamed for our attention. They peddled self-help manifestos and financial guides like gospel. But how audacious does someone have to be to think they know enough to author a book?

I thought back to the kid who barely made it through high school, who scrambled through tech school and university, clawing for a seat at the table of "success." The military sharpened that instinct. I had trained myself to outperform, to people-please, to bury the parts of me that didn't fit the mold of productivity. My worth was my GPA. My paycheck. My rank. I had trained myself to be impressive. But never—never—had I trained myself to be free.

The Air Force was behind me now, but that hunger to please hadn't died. Professors, bosses, peers—I still chased their approval like it meant something eternal. I worked to be stronger, smarter, shinier. But out here, surrounded by pine needles and starlight, I realized I'd spent years invalidating my joy because it didn't earn a salary.

Still—I would need to go back someday. I'd need to rejoin that dance of labor and expectation. This trail, this wild, blissful detour, was a portal. It reminded me that my dreams didn't need to be monetized to matter. That art was worthwhile even if no one clapped. That living well was a protest, and joy was a form of resistance. Hiking had illuminated the version of me I used to be before I traded imagination for ambition. Before I became "respectable." It gave me permission to play again, to wonder. Yes, adulthood demanded responsibility. But I never wanted to be the kind of adult who lost his sparkle. I didn't want to just survive—I wanted to create. To author books. To climb mountains. To kiss the rain and speak to fireflies.

On the PCT, I did.

Savoring the luxury of not having to be "respectable."

. *"When you tell someone to dress for unhindered movement, going naked seems like the best option to me."* —Wataru Watari

23

Dustin and I breakfasted in Lake Tahoe, complete with malt shakes. After we ate, we took a ride to downtown where we found our hostel and showered, did laundry, changed clothes, and relaxed with well-earned beers. I'd been upping my calorie intake, and I felt strong. I saw a nearby grocery store and wended through the aisles to decide what to have for dinner. I decided on a spinach salad, a box of garlic Triscuits, camembert cheese, and a couple bottles of Chianti—one of my favorite go-to bachelor meals. It felt healthy to give my legs and feet a rest. With all the food and drink I could want at my fingertips, I relaxed in a hammock and journaled to music. I missed certain creature comforts, such as beds, healthy food, a clean face, and bare feet. Jimmy arrived at the hostel the following morning just in time to have breakfast with me and Dustin at the Driftwood Café then watch *Jurassic World* at the next-door theater. That after-noon, the three of us walked to the nearby lake where we swam and sipped beers while the sunshine sparkled on our faces. We grabbed food on the way back to the hostel, made dinner, and ate on the balcony as we watched pedestrians amble about to the live street music.

After a full zero day off trail, Dustin and I felt like mustangs penned in too long—our bodies craved movement, our spirits longed to chase the horizon once more. The stillness had been sweet, but the trail called louder than any luxury. Jimmy, ever the trail angel in civvies, grinned as he dropped us back at the trailhead. I hugged him tightly, and told him I'd see him again on my road trip home after the PCT. Just as I turned to shoulder my pack, he stopped me and handed over a small parcel.

It was my brand-new Kindle.

The clouds parted—literally or metaphorically, who's to say—and I beamed like a kid unwrapping his first lightsaber. This wasn't just a gadget. It was a sacred vault. A portable cathedral. A digital spellbook packed with every tale, philosophy, and dream I'd ever wanted to walk beside. Now, I had the freedom to hike with Bryson or Tennyson. Tolstoy or Tolkien. King or Kafka. My mindscape was about to get as panoramic as the Sierra skyline.

I practically floated down the trail from Alda Lake, my feet kissed by the earth, the sun giving me a conspiratorial wink. And as fate, or trail magic, would have it, that morning wasn't just any morning. It was Hike Naked Day.

Yes, you read that right. Hike Naked Day.

The first day of summer, the summer solstice, the holy day of hiker mischief and myth. It's not sanctioned, not commercialized, and certainly not ranger-approved, but it pulses through the bloodstream of long trails like an old folk song nobody remembers learning, yet everyone sings. It's the high holiday of the weird, gritty, ungovernable spirit of thru-hiker culture.

You spend a thousand miles fermenting in your own sweat, mosquito-bitten, chafed, sun-kissed, and deliriously alive. Then, on the longest day of the year, the sky goes full opera. The sun lingers like it doesn't want to say goodbye, the wildflowers sway like they're drunk on honey, and all the hikers you've met—grubby philosophers, wilderness warriors, barefoot sages—suddenly shed their clothing and return to the wild in their birthday suits, boots laced, backs burdened, hearts light.

It's not about exhibitionism. It's not about rebellion. It's about embodiment. To walk naked beneath the open sky, pine needles brushing your haunches, glacier-fed breezes skating across your skin—this is communion. This is the human animal remembering it's part of the world, not separate from it. It takes exactly one hummingbird sighting while your cheeks are flapping in the breeze to remember how sacred and stupidly glorious life can be.

My Kindle nestled safely in its Ziplock tomb, I felt no shame in my naked glory. There I was: Windscreen, hiker, reader, human—liberated of both pants and pretense, standing at the intersection of the absurd and the sublime. We hiked not to escape civilization, but to remember what it had buried: the joy of books read by starlight, the delight of laughing at nothing on a mountaintop, the deep and holy foolishness of walking for months just to see what you'll discover inside yourself. The Kindle in my pack held centuries of thought. The trail made me feel every damn word of it. That's what both the road and the page are really about—not just reaching an end, but feeling so wildly, beautifully alive along the way that you'd do it all over again.

Preferably naked.

It's awkward at first, but after those first few miles I stopped caring because my fellow thru-hikers were either naked too, or high-fived as we crossed paths, because they got it. This isn't about being sexy, it's about us shedding the last layers of societal bullshit and being fully and unironically ourselves. In the high desert or deep into the Sierra Nevada of the PCT, Hike Naked Day has a sun-scorched, dust-blasted flavor tempered by wide views and thin air. There was plenty of space between people, remote ridges, and glacial lakes. There's a risk-reward calculus, but still, plenty of us stripped down anyway, some went as far as to tie on bandanas, whether it was around foreheads or further south, and trek with their equipment swinging proudly. The weird and glorious buck nakedness on trail provides a kind of absurd joy I'll remember long after my last hike. After months spent shedding layers of fear, ego, and expectations, it was surprisingly easy to shed clothes to greet the world exactly as I was.

Dustin and I hiked far enough apart from each other so we both welcomed the experience of absolute freedom without establishing decorum. The summer sun bathed everything in golden light, and with each step I felt more connected to nature. The gentle breeze brushed against my skin just enough to keep the sun's heat from becoming overwhelming. The scent of pine, wildflowers, and earth filled the air, heightened by the lack of barriers between myself and my environment. Just like hiking naked on the Appalachian Trail, there was an undeniable thrill—part exhilaration, part vulnerability as every breath I inhaled was the essence of the wilderness itself. Some thru-hikers embraced the tradition, while others simply enjoyed the spectacle. I didn't see many other hikers, but the few times I crossed paths with someone we would exchange knowing smiles or nods of mutual respect.

Several times that day I reached scenic viewpoints with nothing between me and the endless horizon. For a time, I was raw, unfiltered, and alive as the wilderness reminded me what it meant to be free. Peace settled over me as I gave myself permission to let go of my inhibitions. Taking off my pack for a few hours let my shoulders relax and my feet stretch without tension or tightness. The moment when I completely let go of my concerns and allowed things to happen without overthinking was always worth it. I was learning increasingly than letting go could be one of the keys to better mental health.

We were about 200 miles south of the halfway point, which caused me to think some more about what I'd do after the trail. Does anyone truly desire their life to be orderly, predictable, and all figured out? A Camino Santiago pellegrino of old, Paulo Coelho, said "The boat is safer anchored at the port; but that's not the aim of boats." That reminded me feeling safe is wonderful, but an overabundance of security actually made me fear the unknown. A wide world of adventure existed between staying healthy and certain death, and I loved navigating it. Getting a job sounded like the safest option, but I kept mulling over getting another college degree. I quite liked the idea of being in my home for a while and seeing longtime friends I missed. I felt like a stranger in the United States, and it might be good to familiarize myself with my home country again.

The most worthwhile achievements demanded I venture outside of my comfort zone. I could personally testify to the difficulty of overcoming shyness when performing onstage in grade school, the reluctant decision to invest money for a distant future rather than spend it on something I coveted in the moment, and putting myself out there to experience true love, no matter how mismatched I worried she and I might be. Rewarding experiences were always next door to certain failure and, like most people, I always had a challenging time coping with the uncertainty of taking risks. What if I embarrassed myself by not finishing the PCT? What if I invested my savings in the wrong industries? What if I opened my heart to someone who rejected me for someone better-looking? What if I sucked at writing? I had no assurances against these concerns, but I wanted to try and fail rather than never leave my comfort zone.

Man plans, and God laughs, right? Just when I thought it was going to be another run-of-the-mill twenty-eight-mile day, Nudo's uncle met up with us at a trailhead and shared beers and burgers with us. Fate reminded me how bad I am at predictions as Dustin, Hops, Nudo, and I thanked Nudo's uncle for his kindness and grilling skills. I treated everyone to a pint of ice cream from a nearby general store, then Dustin and I hit the trail, as Nudo and Hops became yet another part of the elaborate mosaic of weird and cool names, come and gone.

After hiking a bit, Dustin and I stretched our sleeping bags out on the soft forest floor surrounded by tall trees to block the wind.

I checked my messages and learned I had an invitation to visit my friend Cathy's sister and her family when in Bend, Oregon. My map showed I was 400 miles away, which meant I would get there in about three weeks. Although I hadn't met Cathy's sister, I replied I would love to take her up on her offer to visit, and I would let them know my progress.

Dustin and I started out at 0515 and traversed under beautiful weather and over logs and streams for thirty-one miles. Not a single cloud appeared all day as I hiked up, down, and along ridgelines through the orange, yellow, and purple flowers carpeting the land. I admired flora I'd never seen before. The miles kept me in a state of perpetual hunger even though I ate enormously. My food pack became noticeably lighter after each break, so I was glad I was going to resupply in Sierra City just ten miles away. As I soaked up the trail scenery I considered what to get another degree in that might complement my business management education and military experience. Should I apply to Wayland Baptist University or someplace new? Should I get a car at the end of the PCT or a motorcycle? So many of my best decisions would have to be sooner than I felt ready for. In the meantime, Sierra City was a pleasant place to rest. Unsurprisingly, I filled my food bag with enough food for the miles ahead, then I filled my stomach with pizza, beer, spinach salad. Before heading out and up the monstrous climb I had that afternoon, I had a pint of ice cream to take the edge off the summer heat. Dustin chose to stay overnight in Sierra City and wait for a package from his parents to arrive at the post office. Powered by calories, beer, and coffee, I devoured the 3,000-foot climb in six miles of peaceful solitude. My mind kept looking to the coming future, figuring out more of the details as I committed to more decisions. Planning concretely for the future was a new sensation after months of simply walking forward. Visions of spending Christmas with my brother and his wife, Thanksgiving with Susan and her family, and exploring more of the United States all appealed to me. I didn't have to dash off anywhere immediately after the trail, and I really did miss so many people in my life. Perhaps spending time away from my family and lifelong friends wasn't the way to go anymore. Taking risks, for me, meant confronting fear, and sometimes that led to failure. Failure gets a bad rap, but I felt like I risked failing daily just by getting out of bed, so I embraced failure as a friend. Since there was always the chance I might not accomplish all I set out to do, I decided I would make more of an effort to enjoy the process of what I did, even if my students chose other instructors to take my place or if academic leadership didn't recognize when a plan came together. Everything I did, either as Chris or Windscreen, involved at least some risk, and that made life delicious. The path less traveled was scary, but it was so much fun. The more plans entered my mind, the more stress I felt, but then I remembered to take a breath.

I woke up early in the campground and gave my attention to the blood-orange sunrise through the fir trees, hiking alone for the first time since leaving Tehachapi. It felt like it had been an age since I recognized any of the names signed in trail journals that populated the PCT. I savored the liminality of the trail two months after Face Jacket and I first stepped onto the PCT, and I planned to camp out at mile 1,235 if there was a reliable water source. The days and nights were warm and although I was nowhere near the desert, it paid to keep an eye out for water. I needed to allow for mistakes if I wanted to grow as a human being. I would rather let my ego take a few hits than live a life without knowing what an unlikely accomplishment feels like, but I also had no wish to taste desperate thirst again.

I saw only one other thru-hiker all the next day. "Do Good" rested in his hammock as I trekked past him at 0900, and I admired his way of doing things. I enjoyed getting ten miles hiked by 1000, and twenty-eight miles later, I noticed a sign to where trail angels lived. I couldn't resist the promise of meeting kind people and took the detour to meet Terry, Nancy, Beth, and Jenny who welcomed me into their home, offered me a shower, a bed, dinner, and dessert. Such encounters remind me, although I didn't mind time alone, I was solidly an extrovert. The wind kissed my clean, sweat-free face while birds above sang from the canopy of trees above. At my feet rested their dog who loved smelling my legs. I stroked her ears and thought about getting a dog when I returned to Albuquerque. Then again, I should wait until I crafted a more long-term vision for my life.

My hosts and I drank beers and waxed cultural as the sun set. I had a great night's sleep on a proper bed, ate breakfast, and hiked twenty-four miles to Belden Town where I planned to catch Dustin. The cloudy weather took the edge off of the summer heat, and other than stopping to collect water from the streams and rivers as I needed to, I hiked eight hours without interruption. I wondered if I'd be able to keep up with Dustin's faster pace and bigger days, especially since he was twenty years younger than me. All I knew was it would be great to see his friendly face again after so many miles.

Belden Town was more of a block of buildings than anything resembling a town, but I was still happy to be there. I refilled my food sack at the general store then grabbed a couple beers at the bar next door. I was the only hiker there, and the two old guys sitting nearby looked at me quizzically.

"Are you a hobo or a bum?" one of the old guys asked.

"I'm a thru-hiker, but I won't judge you if you're the working types," I replied, smirking.

"Have a beer on us!" one of the old guys said after a chuckle.

"Thanks man, you've made this bum a happy man!" I smiled wide and pulled up a seat to drink a beer with my non-hiker friends. I thanked them, then I went to the Little Haven Hostel to find Dustin. I paid for the room next door to him, showered, and changed into dry warm clothes, then joined Dustin in the common room where he was soaking his beaten-up feet and reading *Life of Pi*. Liking that idea, I soaked my ugly hiker feet while reading *Wild* by Cheryl Strayed. There was something meta about reading about someone's PCT adventure while hiking the PCT. The next morning, I weighed myself and saw I was lighter than I'd been in decades at 145 pounds. Dustin and I grabbed breakfast at the restaurant next door and watched the news for the first time in weeks. The Pope could have declared war on the Moon, and we would never have been the wiser. The headlines announced the United States Supreme Court had just legalized gay marriage, which was a rare moment of televised good news.

We climbed the intense uphill trail out of Belden with repaired feet and full bellies. Dustin outpaced me, so I knew I might not see him again for a while. Burney Falls State Park would be coming up in a few days, and I thought about spending a day or two there to celebrate the Fourth of July in style. It was quiet and peaceful at the leading edge of our group. I immersed my mind in the forest with the sounds of wind and water, warmed by exertion while optimism filled me.

Along the mountain ridges my eyes traced the skylines of trees below and I felt an almost irrepressible urge to leap into the sky, to fall, to feel the wind on my body as I fall . . . and fall . . . and fall . . . I felt that urge standing on high bridges, on train station platforms around approaching trains, on towers, on cliff edges, and on both sides of the Grand Canyon. The urge would breathe inside me, as I looked out onto the unsurvivable vista, as I wondered what it would feel like to leap. I'd take a deep breath, then I back away from the precipice. Thanks to the internet, I learned this urge has a name: *l'appel du vide*, the call of the void. Edgar Allen Poe called it the "imp of the perverse," Freud called it the "death drive," and others have referred to it as the "high place phenomenon." I never wanted to act on that urge. I liked to wonder about the consequences of dangerous things and used to interpret the sensation as a deep, inexplicable desire to harm myself, but the surprising reality is that it may be a sign of the person's will to live.

At the PCT halfway marker the next morning I met Pie, another elated thru-hiker. Pie and I hugged in celebration and confessed to each other how difficult it was to wrap our heads around hiking 1,325 miles so far. My legs were intact, my feet were bulletproof, and my constitution had never been better even though my clothes smelled like a young warthog who could clear the Savannah after every meal.

By that glorious midway marker in the woods, I'd transformed. I wasn't the scared soul who left Campo with Face Jacket. I'd endured snow, heat, gear failures, hunger, sketchy water sources, all while thawing from my Camino heartbreak. I knew my pace, my limits, and it was then I made it my goal to finish the PCT by September thirtieth.

Fall in the North Cascades was known to turn savage quickly. If I took too much time, depending on the weather I could sip lake water shirtless one day and posthole in a blizzard the next. Having a target finish date let me pace myself properly, take strategic zeros, and take rest stops so that I wouldn't experience a Sierra-style "just one more pass" tragedy. With feet that often felt like ground hamburger and a pack that smelled like the devil's armpit, a deadline was like a lighthouse to help me push through the suck. I was no longer in the mood to wander; I was heading somewhere. That psychological shift gave me power. Even though I wasn't shouting it from the treetops, having an end date would help me develop an escape plan, shape the beginning of the next journey, and give my hike greater intent.

I'd earned the right to dream with deadlines. I had the rhythm and with a set plan, I enjoyed all twenty-eight miles of trail that day, even though I had to climb over dozens of fallen trees. Each tree crossing was like dancing with sticking-out branches and mounting and dismounting tree trunks every few miles like an indecisive cowboy.

The sun settled in for the night and surrounded by a grove of trees that reached up to the happy sky, and I camped atop a pine needle-carpet. Now that I had a deadline, I remembered to savor the rare freedom of falling asleep and waking up whenever I felt like. I thought about feeling the call of the void as I drifted off to sleep. In Garland, Texas, where I was born, there were no mountains, cliffs, or suspension bridges. Yet even as a boy I felt the desire to soar. I was always climbing the tallest trees I could and often climbed onto the roof of our house. All I wanted was to explore the intensity that lived where my surroundings and my imagination crossed paths.

Only one month prior, I was relaxing at Kennedy Meadows South. It fascinated me that time passed as quickly as it did. I didn't see another thru-hiker all twenty-nine miles, only section hikers and trail maintainers who busted their asses to make the trail navigable for hikers like me. As I navigated around the workers, I thanked them for their time and effort. After several days of hopping and climbing over fallen trees, I was happy to follow the groomed trail to the Drakesbad Guest Ranch Resort, where I had heard a rumor they served a discount breakfast to thru-hikers. I made it there just before they stopped serving breakfast at 0830 and found out the rumor was true. With a belly full of eggs, bacon, and coffee, I savored terrain that was flat. There was a twenty-five-mile water-less stretch coming up I was preparing for, but I wasn't too stressed about it. With just fifty miles to Burney Falls State Park, I felt like I had plenty of time to relax in time to arrive for the Fourth of July.

The next morning, I spent a couple of hours breakfasting at JJ's Café in Old Town. Then, I watered up for the long thirsty stretch. I need not have worried about anything, because halfway up the trail there was a large water cache and some Gatorade trail magic that helped me keep hydrated. I read about Cheryl Strayed's hike twenty years ago in her book, and I felt particularly thankful there were so many water caches in this dry section. Encountering trail magic every few days reminded me of the generosity of complete strangers who went out of their way to support the hiking culture. This would be a slower, lonelier, and more dangerous venture without the kindness of strangers on trail. The weather was wistfully breezy, allowing the summer warmth to shine without being oppressive. Hiking on volcanic terrain and ancient lava felt otherworldly, and the scorched trees all around emanated an eerie circle-of-life type of beauty.

With just seventeen miles to Burney Falls, I wondered if I would encounter familiar faces. Even if I didn't, I could always toast with new friends. I hiked out of Hat Creek Rim the next morning, ending a stretch of trail even drier than British humor. I caught a ride from a section hiker I'd met just that morning, and I treated myself to a yummy breakfast at the Blueberry Patch Restaurant. I then hiked to Burney Falls State Park, where hundreds, if not thousands, of campers had the same thought about celebrating the Fourth of July there as I had. I squeezed through the hordes of tourists and took in the gorgeousness of the waterfall. More people poured in, so after I got my fill of the waterfall splendor, I stopped by the restaurant for lunch. Discovering it was far too crowded and pricey, even for *my* grumbling stomach, so I topped up my food supply at the grocery store. After an hour of meandering through tourists, I ditched my plan to spend my first Fourth of July in three years on American soil at Burney Falls. I decided instead to hike ten miles before bed, putting me in the middle of nowhere, where I found greater peace than I did surrounded by an ocean of drinking, boisterous people with screaming kids (and screaming adults). "Maybe I'm not cut out for civilization anymore," I said to myself as I hiked in peace. It was a sobering thought. Weird, I thought extroverts like me were supposed to crave company. I guess I'm still learning things about things.

The loamy forest floor bounced under my footfalls in a way that felt fun and springy, and the part of me that wanted to drink and party for Independence Day happily gave way to the part of me that loved hiking big days. No parades, barbecues, beers, or fireworks for me on America's birthday, 2015. Instead, I found jubilation in hiking thirty-five miles, only seeing two fresh-faced hikers all day. The trail finally took me up along a ridge over the tree line so I could admire all directions, more than just a hint of scenery through forest. There was so much beauty on the trail, it embraced all my senses. At thirty-six miles, the next day was the biggest day thus far on the PCT. I ate two granola bars and fell asleep under the stars, but at 0400 I was shocked awake by fireworks. After the twelfth raindrop hit my face, it wasn't actually fireworks that woke me up, but thunder. I packed everything away with award-winning efficiency before it turned into a full-on rainstorm.

It was a wet, early start to the day, but I actually enjoyed it, as there were lots of trees around with creeks and streams. I felt alive and refreshed as I hiked in shorts and a t-shirt without bothering to put on my raincoat, which would have only heated me up. The rain rinsed the salt and sweat out of my clothes like hiking through a waterfall. I thought how refreshing it would be to hike naked through the rainstorm but kept my clothes on until lunchtime when the sun came out and dried everything.

I debated whether to push all the way to Dunsmuir that night or take a more relaxed day and head into town in the morning. I was almost out of food again. Although I was jonesing for a hot break-fast, I took an hour-long break at Squaw Creek, whose river was a fine area to relax and bathe in. Solitary journeys through unfamil-iar landscapes beckoned me toward the unknown and unexplored realms of existence. My mind stirred before the grandeur of nature's raw beauty that echoed the ineffable depths of the void. Each step I took into the wilderness resonated with the unspoken dialogue between my soul and the void, inviting me to contemplate even more than I already was. Times and places like this balanced those moments I spent in severe hunger. I found myself missing familiar faces, but a couple of section hikers told me they saw Dustin just ahead of me, which put a smile on my face. On the PCT, at the edge of human existence, my existential dance between the traveler and the void illuminated how the allure of the unknown, as both inner and outer landscapes, converged in harmony. Traveling alone was a transformative odyssey whispering from the depths of my being, compelling me to seek, to explore, and to confront all of the mysteries beyond the horizon.

And yet, I couldn't keep myself from the feeling my chest was pressed wide open by all that was around me, the sensation filled my lungs with desire for more, and to know others experienced the same thing and had even given it a name made me feel like I was less of an anomaly. More than ever, I acknowledged my own will to live, and I wanted to chase that feeling. The call of the void guided me to seek out danger, flirt with fear, and skirt the edges of safety when I knew I might end up paying for it.

Although asking pretty girls to trek with me through Spain, hiking through mountaintop blizzards, and risking extreme hunger and thirst had all been risks with uncertain outcomes, standing on the edge of possibility thrilled me. It's rare for people to dream of leaving their homes to trek for months when no one asked them to. Life involved enough risk without having to go searching for exhausting ways to confront death.

Defying a complacent life and refusing an early death is part of the nebulous free will I wanted to keep exercising. Seeing what existence can mean beyond what I've always experienced is a kind of miracle that let me feel alive more than I ever thought possible.

I wasn't crazy. I was in love with life.

Theodore Roosevelt called Burney Falls the "eighth wonder of the world."

"The sight of it fills one with more conflicting emotions than any other scene with which I am familiar. It is at once weird, fascinating, enchanting, repellent, of exquisite beauty and at times terrifying in its austere-dignity and oppressing stillness."
—Jack London about Crater Lake

24

I had intended to luxuriate in the town of Dunsmuir—one full day and night of comfort, hot food, soft chairs, idle wandering—but the town seemed to exist in a kind of suspended animation. It was like a Western set after the cameras stopped rolling: quaint, lovely, and mostly closed. The laundromat stood open like a silent shrine to civilization, but detergent proved elusive. I would have to settle for a salty wardrobe a little while longer, it seemed.

After striking out at the laundromat, I happened upon the Cornerstone Restaurant, where I waited for it to open like a pilgrim outside a temple. Once the door finally swung open, I entered and had a breakfast so delicious it felt like a benediction—eggs, bacon, hash browns, and the sort of coffee that could bring a ghost back to life.

Afterward, I drifted into the town's modest art gallery, nestled in the historic district like a forgotten jewel. I stood still among the paintings, awestruck. The canvases throbbed with soul. Brushstrokes evoked fog-strewn forests and wild creeks in heatless moonlight. I imagined the artists—all locals, I assumed—pulling inspiration from these very woods and ridgelines I'd just wandered through.

Were any of them hikers like me? Had they stood under the same pines, felt the same hush before a storm, or kissed the same light bleeding through smoke and dawn?

I bought food at the downtown minimart—a humble haul of calories—and devoured a whole spinach and chicken pizza like a victorious gladiator. I chased it with a pint of Haagen-Dazs and watched unfamiliar PCT hikers trickle into town like time travelers from the same mythic road. We smiled at one another, recognizing the same dust in each other's bones, the same freedom in our gait.

But the trail called to me. The town had given me what I needed—calories, colors, warmth—and now I needed movement. I stuck out my thumb, hitched a ride back to the trailhead, and ventured back into the wild under a sky so perfect it felt digitally enhanced.

Then the clouds arrived, dark as spilled ink. Rain fell. Then hail. I hiked thirty-one miles through it all like a drenched prophet with a belly full of pizza and a heart beating in thunderous rhythm with the storm. When the sun returned in the evening, I found a patch of flat ground that felt like sacred real estate—dry enough to sleep on, quiet enough to dream. Thunder muttered above like the gods were telling inside jokes. I lay on the forest floor, wrapped in solitude, knowing I had just lived one of those days I'd remember long after the muscles healed.

Faces remained happy, even under the gray skies and dampened socks. Maybe it was the sweet mercy of no mosquitoes. Maybe it was just the peculiar joy of being alive. The next morning began in sheets of rain that soaked the world in silence, and I hiked through it until the sun cracked the clouds open around 0900. Twenty-eight more miles melted beneath my boots like a prayer whispered repeatedly. I was closing in on Etna, with only twenty-six miles to go.

Hiking in the rain can turn a saint cynical, but I chose laughter. The trail had long since taught me that suffering is inevitable, but misery is optional. My raincoat sent water directly into my face like it was auditioning for a slapstick comedy. Puddles launched assaults on my socks with malicious glee. My glasses fogged up until I looked like a librarian lost in a steam room. I could've cursed it all—but instead, I laughed the kind of loud, echoing, solo traveler laughter that no one else hears but the trees.

Then it hit me—this wasn't a flaw in the plan. This was the plan. Humor wasn't just a defense mechanism. It was my compass. It had led me to take bold steps into unknown terrain: working in Saudi Arabia, launching myself on an atheistic pilgrimage through the spiritual architecture of the world, walking across two countries in search of nothing more (or less) than truth.

Humor was how I rewired my brain to see the absurdity of fear, the comedy in anxiety, the wild invitation behind every detour. Leaving my climate-controlled home in Albuquerque for this muddy, mosquito-filled, rain-drenched life wasn't madness. It was alchemy. It turned discomfort into delight, uncertainty into revelation.

I used to think intelligence was all about grades, titles, paychecks. Real intelligence also looked like smiling in the rain. Like being curious enough to chase joy. Like choosing not to let fear win. I let go of cynicism because it was heavy. I replaced it with lightness, even in a thunderstorm. Gratitude, hope, a dash of the divine— and always, always humor. That was my travel kit. That was my trail magic. In those wet miles, I understood something precious: the path to meaning winds through laughter just as surely as it winds through pain. And if you're lucky, you get both in a single day—and call it a good one.

At my first break that morning, I sprawled out across the gravel lot of a remote trailhead, wet gear flung in every direction, socks steaming in the sun like flags of surrender. I tore into my food like a starving philosopher and welcomed two section hikers, Lucky and Bad Wolf, who joined me in that glorious ritual of airing out the damp, the sweat-soaked, and the stench-soaked.

I already knew I'd need to resupply in Etna. My appetite was a roaring bonfire that consumed calories with a spiritual fervor. The sky overhead darkened with clouds that threatened without delivering—an eerie calm, as if the trail itself was holding its breath. That night, I set up camp with a couple from San Francisco, aptly named Pinky and The Brain, whose dry wit made the miles feel lighter. For only the third time on the Pacific Crest Trail, I raised my tent, not out of necessity, but a cautious nod to the storm gods that had toyed with me so often.

The following day the heavens let loose. Chilly rain swept across the Russian Wilderness like a curtain of memory and mystery, blinding the eye but sharpening the soul. The views, hidden behind gauze-thick mist, remained ghostly figments of the sublime—landscapes I could only imagine in the pauses between thunderclaps. Still, I pressed onward through twenty-six miles of soaking solitude, arriving at the Etna trailhead with a grin that no weather could wash away.

I got a ride into town with K-Mart and Mr. White, two hikers with trail names fit for a 1987 indie film about a meth dealer set in Garland, Texas. We made our way to the Hiker Hostel, a hallowed space of lofty ceilings, warm welcomes, and the unmistakable scent of trail mix and shampoo. Inside, I reunited with a cavalcade of characters: No Tent, Camel, and Hog. Each name, a story.

As the hostel filled, hikers combined laundry loads like it was communal alchemy. We invaded the local grocery store with the urgency of Vikings and returned with packs swollen and spirits lifted. I fired off messages to friends and family from that small, miraculous pocket of cell reception. To Karen in Bend, I wrote that I was just 400 miles away—a number that once seemed Herculean now looked like a victory lap.

Then, like the closing of some beautiful cosmic loop, Dustin arrived.

Our reunion was effortless—two wanderers drawn again into each other's orbits. We celebrated over pints at the town's brewery, whose weathered wooden storefronts and one-street-town charm exhaled a peace I hadn't realized I'd been craving. As I strolled past porches and pickups, I kept seeing a mysterious green-and-gold flag. It tugged at my curiosity until I couldn't help but ask.

That's when I learned about the State of Jefferson.

This wasn't just some novelty for locals to sell on mugs. It was a living, breathing vision, a cultural heartbeat. The bartender poured beers and history in equal measure, explaining how the people of this forgotten northern territory wedged between Sacramento and Portland felt cast adrift by politics, and yearned for sovereignty rooted in rugged self-reliance. In this town nestled between ancient pines and volcanic ridges, where every face had wind-scarred wisdom and every handshake felt forged in fire, the idea of breaking away from a system that didn't serve them felt less like rebellion and more like survival.

Dustin and I raised our glasses to Jefferson, then drained them. That night, back at the hostel, we joined the circle of headlamps and stories under the eternal gaze of the stars. The cosmos listened. We passed beers and firelight, trading tales of pain, humor, near-misses, and tiny victories. In that moment, the trail wasn't a line on a map—it was a living organism, stitched together by souls like ours.

After sleeping like royalty in actual beds, Dustin and I parted again, each recommitted to our own pace, our own hike. Like all good hikers, we respected each other's solitude. The sky was mercifully dry as I hiked twenty-nine miles and collapsed in my tent atop a craggy hillock that looked like it had been imported from Scotland—a lonely altar to distance and devotion. Below me, Seiad Valley awaited, twenty-seven miles away: the final outpost before the border, the threshold between California and Oregon.

I reached Seiad Valley on July 12th. A loose, dusty town with a kind heart, it offered everything I needed: a store, a restaurant, laundry, and enough fellow hikers to fill a village. My Etna crew had reconvened, and we sank into the moment together like pilgrims come home. I planned only a quick stop—but the vibes were too good, too unspoken, too rare. That night, the restaurant—usually closed on Sundays—opened just for us. We feasted. We tipped generously. Around the fire, names like Ronin, Magic, Polka Dot, Flying Fish, Stone, Concrete, and Thermometer lit up the night like constellations. We passed wine, told lies, sang softly. My feet blistered, but my heart felt invincible. In that sacred stillness, I dissolved into something bigger than myself. I wasn't young or old. I wasn't even entirely human. I was the forest. I was the fire. I was the song.

For a fleeting heartbeat, I touched something infinite.

The next morning, I stood at the edge of Seiad Valley, gazing up at the brutal 7,000-foot climb ahead. I didn't flinch. I was ready. That day, I hiked only twenty-four miles, cowboy camping under a flawless sky. I wanted to feel the pulse of California one last time before crossing that invisible line into Oregon. The stars blinked overhead like ancient witnesses. Though I would soon walk out of California, I knew California would never walk out of me.

I hiked a cool thirty-three miles the following day. This left me seven miles to hike to the trailhead and hitchhike to Ashland, my first trail town in Oregon. The holes in all my socks were so big, I couldn't tell which end was which. Even my shoes only clung to my feet purely by wishful thinking. I hiked across the border of California into Oregon and signed the trail register at the state border. I noticed Dustin had signed in two days prior, and was thinking about how fast he must've been hiking when out of the corner of my eye, about twenty feet away, I saw a black bear.

If I had grown up in the Pacific Northwest, seeing a Black Bear wouldn't have been worth mentioning. But because I grew up in Garland, Texas, encountering a bear was sensory overload. Growing up in a place where danger meant termites, fire ants, and cockroaches, I was unprepared for a several-hundred-pound forest monster lumbering through the pines like it owned the place (because it did).

Yet, there was this weird calm to it. The bear didn't charge me or foam at the mouth like in a cartoon. It seemed content sniffing a log, doing ursine business as my Texan instincts fired like a security alarm.

I was astonished it took no notice of my heart pounding while I stood frozen and sweaty, jelly-kneed, and closer to it than I wanted to be.

It foraged snout-deep for breakfast in a fallen fir tree as I kept still, my eyes latched on to it without blinking. I felt naked. I'd like to think my calm and stoic response was due to my oneness with nature, but if I had to be honest, it was more likely complacence in the face of danger.

As if in a badly written cliché, I stepped on a twig and startled the poor bear. In that microsecond the bear and I locked eyes and I knew if it had decided to eat me, it would have. If it knew how laughably defenseless I was against the weakest of its actions, it might have finished its breakfast with all 5-foot-6-inches of me. It wouldn't have cared in the slightest that I was, and always have been, sympathetic to the causes of all bearkind. Fortunately, the bear lumbered quickly away from me, deep into the thick forest. That moment I spent staring face to face with that hungry bear could have been beset by fear, illusion, and negativity. I wasn't actually complacent in that moment, my humor helped to make up for my ignorance of what to do when the universe put a bear in my path.

The Bhagavad Gita speaks about how we can act in our lives without attachment to the result. Shakespeare wrote no matter how painful or pleasurable something appears, it is only an understanding that comes from our own thoughts and perceptions. Even when all seems deadly and hopeless, humor even lent a hapless smelly hiker like me moral and spiritual value. Humor surprised me by being an effective coping mechanism in that stressful and frightening encounter. There was a ton of residual tension and fear hit me once the bear and I went our separate ways, and I could feel my humor helping to dissolve tension. It let me step back from the intensity of the experience while the absurdity of the situation helped me to shift my perspective from feeling like a victim of circumstances to someone who could see the lighter side of things. It reframed the experience in a more manageable light while releasing endorphins to manage my emotional response. Instead of panicking, overreacting, and screaming my way into the jaws of that California black bear, humor allowed me to perform and relax effectively. That I relied on my humor this way didn't mean I dismissed the seriousness of nearly being eaten. Having a sense of humor might have been key in the bear encounter becoming part of my life story, instead of being part of my death story. Maybe the bear left me alone because I smelled like hikertrash. Maybe it's Maybelline.

After my near-bear experience, I was blessed with a great night's sleep and started hiking at 0600. I caught up to Bobaroo and hiker couple Caboose and Cutfinger. We chatted our way through six miles as I hiked on disintegrated husks that used to be shoes. Cutfinger and Caboose were celebrating their last day on the PCT, so we all hitchhiked to a restaurant called Morning Glory where we ate breakfast together. Afterward, I tossed my shoes out and sauntered through town wearing crocs and ran into Mr. White and Camel, who suggested we split a room in the Best Western. We checked in and took turns showering off our trail dirt, then we resupplied our food at Albertson's.

That night I planned out the upcoming highlights and messaged my Bend benefactor I would be able to meet her at the Shelter Cove Resort in about eleven days. That would allow me to enjoy a thirty-mile-a-day pace, including a detour to Crater Lake. The Oregon trail looked to have reliable water, manageable terrain, and barely any dysentery. I found a great outfitter in Ashland where I bought a new pair of shoes that wanted to hike Oregon on my feet, no one else's. That evening, I joined Magic and Polka Dot for dinner at Caldera Brewery where I had a couple cheeseburgers and a couple pints of beer while live music filled the streets. After such a great evening in Ashland, I decided to spend one more day being clean, and so I took a spontaneous zero. I ate lunch with Hog the hiker at Morning Glory where we exchanged stories about our trail experiences. It had *been* a long road, we agreed, getting from there to here. Having hiked the Appalachian Trail and the Continental Divide Trail, Hog was about to complete the last of America's three long trails. I liked that idea that I might become a Triple Crowner someday.

I checked out of the Best Western and stayed at the Ashland Lodge with other fellow hikers where I swam, sunbathed, read, and processed the miles behind me. I ate one last dinner with Hog, Bobaroo, Tinker, Magic, and Polka Dot at Standing Stove Brewery, where I ordered a lamb burger with spinach followed by a marionberry cobbler which went so perfectly with the pints of stout I ordered. I enjoyed having the metabolism of a hiker.

I was on trail at 0600 with the energy of a rabid teenager. The trail was flat, and the weather was bright and breezy. I hiked thirty-two miles, and I hiked thirty-four the day after. So much for keeping a relaxed, easy-going pace, but it seemed like the terrain itself wanted me to hike big miles. I camped out with Ronin, Magic, Polka Dot, a couple section hikers, and about 30,000 mosquitoes thirty-seven miles south of Crater Lake. I visited it back in 2009, and its beauty haunted me ever since. The weight of the trail was noticeably light. The miles ahead were like the pages left to read of a book I couldn't tear myself away from. I had completed two-thirds of the PCT, with 860 miles before I would have to reintegrate into normal civilization. I felt no dread, just elation and contentment.

Although I didn't yet feel connected to my future or how best to find my normal self after this adventure, I'd never felt less fear about such things. Instead, I felt limitless gratitude about getting that rare chance to be up close and personal with nature. It wasn't until I was in my early thirties that I started to explore the wilderness. In Walden, Thoreau laid out his valid concerns about the degrading influences of unrestrained society and industry. I believed this was my first foray into naturalist literature that poignantly illustrated to me the many benefits of getting familiar with nature. Thoreau was also a traveler who discovered a powerful love of hiking. I reveled in his travel writings, unable to get enough of the meaningfulness of the wilderness, and how nature was intensely spiritual, morally vital, and dangerously underappreciated. It had me thinking of a world beyond the concrete container of my civilized life and might have been the first step I took toward becoming Windscreen.

No conversation about the American wilderness is complete without mentioning John Muir. I could only imagine what his life had been like living on the Western frontier. The way he waxed transcendental, like some romantic who articulated a nature-centered spirituality, paralleled my own journey in faith. Muir let the natural experience guide his personal and spiritual transformation, and I thought I could do well by doing the same. In this overworked and over-materialistic world, Muir realized that mountain beauty and forest time was not only pleasant, but it was noticeably healthy for the mind, body, and soul. Without John Muir's persistence and direct involvement with land preservation, there might not be any national parks today. I respected the spiritual and aesthetic values regarding the American wilderness that challenged the idea the nation's resources should be exploited for human consumption, and Muir helped to recalibrate social perspectives to see how scarring the land for private enrichment was shortsighted and unhealthy. Beauty, Muir insisted, was as vital to human sustenance as oxygen and food. He helped to popularize the philosophy human qualities of life can be provided for without ravaging the planet. Cultivating higher sensibilities than those held by previous generations, and I owed John Muir for shaping my life.

I was unable to hike small days while in Oregon. I didn't know if it was the weather, the landscape, or both, but the trail invigorated me. I began the day thinking I might just do a twenty-seven-mile day, but then I made a command decision and pressed on to make it a thirty-seven-mile day instead. It was with deep satisfaction when I rested on a picnic table outside the Mazama Village general store, where my new hiker friend Camel and I resupplied our food sacks. Camel had the wonderful idea to night-hike a quarter-mile further, cowboy camp, and wake up at 0400 to hike up to the caldera to see the sun rise over Crater Lake. I had reception at the Mazama General Store, so I read that Karen would pick me up and host me for a couple of days. I replied with gratitude and shut my eyes under the glowing stars. When life is already a dream, where does the mind go during sleep?

Camel and I rose without hesitation at 0400, driven not by obligation but by reverence. The world was still dark, hushed, and sacred—the kind of silence that feels like a held breath before a miracle. With headlamps dimmed and anticipation as our fuel, we climbed the steep trail that curved like an offering bowl around the ancient caldera. Our boots pressed into volcanic ash and pumice, the ground still dreaming beneath us.

As we crested the rim, the world changed.

The sky to the east began its slow exhale, and Crater Lake— the indigo eye of an ancient god—greeted us in silence. By 0530, we were perched lakeside, facing the coming sun, watching the alchemy of morning unfold. Deep amber, gold, and violet spilled across the lake's still surface, dancing like spirits awakening from slumber. The palette defied description—like someone had shattered a cathedral's stained-glass windows and swept the fragments across the water.

We said nothing. There are moments on trail when words feel like a trespass. The silence between us stretched out infinitely, becoming not emptiness, but fullness. The air held still. Even the birds waited. Time passed in a dreamlike drift, and then, as if summoned by myth, a hiker appeared on the path behind us—Howdy Doody, with his wide grin and trail-worn boots. The three of us fell into an easy rhythm, drawn not only by camaraderie but by a singular scent that sliced through the mountain air like poetry—bacon, eggs, and coffee. The Crater Lake Lodge sat ahead on the rim like a mirage carved from stone and luxury, its dining room glowing in the early light.

We wandered in like druids into a cathedral, our crusty packs and dusty legs a stark contrast to the crisp linens and steaming teapots. But no one blinked. The servers had seen our kind before—the weary, the wild, the wonderstruck. We feasted. And I mean feasted—like Olympians returned from war. Fluffy pancakes the size of frying pans, eggs that melted like butter, and coffee rich enough to call a friend. We laughed, devoured, and reminded ourselves what it felt like to be human again, if only for a single, decadent hour.

Then, with full bellies and spirits lighter than our packs, we hiked the Rim Trail as it hugged the lake closely. Eventually, the lake slipped from view, and we entered the long, thirsty corridor of the twenty-six-mile waterless stretch. The wind sang in the pines, and we answered it with our footsteps, soft and steady. I sang trail ballads to the trees, nonsense songs and fragments of memories I hadn't known I still carried. It was the kind of stretch that strips you down—not just your body, but your mind, your illusions, your defenses.

By day's end, I stumbled upon a campsite kissed by the music of a pristine creek. The sound wasn't just water—it was liquid hymn, flowing over stones polished by eons. I knelt and drank deeply, letting the cold clarity wash through me like absolution. The contrast between the morning's fire-colored lake and the twilight murmurs of this stream felt like poetry designed just for me.

That Crater Lake breakfast had powered me through a full day of myth and muscle. As I curled into my quilt, I counted the miles that remained—just fifty more until I would see Karen in Bend. The math was simple, but the meaning was anything but.

I drifted off with the lake still burning behind my eyelids—its color etched into the memory-vault of my soul. I hoped I'd never forget it. Not just the sight of it, but the feeling—that early morning holiness, the taste of sunrise, the hush before speech. The jewels of this trail weren't made of gold or crystal. They were made of light, silence, companionship, and the ache of feet that have walked far enough to reach the edge of the world . . . and know there's still more to come.

I spent the next day rationing my water effectively so I could cover the thirty-seven miles to Crescent Lake before sunset. Once there, I rewarded myself with a refreshing swim then walked around the campsite until I found an empty spot. I was about to tuck into my food bag and have a well-earned dinner at the picnic table when a camper broke from his raucous group and ambled my way.

With breath that smelled like a cheap brewery, the guy slurred, "What brings ya here?"

"Oh, hey. I'm hiking the PCT—"

"Where's your car?" he interrupted.

"It's in my garage in Albuquerque," I replied, wondering where he was taking this conversation.

"You can stay if you don't bother anyone."

"So, if I keep quiet, kinda like I was doing, I can stay here?"

He clapped my sweaty back. "You're welcome!"

"Thank you."

He stumbled back to his party. Ten minutes later, another camper from his group came over. "You have to go."

"I do?" I arched my eyebrows, smelling even more beer on him than I did from his friend. "Your buddy told me I'm welcome to stay here," I replied politely, feeling that my time there was wrapping up.

"Nah, man, you gotta get out."

"You got it, Chief." I said.

I knew I must have looked like a homeless bum to him, but I was taken aback. He simply didn't care what my story was; he just wanted me gone. I wasn't about to escalate things, so I packed up my things and headed back on trail.

Their unfriendliness hit me sideways. After acclimating to a culture where every hiker shared water, snacks, and stories like family, the idea of being told to leave a campsite by a few belligerent drunks was like finding a rip in the fabric of the trail's kindness. All I wanted was to curl up under the stars, and even trade laughs with strangers-turned-friends. Instead, they met me with puffed-up bravado and insecure energy that jarred me. I told myself it wasn't a big deal; they were entitled to their space and weren't required to share anything. The trail had made me open, trusting, and willing to share a Snickers bar with someone just because they look tired.

This experience was against the code of the trail, and there was shame in not understanding the unspoken agreement of looking out for each other. I felt anger, confusion, and the hurt of betrayal. People did worse to each other; I wasn't blind to that. Best to my knowledge, no one ever killed me, so I tried to get my bearings and hike on, feeling like a stranger on a trail that had felt more like home until recently. Far enough from that disappointing venue I felt calm enough to manage a bit of gratitude. The PCT had just taught me that peace is fragile, and that kindness is sacred.

Hiking made me feel better, and my overthinking melted into quiet disappointment. I hiked with my headlamp on, searching for a suitable place to lay out my sleeping bag. After an hour, I found a comfortable place to cowboy camp where no one would take offense.

I wondered what John Muir would have thought about what happened at that campsite. People like him defended the sanctity of nature and its connection with humankind and passed The Wilderness Act in 1964 so people could experience true wilderness.

The drunken, territorial entitlement like I saw ran, to me, hard and jagged against the grain of John Muir's entire philosophy. Muir saw wilderness as a temple, a place to be small, humble, and reverent. He didn't believe nature was something to dominate or claim, but something to commune with—a space where human ego was brave enough to relax and let wonder flourish in its place. He spoke of being part of the landscape, not the boss of it. To Muir, a night under the stars was a form of prayer. Was I out of place thinking drunk campers treating public land like it's theirs to control was akin to stomping on what Muir stood for?

The trail, in my experience, was one of the world's last great equalizers where every soul felt welcome, and every granite spire and alpine breeze was to be shared. The behavior I witness that evening pissed on the altar of the church that people like John Muir had spent their lives building.

The following morning, I was back in good spirits. By the time I arrived at Shelter Cove Resort I was positively giddy. I saw Bogey, Howdy Doody, and a fresh face called Penny Lane. As I waited for Karen to pick me up for a respite in Bend, we four thru-hikers reveled in the joy of having made it to Oregon. I was glad I didn't have to rely on the store here as a resupply point, but it was a fine place to drink a beer or three.

Navigating between human sustainability and the solidarity of nature was, and still is, an unending dance that strives to permit our species to coexist with Mother Earth. The foundation upon which naturalism finds expression continues, thanks to the truths espoused by enthusiasts like Thoreau and Muir. Such truths reminded me my thoughts are not alien in this world. We belong. I belong.

Mt. Hood: Voted Most Likely To Erupt

25

Spending time with Karen and her husband John was like stepping into a warm hearth after wandering for months in wilderness. Their kindness felt effortless and abundant, like Bend's sunshine filtering through tall pines—constant, golden, and true. They welcomed me not as a guest, but as kin. They drove me to resupply groceries, brought me to REI like a pilgrim entering a temple of gear and hope. In return, I insisted on treating them to Red Robin—because sometimes a bottomless basket of fries can say what words cannot.

When Karen dropped me back at the PCT, my feet felt brand new. My pack was full. My spirit was light. The sky was an open vault of blue. Somewhere along the path that day, between the rhythm of poles and the hush of pine needles underfoot, I suddenly realized I wanted to go back to school. The idea of getting another degree bloomed like a wildflower in my mind, fragile but radiant. It was a far cry from turning wrenches and teaching aircraft systems, but wasn't that the point of walking from Mexico to Canada? To crack open the shell of old identities and listen for what sings underneath?

The following day, the trail gifted me one of those magical detours only the PCT can offer. I came across Elk Lake, a shimmering sapphire nestled like a secret among the forest. The smell of grilling burgers wafted through the air like perfume from the gods. I joined Bogey and a hiker called White Rabbit at a table near the water—dusty, sunburned, and blissfully ravenous. We devoured burgers and cold beer like it was a religious rite.

Then the unexpected happened—something only the PCT could orchestrate with such disarming grace. A group of vacationers approached us—Rod, Bob, Laurie, and Deb—beaming with curiosity and reverence, as if we were mythic creatures they'd read about in books. "Are you really PCT hikers?" they asked, eyes wide, voices giddy.

We braced for awkwardness or judgment—but what followed was pure trail magic. They didn't want us to leave. They wanted us to come with them. To hop aboard their pontoon boat, drink beer, float the lake, and share our stories. At first, the offer felt surreal—too good, too cinematic—but the sparkle in their eyes was genuine. We looked at each other, grinned like teenagers getting away with something deliciously wrong, and climbed aboard.

The afternoon became a sunlit fever dream. Bruce Springsteen and Lil Jon blasted from speakers as we sailed across Elk Lake like gods on sabbatical. We toasted our blisters. We swapped trail myths for their lakeside legends. The pontoon became a confessional booth, a dance floor, a floating campfire of connection. Every question they asked about bears, food, distance, and life beyond the trail dripped with admiration.

When they invited us to dinner at their rental cabin, it was an easy yes. We broke bread like old friends and laughed under the stars until the fire turned to coals and sleep claimed us one by one. It felt like an ancient rite of hospitality when strangers become kin for a night and part ways with hearts a little fuller than before.

The next morning, we woke up with the sun and the smell of bacon. We helped clean up camp, gave heartfelt thanks to our hosts, and returned to the trail with smiles so wide they nearly split our faces. I felt buoyant, restored—not just physically, but spiritually. There was still goodness in the world. Sometimes it floated by on pontoons.

That day, I hiked twenty-five miles with ease, my soul still ringing from laughter and music. The Oregon wind whistled between the trees like a blessing. The following day, I surged with energy, hiking thirty-three miles and passing the 2,000-mile marker—a number so absurdly large it felt like myth. Rain soaked me all day, and I barely paused, too hungry for miles, too alive to stop.

I cowboy camped beneath a spray of stars, the Milky Way smeared across the heavens like a cosmic compass. The silence of the high Oregon wilderness wrapped around me like a cloak, and my food bag hung half-empty beside me, a testament to my constant hunger—for miles, for meaning, for more.

The next morning, I woke to find my world frozen. A thin sheet of ice had crystallized across the meadow, including my face and sleeping bag. My bladder urged me to move. My warmth begged me to stay. Eventually, nature won—as it always does—and I emerged like a reluctant bear from hibernation, shivering but smiling.

At Olallie Lake, the charm of the little rustic resort was a balm. I dried my gear, restocked my food, and met a hiker named Ryman—thirty-nine, like me. The first hiker I'd met who was my age. We hiked side by side through an Oregon dreamscape, talking about life, trail, and everything in between. He would soon reunite with his wife at Mount Hood, but for now, our paces synced and our stories wove together like creek water over stone.

I looked ahead to Mount Hood, and behind to Crater Lake. I thought about airports and classrooms and passport stamps. I thought about home and what that even means. But mostly, I kept walking—because that's what long-distance hikers do. We carry our lives on our backs. We walk into our future with each footfall. Sometimes, people even invited us onto a boat.

We camped out after a grueling thirty-two-mile day, our legs carved from fatigue and willpower, when we got word from some southbound hikers that the Timberline Lodge, perched high on the sacred flanks of Mount Hood, offered free accommodations to thru-hikers. That sentence alone could raise a blistered pilgrim from the dead. But for me—someone with a backpack full of duct tape, granola, and an unholy love of Stephen King—it meant something more. This wasn't just any stop. This was The Shining hotel. Stanley Kubrick's bone-chilling monolith of snowbound horror. The chance to sleep beneath the roof that once echoed with the haunting type-writer clatter of Jack Torrance? It was like crossing into myth.

My shoulders ached like someone had hung planets from them, and mosquitoes were throwing a blood rave on my neck, but none of that mattered. I was closing in on Cascade Locks, the threshold of Washington State, and I could taste it in the wind. That sense of arrival, that pull of a distant finish line—it lit a fire deep in my gut that no ache or sting could extinguish. I wasn't just hiking through Oregon. I was closing a chapter in the grand saga of my own becoming.

The trail, like life, didn't always offer guarantees. Even with all my effort, planning, and ferocious mental tenacity, it still often felt like the universe was politely ignoring my aspirations. There was something undeniably encouraging in the simple fact that I was still moving forward, mile by hard-earned mile. Order might never be permanent, but it could still be carved out of chaos, if only temporarily. That carving—that act of creation through motion—was enough.

The Air Force had trained me in the art of precision and control, but it also taught me something far more vital: how to thrive in uncertainty. How to let time unspool without rigid structure. How to breathe inside the blur of the unknown and not collapse. It took years to understand that flexibility was a superpower, not a weakness. That letting go of the plan didn't mean failure, it meant faith. Not religious faith, but something grittier. Wilder. The kind that's earned in lightning storms and long silences. I'd had more than a few moments in life where my carefully drawn maps were set ablaze, times when I felt the pull of emotional gravity trying to suck me into despair. What the trail taught me was that if I could learn to dance with chaos instead of resisting it, it wouldn't break me. It might even show me the way.

The PCT didn't hand me answers. It handed me perspective.

I realized that I couldn't control the storm, but I could choose how to move through it. If I moved with grace, with curiosity, with a bit of rough-edged joy, I could see that chaos was just transformation in disguise. As I neared the border with Canada, the gravity of my own thoughts intensified. I felt like I was getting closer to knowing what I wanted—not just after this trail, but in life. I distilled the answer into something sharp and unshakable: nature, education, travel, laughter, connection, and, if I was lucky, being a force for good. That wasn't a final destination, it was a compass heading.

Hiking to Canada was the easy part. I found myself stopping more often—not out of exhaustion, but reverence. When I paused to admire the Oregon Cascades or chat with a fellow hiker over trail mix and Clif Bars, I remembered that beauty didn't require order. It required presence. The chaos of the natural world wasn't a mess. It was a masterpiece. From the fractal intricacies of pine needles to the sudden hush that falls before a storm, everything worked because everything connected. It wasn't just a system—it was a symphony. That sacred thread of interconnection—that sense that everything belongs—was the soul beneath John Muir's writings. It was the unspoken liturgy of the PCT. It was in the shared silence of a star-soaked night, where headlamps flicker like fireflies. It was in the tiny, monumental act of handing someone your last tortilla because you know they need it more. The PCT, in all its brutal, breathtaking glory, was just as holy as the Camino Santiago.

That awareness gave me a clarity I'd never found in a pew or a pulpit. Catholic school had taught me how to kneel and obey.

Hardline Islamic culture had tried to cage me in orthodoxy. The trail taught me something those places never could: you don't need a building to find the divine. You don't need a prophet to access your own damn soul. The trail didn't care what I believed. It didn't want me to follow. It wanted me to listen.

That's why the resentment I carried toward organized religion began to dissolve. Not because I rewrote the past, but because I had begun to transcend it. I finally saw that sacredness wasn't something handed down from a pulpit. It was something rising from the dirt, sparkling from the ice on my sleeping bag, shining from the eyes of strangers who shared nothing but kindness. Chaos wasn't litter. It was the pulse of the universe. The howl of transformation. The fierce, beautiful reminder that everything changes—and that's exactly what makes life so precious. I didn't need to escape civilization forever to understand this, but I did need to get far enough away from its noise to hear the truth behind it all.

Of course, I still made plans. I still dreamed. But I let go of the illusion that I could master the future. Instead, I chose to dance with it—even if it meant spinning through absurdity, through pain, through glorious unknowns. On the trail, just like in life, it's not about staying clean or sticking to the script. Somewhere between the silence of the PCT and the cathedral bells of the Camino, I let go of a persistent illusion: the belief that I could out-plan the future. That I could navigate life with the right combination of ambition and tactical optimism, the way I navigated the trail—with humility and integrity.

Spirituality isn't owned by any one system. It shows up in motion. In struggle. In kindness. In beauty. The more I let go of mastering the future and began to dance with it, the more I understood that the sacred was wild. It couldn't be legislated, suppressed, or dictated. It simply was—whether in a cathedral or under a tarp. Just because Catholic dogma and Saudi-style Islam didn't bring me spiritual truth, it didn't mean I needed to cut the cord to the divine.

As a spiritual explorer who grew up under very vertical religious frameworks, I tried to find nourishment by managing life with bureaucratic efficiency, scheduling the sacred, controlling the outcome, optimizing the unknown. When that didn't work—when chaos laughed in my face and rearranged all my tidy little plans—I didn't know what to do with myself.

But the trail knew exactly what to do with me. The Camino didn't hand me a syllabus and the PCT didn't give me lectures, but they both whispered the same lesson: Stop trying to own the future. Dance with it instead. I let go of the idea that chaos was the enemy. I started to understand that entropy wasn't punishment—it was transformation.

Nature isn't neat.

Neither is healing.

Neither is hope.

The three of them are beautifully connected—and that connection became my new sacred. I wouldn't pretend to follow faiths I didn't believe in anymore. Nor would I declare myself spiritually unaffiliated or constitutionally anything. I just needed to show up— with feet on the ground, a pack full of compassion, instant mashed potatoes, and a growing sense that this wild, weird world has room for me . . . even if I didn't have it all figured out.

I may not master the future.

Let the mess come.

Let the trail twist.

"In all things of nature there is something of the marvelous." —Aristotle

26

The next morning, I hit the trail with the kind of resolve that only comes from sore feet, low food, and the siren call of Timberline Lodge echoing through the mountains like a promise. I was moving by 0545, headlamp still cutting through the forest mist, taking just one break to water up. No time to dilly-dally, not with history, architecture, and pizza awaiting me at elevation.

The trail wasn't about to make it easy—every step a suction cup trying to reclaim my feet. Still, I pressed forward like a man possessed, muscles screaming but spirits soaring. By 1630, I crested the final rise and laid eyes on Timberline Lodge, a fortress of cinematic grandeur perched like a crown on Mount Hood.

My legs burned like hellfire, but my geeky little heart lit up like a slot machine. I'd seen this lodge in Stanly Kubrick's The Shining a dozen times, and now it stood before me, more majestic than the screen had ever allowed. I walked the perimeter first, reverent as a pilgrim circling a shrine, soaking in the wind-whipped silence before stepping through those famous doors. The inside didn't disappoint. Vaulted ceilings, massive stone fireplaces, and the kind of craftsmanship that makes you believe in magic again. I was very aware of my hikertrash status—sweaty, dusty, rocking a thousand-mile stare—but reverence outweighs shame, so I strutted through the corridors with the silent pride of someone who earned their place with blistered feet and big dreams.

Downstairs, I ordered a Red Rooster pizza and two pints of Oregon porter—for "nutritional balance," of course. A vacationing couple from Canada seated nearby watched as I absolutely annihilated my meal with the gusto of a starving Greek god.

"Where did you hike from?" the wife asked, wide-eyed.

"The Mexican border," I said, wiping marinara off my lip, not entirely sure they'd believe me.

"Can we join you?"

"I'd be honored," I replied, genuinely touched by their warmth. "Please forgive my appetite. Would you like a slice?"

"We just ate, but thank you," said the husband, smiling.

We spent the next hour talking about trails and travels, swapping border-crossing sagas and road-trip dreams over pints. When they finally left, I thanked them with a full heart. Half an hour later, when I asked for the check, the waiter just smiled and said, "Your Canadian friends already took care of it."

Trail magic, baby. It never gets old.

Upstairs in the grand bar, I found Ryman posted up with a couple of fresh-faced hikers. I slid into a seat and got to know Bear and Beaver, a young couple nearly finished hiking across their home state of Oregon. They glowed with the same strange mix of exhaustion and joy that all trail-worn souls share. Ryman's wife joined us later, and we closed the place down together—laughing, storytelling, sipping slowly on drinks like time had agreed to pause for us.

We camped that night beneath a canopy of stars, near the Timberline hiker site, our tents glowing like fireflies against the snowy backdrop of Hood. I woke up at dawn buzzing with excitement for the breakfast buffet, sipping coffee in the grand lounge while the sun painted the Cascades in gold.

When the restaurant doors opened, I walked in with reverence—and a hunger I wouldn't wish on my worst enemy. The buffet defied belief. Eggs in every style. Ham, sausage, hash browns, pancakes, fruit, canapés, and biscuits as far as the eye could see. Our table of hikers consumed ungodly quantities of food while polite tourists looked on in open-mouthed awe. Taking a zero was tempting. I could have lounged for days in the deep leather chairs, journaling by the fire and watching snow twirl outside like confetti from Olympus. But the trail called. With only 500 miles left and flawless weather, I was free to tune into subtler shifts, the tectonic kind inside my own spirit. I felt both triumphant and tender.

I followed the Ramona Falls Trail, took a lunch break by the water, dipped my head in its ice-cold clarity, and stared up into treetops that swayed like sages. That afternoon I walked beside a gentle stream pulled straight from my dreamscape. By sundown, I'd clocked 25 miles, putting Cascade Locks within striking distance.

Southbounders had whispered to me of the Eagle Creek bypass—a side trail not to be missed—and they weren't wrong. It was a parade of beauty. I grazed on wild blackberries and raspberries all day, the sunshine bouncing through the trees like spotlight beams. Oregon, as if knowing our time together was short, threw its full splendor at me—waterfalls, moss-drenched cliffs, and the kind of light that makes your soul kneel down in gratitude.

And then: Tunnel Falls. A waterfall to walk behind. I couldn't believe it until I was inside the rock passage, feeling the cool mist as the waterfall roared just feet away. I lingered there like a monk at a sacred well. Eventually, more day hikers arrived, and I peeled myself away before the magic vanished.

A few hours later, I arrived at Cascade Locks. I stood at the edge of Oregon and looked across the Columbia River into Washington, letting out a deep sigh that seemed to come from somewhere ancient inside me. The third and final PCT state. I'd made it here weeks ahead of schedule thanks to big miles and the invisible generosity of trail angels and water caches.

I checked into Shrek's Hiker Hostel and crashed in a kind of blissful delirium. A zero day was in order. I met a couple other hikers—Freedom Train and John the Baptist—who radiated that same sacred exhaustion. We were the lucky ones.

Everywhere I looked, beauty bloomed—vivid, unapologetic, endless.

And I knew: I didn't want to rush anymore.

Not through Oregon.

Not through life.

For once, I didn't feel the pressure to solve or systematize that truth. That was the sacred reality of chaos—raw, infinite, untamable. The mind can't overthink when staring into the abyss of everything; it can only feel. And it was there, while steam rose around me in the hot shower at Shrek's Hiker Hostel—half-naked, sore, and euphoric—that I made a quiet vow. Before reaching Stevens Pass, I would choose a plan of action for what came next. I had lived in chaos long enough. And while it had served its purpose—breaking down the old, calcified parts of me—any further stalling would turn from liberation to avoidance.

I wouldn't let perfectionism stall my growth. I'd learned that much. The spontaneous magic of the Camino Santiago and the raw elemental wildness of the PCT had rattled the dull machinery of my past life and sparked something truer. But the time was coming to seek a new kind of spiritual richness—not in abandon, but in intention. Surely, I could still walk the knife's edge between freedom of chaos and responsibility of design. Surely I could earn a wage without selling my soul, and live with conviction without losing curiosity. That, I believed, was what the indifferent universe wanted from me—to want something of my own. Not because it cared, but because it didn't. In that divine indifference, I found my window of freedom.

No matter how many roads I imagined, all the overthinking—the endless ifs and maybes—kept bringing me back to one elemental truth: I felt most alive when I used my body and mind to create something out of nothing. Whether that was hiking through fire-season ash, writing under a pine tree, or improvising a plan on a dusty roadside, that spontaneous yet purposeful energy was where I met my best self. It was where I remembered who I was before the world told me what I should be. Every time I stepped forward on the trail, I reclaimed a little piece of my agency from the teeth of chaos. I was thankful for that intention, rare and radiant, shining like a headlamp in the dark.

I spent two restorative days in Cascade Locks, the borderland between Oregon and Washington—a liminal paradise for weary hikers. Everyone there agreed: it was the perfect place to rest and gather strength before launching into the third and final state of the PCT.

One morning over breakfast with Bear and Beaver, she told me she ran a small business crafting custom journals. My ears perked up. I asked her to make me one with extra pages and a PCT-inspired illustration on the cover. We traded information, and I paid her on the spot. It felt symbolic, investing in something that would hold the next chapters of my life, not just on paper but in spirit.

Later that day, I took advantage of the café Wi-Fi and started researching graduate schools in New Mexico. I was surprised at how natural it felt. After so long dancing with uncertainty, taking actual steps toward my future felt like laying stone across a river of doubt. As a reward, I strolled to a local art gallery and then lay down on the warm, grassy riverbank of the Columbia Gorge. I looked to the sky, open and impossibly blue, and imagined the ancient glaciers carving this land into the breathtaking cathedral it had become. Beauty like that demanded reverence.

That night, I met up with old friends and new trail family at Thunder Mountain Brewery. We drank to miles and madness. A wiry hiker named Falafel joined us, fresh off a fifty-mile day. Fifty.

It was rare and Herculean. My biggest day was forty miles, and that nearly broke me. I couldn't help but admire his fire. We toasted to his feat like it was a religious rite. In a way, it was.

On my final morning in Cascade Locks, I had one last breakfast with Bear and Beaver, then walked with them across the Bridge of the Gods—the literal threshold into Washington. It was their finish line and my fresh beginning. I hugged them, then kept moving north.

Columbia River Gorgeousness.

"Of all the paths you take in life, make sure a few of them are dirt." —John Muir

27

The trail didn't ease me back in. I hiked twenty miles that day to cowboy camp under a watercolor sky that still smelled like river wind and pine bark. The next day, still high on vitality, I logged thirty-five miles. I started Thinking, Fast and Slow by Daniel Kahneman, a book that made me laugh at how strange and silly the human brain really is. It lit up new synapses in my mind while my feet traced ancient terrain.

I encountered a handful of hikers—four southbound, two northbound—and the sparse traffic reminded me that the end was creeping closer. I savored the impossible beauty while I still had it. The perfect blue sky, the golden hush of late summer sun, the cathedral stillness of Washington forest . . . all of it endeared me instantly to this new, mysterious state.

The next morning, the temperature dropped sharply. I layered myself up in my down jacket, gloves, and the beanie Susan had given me way back in Big Bear. At lunch, I encountered a trail angel stationed like a minor deity beside a portable grill. He greeted me with a knowing smile and offered up burgers and hot dogs, juices and beers, and a cooler full of Little Debbies. The smell alone was erotic. I ate like a man who'd been living on dreams and Clif Bars. With my belly full and heart fuller, I thanked him and hiked on, finishing out a 32-mile day that ended in a quiet meadow perfect for cowboy camping.

That night, leaning against a tree, I cracked open Kahneman's book again. As the last light died from the sky, I read about how the brain processes reality. It felt ironic, reading about cognitive illusions while living inside a living dream. I was about sixty miles from White Pass and found myself wondering: what the hell does "normal" even feel like anymore?

All my life, people told me what it meant to be stable. That a person should follow rules, live safely, bury emotions, and worship productivity like it was God. Strength was defined by denial. Power was measured in paychecks. Hiking had exposed that entire script as a polite fiction. The madness of the trail—the emotional depth, the irrational joy, the open wonder—was the kind of insanity I never wanted to lose.

I didn't want to "get back to normal." I wanted to keep dancing to the wild music of the universe.

The next day, I hiked thirty-four stunning miles that felt more like gliding than walking. And then—Goat Rocks. The trail turned mythical. The climb was sharp and sharp-edged, but the views were the kind that make you forget your legs even exist. I moved with unreasonable energy, fueled by spirit alone. I subsisted that entire day on just four Clif Bars, like some kind of minimalist pilgrim high on life.

At White Pass, I met Jan from the Netherlands. He was fifty-three and believed the trail should be savored slowly. When he found out I was hiking over thirty miles a day, he frowned like I'd just kicked a sacred stone. "It's wasteful," he said. "Frantic."

Then he asked if I'd split a hotel room with him.

I paused. "Sure," I said, "as long as you keep your negativity to yourself."

I stocked up my food bag like I was provisioning for a mission to Mars—150 miles to Snoqualmie Pass, a stretch of trail that felt less like a walk through a state and more like a journey through an ancient, breathing cathedral of earth and sky. Jan and I split a pizza and bought a six-pack of beers that tasted like liquid starlight after so many days of trail food. We swapped thoughts about the strange, sacred power of Washington's wilderness—the way it held you in a kind of reverence whether you deserved it or not.

Even after all those miles, I welcomed rest like it was an old friend I hadn't seen since the womb. My feet—those magnificent, scarred, ten-toed miracles—had carried me like silent champions through desert, fire, ice, and altitude. I'd expected them to mutiny, to blister and buckle and break down. Instead, they rose with the same defiant grace as the mountains I'd climbed. I owed them a debt that couldn't be measured in massages or new socks—only in the deep, wordless gratitude that comes when your body holds up under the weight of your most outrageous dreams.

I had Wi-Fi. I had water. I had food.

"Who could ask for anything more?" I whispered to the stars I couldn't see yet, and meant it.

I sent word to my loved ones, those constellation points in the map of my life. Then, like a long-lost cosmic alignment, a message popped up from Handwalker. He was on his way. I hadn't seen him since Kennedy Meadows South, and in trail time, that's prehistoric. I decided to stay an extra day, to wait for him. Meanwhile, the trail, never one to offer smooth sailing for long, hinted at something ominous—wildfires up north, thick with uncertainty and smoke. The rumors carried weight like distant thunder. I vowed to hike on, cautious, watchful, hungry for resolution but not at the cost of my life.

When Handwalker arrived the next morning, we hugged like brothers. Our joy was kinetic, flowing fast and easy. Someone offered a shot of whiskey—Thermometer, that eccentric trail legend from Japan. Normally I'd pass, but celebration demanded a toast, and I savored the fire in my belly as we set out to hike twenty-six miles under skies that seemed painted by the gods.

The terrain was tender, the air kissed by perfect temperature, the water exactly where the trail notes promised it would be—miracles, all of it. Hiking with my friend under those benevolent conditions felt like something out of a dream curated by the universe itself just to reward us for surviving this long. We spoke all day, unable to stop, trading stories like secrets from parallel universes. The PCT had fed us experiences that were too vast and numerous to recount. It had turned us into archives of wonder.

That night we cowboy camped beside Dewey Lake, the cosmos swirling overhead, each star whispering a different version of infinity. I let myself feel it—really feel it—the electric truth that I was part of the universe, that I was made of its dust and light, and that this hike was my pilgrimage to rediscover it all. Freedom didn't just mean going wherever I wanted. It meant reclaiming myself from the scripts written for me by generations of "normal." It meant choosing joy, wonder, and truth over stability and approval.

The next morning, I started early. We'd agreed Handwalker would catch up. I stepped off-trail for a bathroom break, and that's where he unknowingly passed me. All day, we hiked like wild men possessed. I raced to catch up. He raced ahead to find me. Southbounders along the way told each of us that the other had just gone by. It was hilarious cosmic miscommunication, and I accidentally racked up my second forty-mile day on trail. He did forty-four. I collapsed under a clouded sky, my muscles electric with exhaustion, and my soul grinning like a madman.

By 0430, I was back on trail. A stream break, and then—

"Windscreen!"

I turned, and there he was. "Handwalker! Man, you're a freaking hiking machine."

We laughed, hugged, swapped stories of our misfire.

"How about we cruise a light thirty-two into Snoqualmie Pass today? That enough for you?" I suggested.

"Let's go, old man!"

At Snoqualmie Pass, we devoured food like warriors back from battle. The water pitcher was our Holy Grail. The food? Mediocre. The satisfaction? Divine. Flower, another hiker, joined us, glowing with relief to have company after tough days. Her feet needed healing, her spirit needed lifting, and we were happy to provide both. She invited us to crash on her hotel room floor. That six-pack on the balcony, shared under the rain-heavy sky, tasted like childhood and deliverance.

The storm crashed in the next morning, and we watched it like monks observing a holy rite. The trail called. Wet socks or not, we went. Maybe the rain would douse the fires. Maybe not. Southbounders tipped us off to the Goldmeyer alternate—farther from the fires, with rivers and greenery as rich as Eden. We followed their advice, feeling the heat in the wind, the smoke like prophecy on our skin.

Twenty-six miles later, we made camp near a burbling stream. The night was calm. The air? Blessedly breathable. Morning came, and with it the quiet stirrings of grateful hikers sipping coffee and sharing news like ancient travelers at a desert well.

We kept moving, alert to change, but swept up in the momentum of the final act. Twenty-nine more miles, ending at Mig Lake under a sky on fire. The sunset was pure myth—crimson, gold, violet—splashed across the surface of the lake like an altar to all our miles. We met older hikers there who confirmed what we feared: Stehekin was unreachable. Fires were closing in. We'd made it this far. Carried by the unrelenting rhythm of our legs, the faith in our feet, the electricity of our friendships, and the mad poetry of the trail. If I had to stop here, I could still call this hike complete in the ways that mattered. If the trail had more to give, I would meet it in full—with eyes open, heart thumping, soul ablaze.

The next morning, the trail gave us an effortless seven-mile stroll to Stevens Pass—as if easing us toward the next chapter like a loving parent does a child at bedtime. From there, we caught a ride to a place every PCT hiker knows by name but can't understand until they arrive: The Dinsmore's Hiker Haven.

If Valhalla had a washing machine and a box of powdered Gatorade packets, it would look like the Haven.

The Dinsmores, two salt-of-the-earth saints in flannel and denim opened their home, not just physically, but spiritually, to the odyssey-weary. Their barn-sized shelter felt like a trail monastery: bunk beds lined the walls, couches sagged with the weight of shared stories, and the air hummed with recovery, reflection, and just a little foot funk.

After showering off layers of trail dust that held entire memories in their grime, we washed our laundry and watched as a dozen other hikers filtered in. These were no strangers, even if we'd never met before. They were our species—sun-worn and wild-eyed, drawn to the glowing hearth of this command post nestled in a town smaller than some trailheads. The Dinsmores had posted weather maps, fire reports, and trail alerts on the wall like the Oracle at Delphi, helping us decode the chaos that now plagued the Pacific Northwest.

Forest fires. Big. Close. Zero chance of hiking north in the next couple of days.

Like the patient warriors we'd become—we accepted it. We adjusted. We rested.

That evening, a gaggle of us hitched to Baring for food, and the moment I stepped inside, the humble roadside diner became a homecoming eruption. Ryman! Howdy Doody! Freedom Train! Tinkerbell! So Far! The energy was electric, tearful, a spontaneous combustion of joy and disbelief. Laughter. Hugs. Toasts. The air smelled of bacon and possibility. That meal may have only been eggs and toast, but to us, it was Michelin-starred euphoria on ceramic plates.

Later, I found a discarded pair of trail shoes my size in the hiker box. My ragged shoes had been hanging on by willpower and duct tape. This was divine intervention in rubber and mesh.

While most hikers took naps or dozed under quilts of exhaustion, I logged into Wi-Fi and browsed universities, because of course I did. I found myself back at Wayland Baptist University's site, the place where I earned both my bachelor's and master's degrees. They were launching a doctoral program. I blinked at the screen, half-laughing. What could be more absurd than an atheist named Christian earning a doctorate from a Baptist school? Yet, somehow, it all made sense. The trail made you believe the impossible was possible.

I finished Thinking, Fast and Slow and felt like I'd upgraded my brain firmware. Then I casually clicked a Craigslist ad for a motorcycle in Puyallup—something sleek and thrilling to carry me through the next chapter. And just like that, I realized my Windscreen alterego was dissolving, sloughing off like dead skin after a month in trail runners.

The PCT and I were breaking up, and it hurt.

That night I slept in a real bed under a soft roof while rain whispered on the outside walls. I dreamed of cities and T-shirts and clean fingernails. Of clocks and people who asked how your day was going and meant it. The change was coming—not violent, not abrupt, but tectonic, and I felt it deep in my bones.

By morning, more hikers had arrived—tents popped up on the Haven's lawn like flowers after a spring rain. The fire updates, however, grew worse. The verdict came down like trail thunder: We couldn't hike north from Stevens Pass. Period. The PCT was closed.

Handwalker and I unfolded maps, compared GPS points, checked rumors like war generals mapping a retreat. We decided to hitchhike around the fire zone, then rejoin the trail where it was safe.

I thought of the Pyrenees snowstorm with Francessca on the Camino. I remembered almost dying with Roger near the icy tomb of Mount Baden-Powell. Maybe I wasn't lucky or unlucky—maybe I was just unrelenting.

We thanked the Dinsmores like they were the angels they were, then hitched to the Skykomish bus stop, bought tickets to Wenatchee, and then on to Peteras. From there, the journey became a road-trip fever dream: we hitchhiked to a ghost town called Crater, then on to the mountain-cute village of Winthrop. One ride led to another—strangers who'd never heard of the PCT welcomed us with open doors and dusty pickups.

At last, we reached Mazama. Another resort. Another café. Another portal in the matrix of this mystical trail world.

After a final hitch, we arrived at Rainy Pass, and the PCT, sweet and endless, beckoned us back like a lover who didn't care that we'd strayed.

We hiked for an hour, lungs full of clean air, minds buzzed with purpose, until we reached a campsite that offered a panoramic view of the infinite: forests, mountaintops, galaxies above the trees, the golden bruise of sunset.

The next morning was our final day on trail.

Handwalker and I, walking side by side beneath sapphire skies, felt the gravity of the moment press softly on our shoulders. The streams sparkled like blessings. The vistas swallowed language. And then, there it was: the northern terminus monument. The hallowed totem. The Mona Lisa of the long trail.

We stood before it like monks before a shrine. No more fear of injury. No more fear of failure. No more fear. Just awe.

I opened the box of wine I'd purchased at Mazama, toasted our victory, and took photos that would never do justice to what our hearts felt. Then—because momentum is a law of the universe—we walked onward. Across the border. Into Canada. Into our final night on the PCT.

At the last campsite, cradled beneath the old-growth arms of the northern wilderness, we slept like children at the end of a long, enchanted story.

The next morning, we hiked five miles to Manning Park, the Canadian resort. No mosquitoes. No dew. No rain. No problems. Easiest part of the hike, by far. We had three quiet hours to wait for the bus to Vancouver, and so I did the only thing that made sense, I walked slowly. Deliberately. I let each step linger. I wasn't hiking anymore; I was honoring. I drifted through the final stretch of trail like smoke through tall trees, letting the hush of the wilderness press gently against my skin one last time.

I tried to memorize everything: the feel of pine-needled dirt beneath my feet, the way the air tasted like memory, the hush of branches swaying above me as if the forest itself was whispering goodbye. I was saying farewell not just to the trail, but to the life I'd lived on it. To the freedom that had become more than a condition—it had become a truth.

What would I do without the trail?

That question pulsed like a distant drumbeat in my chest. But even as grief tugged at me, something higher lifted me out of that fog. My heart rose, light, like a bird finally trusting the wind. My spirit had begun to shift. There was hope. And not just hope for the future, but hope in my life.

I made a conscious choice in those final hours: not to mourn the loss, but to hold the joy. The trail was not being taken from me. It had been given without conditions, and now I had to be brave enough to carry its gift into the unknown. Like all travelers, I felt the familiar ache of separation, that hard-to-name melancholy that follows any great journey. This time, I didn't resist it. I let it pass through me like wind through a tent flap.

I had spent months training my mind on the trail—not just my legs. I had practiced replacing cruel thoughts with kind ones. I had learned to choose gentleness over judgment. I found the courage to let go of pain I had carried for decades, pain that had become too familiar to name. Letting it go didn't just lighten my step—it opened me. It made space for compassion. Not only for others. For myself.

At the Manning Resort, Handwalker ducked inside to use the bathroom first, and I stood outside beneath a cathedral sky, hands in my pockets, already feeling the trail retreating behind me.

Then I heard my name: "Windscreen!"

I turned, and there was Dustin—real and grinning. We had last seen each other in Etna, Northern California—a lifetime ago. Dustin hugged me with the force of shared survival. All the miles, the storms, the sweat, the laughter—they surged back in an instant.

"Man," I said, overwhelmed, "I'm sorry I couldn't keep up with you. I'd hike anywhere with you."

"Man, you too," he replied, and the simplicity of it—so male, so humble—hit me hard.

Gazelle—whom we hadn't seen since Tehachapi—invited me and Handwalker to visit her hometown of Vancouver. Of course, we said yes. There was a strange elegance in a fellow thru-hiker ushering us back into the world.

Handwalker and I stepped away from the PCT not with closure, but with continuity. The dance would be different now—but the music wouldn't stop. I used to flinch from silence. I used to fill it, fearing it meant emptiness, wasting, loneliness. The trail taught me silence wasn't hollow—it was holy. I had learned to crave it. Liminal peace. That sacred hush of no deadlines, no alerts, no roles to play. I stopped fearing it.

As I learned to spend time alone, I found the space to make sense of things I had never dared to sort through. I found clarity. Stillness no longer meant wasted time—it meant distilled time. It gave shape to my chaos and purpose to my thinking. When I returned to the world—when I rejoined civilization—I didn't want to lose that. Not the wild. Not the silence. Not the sacred hush that kept me centered. The world is noisy, but I didn't have to be.

As we waited for the bus, I visualized the life I wanted next. Not to escape the trail, but to keep its spirit alive in me. The way I speak. The way I listen. The way I walk through this world. Thanks to the wilderness, I had tasted the absolute high of freedom, and now I was ready to return. Not to what I was. But to who I had become. I no longer feared change. I welcomed it.

In that space—cradled by silence, wrapped in memory, touched by the last breath of the trail—I realized I had found what I never expected: peace, and a deep, emotional strength that rose not from victory, but from surrender.

All it took was time.

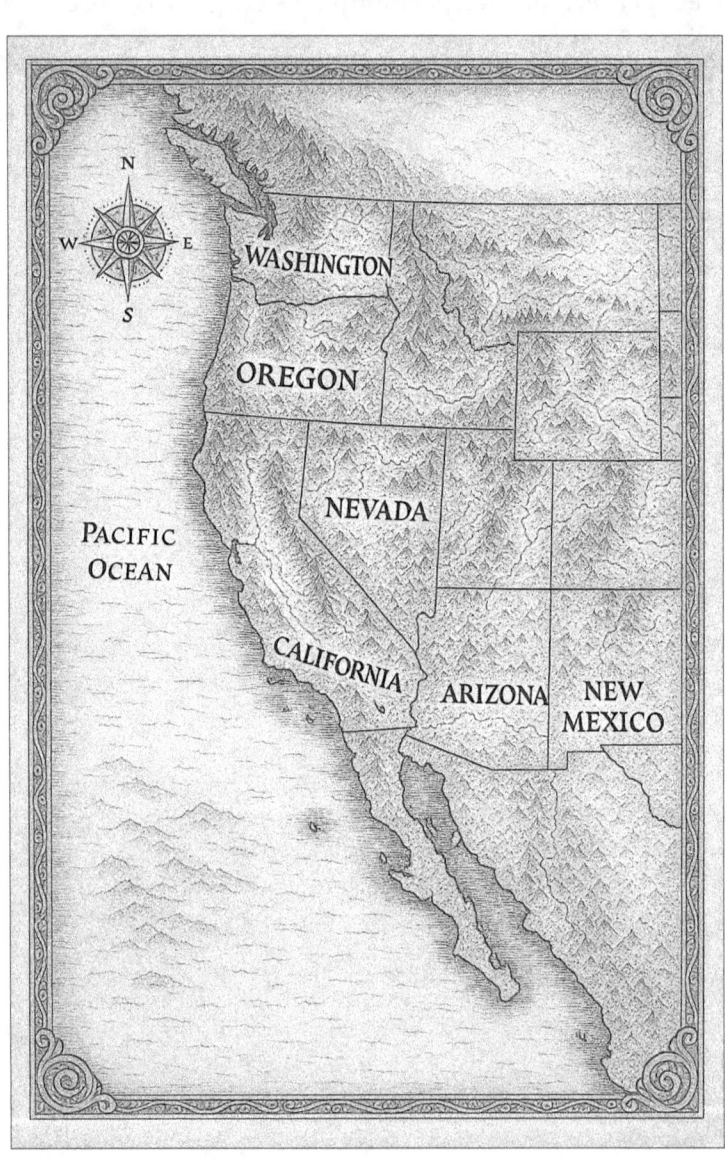

PART 4

Arriving Alive

*"Every man, woman, and child on this earth
is a wandering pilgrim in his or her own way,
each searching for a belonging place. That sense
of belonging is found only as we care for one another."*
—Seth Adam Smith

*"When I'm riding my motorcycle, I'm glad to be alive.
When I stop riding my motorcycle, I'm glad to be alive."* —Neil Peart

28

On 19 August, Handwalker and I took the four-hour bus ride from Manning Park to downtown Vancouver. Figuring we should indulge in some Canadian culture, we visited the Museum of Art like a pair of civilized people instead of the hikertrash we'd been for over four months. We managed to contact Gazelle and had street tacos and fruit smoothies for lunch. Andy and I then bought our bus tickets to depart for Seattle the following morning, then I contacted my motorcycle seller to buy their motorcycle, a Honda Nighthawk 750.

Walking around the city was fun, but I noticed how impatient I became at crosswalks, not to mention how being among such slow-moving people ignited a new kind of frustration. I saw a candy wrapper resting on the curb, unnoticed by everyone except me, and immediately remembered plastic bags caught in the Saudi Arabian winds like ever-present ghosts with nowhere to go. Even after months surrounded by unblemished nature, memories of unbroken streams of trash alongside roadsides and near mosques came to mind with living color. I thought of how the litter felt offensive; not just ugly, but disrespectful. Over time, I stopped reacting. It became a part of the background as I walked around it, same as everyone else.

The part that stung me was, I suddenly realized as I looked at that lone Canadian candy bar wrapper, it was exactly how I'd been carrying my own internal mess. My judgments. My resentments. My biases about religion, culture, and belief. I told myself I'd left the worst behind me—Catholic school discipline, the authoritarian strain of Islam I observed in the Kingdom—but I hadn't. I was still carrying pieces of all of it: quiet bits of superiority, defensiveness, even a kind of pride in not believing what others around me did. I had been priding myself on being more awake, more liberated. It hit me on that busy Vancouver intersection that freedom without awareness is just another kind of prison. I had my own garbage to account for. I was guilty of judging the visible mess while ignoring the mess inside my own heart. Wasn't that the classic human hypocrisy, to call out what was on the surface while keeping blind to what's buried?

Self-improvement wasn't just meditation and gym sessions and better choices. It included crawling into the parts of my mind I'd rather keep boarded up and ask myself "What am I still clinging to that no longer serves me? What am I so used to seeing that I don't even recognize its damage anymore?" It took a break from normalcy and civilization for me to realize certain shortcomings and biases I'd permitted to take root. The litter I saw in Saudi Arabia wasn't just a metaphor. It was a mirror. It showed me how numb I'd become to the clutter in my own heart. It showed me that awareness isn't enough—I had to do something about what I saw. Pick it up. Sort it out. Take responsibility. Not once, but every day, and always. This realization was yet another gift Windscreen brought into my life as I was transitioning back into Chris. I had a long way to go, but I didn't want to keep pretending the mess wasn't there. I would always have mess to clean up, just like there would always be litter to pick up no matter where I went, but the work would always be worth it.

"The light's green, Chris" Andy nudged me from my moment of enlightenment.

It was odd calling each other by normal names. After so much time living simply and focusing on only a few basic needs—walking, eating, sleeping—the return to modern society was a little overwhelming. The constant noise, traffic, and crowds jarred me. The city's artificial lights, loud voices, and digital screens everywhere I looked felt intrusive and unnatural. I enjoyed returning to the cleansed body of Chris, but I would miss being Windscreen.

The next day Andy and I spent the bus ride from Vancouver expressing how powerful the hike was for us and crossed the border into the United States. When the bus pulled into Seattle, we disembarked and collected our things.

"I guess this is it" Andy said as I lifted my bag out from the luggage compartment.

"Yeah. Kinda surreal; we just go back to our lives."

"Back to what, though? I don't even remember how to be normal. Like . . . do I just wake up and not walk twenty miles?" Andy wondered half-seriously.

"And eat a reasonable amount of food? Like, do I still get to inhale a full pizza in one sitting?" I said, already missing the ability to eat anything I wanted without consequence.

"If not, where's the fun in that?"

Hiking 2,650 miles through deserts, glaciers, and volcanoes wasn't nothing. We dodged rattlesnakes, snowstorms, and mental breakdowns. I felt that talking about transformative moments on trail would be unrelatable to most people. I watched mountains rise and vanish. My soul sang in the silence of 30-mile days. I braced for the ways I might feel alien. I struggled to talk about what really mattered because it wasn't about blisters and bears. It was about how the trail cracked your worldview open, how I found more truth than ever, and how my soul clicked into place. People would be disappointed if all they wanted a highlight reel, because I wanted to talk about my spiritual reckoning. Would I have to choke back the deepest parts of myself?

I was overthinking again. I knew friendships survive and grow. My loved ones already knew I didn't walk 2,650 miles just to stay the same. Friend and loved ones that try are the trail magic of the world. In that way we would manage to be parts of each other's journey.

"I guess this is where we say something meaningful." Andy said as he got ready to board his bus for Phoenix.

"Something deep and profound." I agreed.

"You got anything, Windscreen?"

"Nope."

"We'll see each other again, right?"

I reached out my hand. Andy shook it, then pulled me into a tight hug.

"Take care of yourself, Handwalker," I said.

"You too, Windscreen. Maybe sometime . . ."

"Another trail?" I suggested.

"Another trail."

I boarded my bus to Olympia, and an Air Force buddy Dave picked me up and took me to go look at the motorcycle, which was exactly what I hoped it would be. For a twenty-year-old motorcycle it ran well, and had no rust. I transferred money to the owner's bank then I followed Dave on my motorcycle to his home. Dave introduced me to his wife and kids; then, we had dinner and I crashed for the night.

The attire that served me so well on two hiking trails would not do well for my road trip, so I bought a helmet, motorcycle gloves, jeans, jacket, and boots. After walking everywhere for the last several months, moving at the speed of traffic was terrifying. I focused on riding safely and paying attention to the traffic as the concrete sped under my feet sped at warp speed. Even riding just forty-five mph caused me to squeeze my legs nervously against the fuel tank. In this world, everyone traveled in comfort for hundreds of miles. Effortlessly.

At Dave's house, I crossed a quiet threshold. No blisters, no dust on my legs, no distant summit in view—just the soft click of keys as I submitted my application to the doctoral program at Wayland Baptist University, the same institution where I'd earned my bachelor's and master's degrees. It was the first step of a new kind of adventure, one rooted not in distant landscapes but in intention, stillness, and discipline. As I submitted my application, there was a sweetness in that kind of beginning, one so quiet and unceremonious yet so deeply full of hope.

I took Susan's advice—given so long ago in Big Bear when my thoughts ran as wild as the mountains around me—and made my way to Whidbey Island. I roared north on my Honda Nighthawk, its engine now an old companion, and rode across the mainland like a drifting ember carried by wind and fate.

I greeted Janis with a big hug as though we'd met in a prior life. She brought homemade pastries. They weren't just off-the-shelf desserts—they were offerings of hospitality in a most delicious form.

Then I saw Whidbey Island.

The air shifted as I crossed over Deception Bridge—salt and pine on the breeze accentuated the scent of sunbaked earth and far-off tides coalescing into something primal. The sky was a canopy of clouds and cobalt, cut by the majestic silhouette of the Cascades to the east and the Olympians to the west. Golden fields rolled into dense evergreen forests that met jagged cliffs, where the earth plunged into waters that shimmered with a quiet, ancient knowing.

I didn't just admire the place—I belonged to it.

Janis and I talked about our upcoming reunion in Las Vegas, where she'd celebrate her birthday with Susan and Chad. The knowledge we'd see each other again gave our goodbye a softness. I hugged her in gratitude—not just for the pastries, but for showing me around Whidbey Island in all its splendor.

With the Pacific Coast Highway (PCH to travelers like you and me) unwinding ahead of me like a ribbon of memory, I followed it south through the lush wilderness of Washington and into Oregon's cliff-lined majesty. I stopped when something called to me—ocean vistas, Cannon Beach, a lonely diner, Rogue Brewery, a stretch of woods whispering secrets I didn't want to forget, and even a couple lighthouses.

I met up with Magic Bag and his girlfriend in the Redwoods of California, We walked like children beneath towering elders, those ancient trees holding centuries of silence in their rings. We dipped into streams so clear they reflected the sky itself. I felt once more that I could never run out of awe for this planet's splendor. I joined Lake Tahoe Jimmy in Napa Valley, where wine flowed and stories did too. We raised a glass to the old Kindle he'd brought to me, and I let him know about the books that accompanied me along the PCT.

Departing the PCH, I veered east onto Highway 50 aka "America's Loneliest Road." On that stretch of road there was no shade, no skyline clutter, just the endless, trembling shimmer of heat. I sped across the Great Basin, through towns that barely existed: Austin, Eureka, Ely—little outposts barely tethered to the century. Every fifty miles, if I was lucky, a gas pump, a neon sign, a server who'd ask where I was heading, then nod as if they already knew. The metal of my bike scorched the skin if I touched it in the daytime. The hum of my tires against asphalt and the wind singing in my ears kept me company as I rode through the beautiful and desolate terrain. Once again, I was just a passing shadow in a landscape that couldn't care less. I loved it for that.

I met up with Kevin, another Air Force buddy, and spent a couple days exploring Great Basin National Park, then carried on toward Las Vegas where I stayed with Susan, Chad, Connor, Grace, and Janis. We celebrated Janis's birthday with balloons, laughter, and the kind of closeness that only forms after long separations and important friendship.

From there, I rode to Phoenix, swapping stories and planning futures with Andy (no longer called Handwalker). We talked about jobs, next steps, and dreams. In Flagstaff, I stopped for dinner and, to my astonishment, reconnected with Cletus, a friend I hadn't seen in over a decade. He'd seen my post, reached out, and suddenly we found ourselves laughing like no time had passed at all. The trail hadn't just given me clarity—it had given me back people I once thought lost.

Five months after returning home for just one week between the Camino Santiago and the PCT, I walked into my house, kicked my shoes off, and went upstairs where my bed waited for me. No pine needles here. No mosquito net needed. No sleeping pad separating me from the chill of the earth. Just softness.

I lay down—not as the person who left, but as someone fuller, slower, wider in spirit. I had traveled thousands of miles on foot and thousands more by motorcycle. I had witnessed the sacred and the absurd, the chaotic and the divine. I had tasted silence and spoken prayers I didn't know I knew.

After leaving each Air Force base and deployment, after hiking the Appalachian Trail, even as recently as completing the Camino Santiago and PCT, life reminded me of a bittersweet truth—bonds forged through shared experiences, miles of heartfelt conversations, and the unspoken camaraderie of the trail can stretches over time as communications happened less and less frequently as priorities shifted. I had to remind myself this was not a denial of love or friendship—but simply the nature of life's ever-changing landscape. When it came to relationships, I still found litter I wanted to tidy up. I realized that I unknowingly closed parts of myself off whenever I felt down.

Despite my best efforts to be open-minded, in certain ways I still built my personality around my biases and told myself it was accumulating wisdom, having standards, and "not settling." I had a tough time believing that someone could show up and mean what they say, stay when things got messy, and love me for real without using that love as leverage. When it came to romance, I always prepared myself for the worst because it felt safe. Safer than hope. I never noticed how I carried this bias against goodness like a backpack—quietly, unconsciously, like a constant weight. I missed out on connections because I thought I was protecting myself, and I underestimated my blindness to love. I still managed to point a finger at external chaos while my internal world flooded with emotional debris. I had my work cut out for me, and would spend the rest of my life working on these parts of myself.

Self-improvement isn't all cold plunges and wholesome affirmations. It's about sorting through the wreckage and asking, "Where did this come from? Do I still need it? Who taught me to be afraid of love?" It's admitting I wasn't as healed as I wanted people to think I was. While that realization meant I wasn't as close to the finish line (or northern terminus?) as I wished I was, I respected the authenticity and self-respect of picking up the trash instead of just stepping over it.

Realizing that I alone wasn't enough to accomplish what I wanted, I started going to therapy. Surprisingly, it was like when I decided to hike the PCT. When they found out, people would nod their heads and say things like, "That's amazing. Good for you." Therapy, like the Camino Santiago and the PCT, showed me aspects of myself I'd never seen before, and took me through moments of awe that transcended words. Therapy gave me blisters in places I didn't know could blister. The healing journey took me through moments of shock and turmoil. Just like the wildernesses I pushed through on trail, I tackled my inner demons without distractions to numb the pain of facing certain truths. Just like Jean-Luc Picard said in Star Trek: The Next Generation, my first duty should be to the truth, whether it's scientific truth or historical truth or personal truth.

I didn't just unpack my baggage—I dumped it all out, time after time, finding more with each session. I talked about things that I'd buried like so much trail poop, thinking nothing would or could resurface. I learned about the pain I'd been carrying for so long "just to get by" while I bullshitted myself into thinking I was being healthy and strong. Underneath the pain and fear and survival mechanisms, I began to see the part of myself that wanted to live openly, that wanted to love without armor, the part that wanted to be free. I chose to walk through my own wilderness not because I enjoyed suffering, it was because I believed something better waited for me on the other side. Just like how the trail wouldn't alone fix me, therapy wouldn't either. Both would strip me down to my naked self until I recognized who I was, and that was worth every damn step. Maybe it's personal growth. Maybe it's . . . no, it's definitely personal growth.

Rest in Peace, Zachary Clay "Face Jacket" Joiner.

29

After completing the PCT in 2015, Wayland Baptist University, where I'd once earned my bachelor's and master's degrees, accepted me into their Doctoral Program. The Pacific Crest Trail had tested my physical discipline, and academia would test my mental discipline. Instead of wide-open skies and dirt paths were tight deadlines, academic jargon, and a gnawing doubt that I didn't belong in the marble halls of scholarship. Wandering through hunger, weather, and solitude was one thing, trudging through dense research and second-guessing every word I put my name to led me to wonder if I wasn't an intellectual fraud. Each step I took was unsure, and every academic paper another night in the cold with no guarantee I was even headed in the right direction. I clawed my way forward making certain my grades were high enough to qualify for the financial backing of the G.I Bill. I buried myself in research, second-guessed every sentence I wrote, and questioned whether the trail had made me physically strong but intellectually fraudulent.

I kept highlighting terms in my business reading like "transformational" and "authentic," but nothing inspired me. These captains of industry weren't the kinds of leaders who got me through tough times. The leaders I trusted didn't speak in jargon. They laughed. They made me laugh. They broke tension with a joke, not a reprimand. It hit me: humor wasn't a detour from leadership—it was the path itself.

There it was, I knew what my dissertation topic should be. Realizing that I could pontificate on the merits of humor all day every day struck me like a bolt out of the blue. I went from drowning in academic journals to caring about the compassion of humor and the currency of efficacy in leadership theories. Suddenly, I became energized. I dove headfirst into the very research I'd bemoaned for the first couple of semesters. I wanted to see if I couldn't academically support that humor wasn't just fluff or a casual footnote in leadership philosophy. I felt deep in my core that humor, positive-based humor in particular, could build bridges, dissolve hierarchies, and create safe space. The best leaders wielded it instinctively, but I felt that few understood its power. I told my professors that I wanted to write my dissertation on the efficacy of humor in leadership, and they approved my dissertation topic.

Even though writing academic papers could feel like singing at gunpoint, writing had long been a passion of mine. In choosing to study humor, I was studying my coping mechanism, my armor, my way to connect with others. It had gotten me through my challenges in the military, in Saudi Arabia, through heartbreaks, and through trials on the trail. Humor wasn't just entertainment; it turned wounds into character and failures into pride. I got to work showing, plainly, that humor wasn't a soft skill. I saw it as a vital facet to intelligence, a language of qualified leadership, and even a philosophy of resilience. I'd been using it deliberately for decades, not to distract, but to face the world head-on. Whether managing a team, surviving a soul-crushing job, or nursing a rejection, humor had always been my way of staying grounded, staying kind, staying me. The real leaders in my life told jokes. They laughed with people, not at them. They didn't preach; they connected. That realization hit like a warm cup of coffee in a cold tent: humor wasn't a distraction from leadership, it *was* leadership. When applied with compassion, humor could build trust, open minds, and reframe failure. It was persuasive. It was connective.

What started as a lightning bolt became a bonfire. My research consumed me in the best way for the next few years. I found studies on how humor could improve workplace morale, ease trauma, amplify memory retention, and even disrupt toxic power dynamics. It was everything leadership theory claimed to want—delivered in a form most scholars ignored. My dissertation was more than academic, it was personal. Writing it helped me peel back the armor I wore, and see that honest and inclusive laughter was how I made sense of the world.

On June 23, 2018, tragedy struck. Face Jacket was drinking with friends when one of his companions brandished a gun. In a senseless turn of events Face Jacket lost his life. He wasn't even thirty yet, a full decade younger than me, just getting his feet under him in the world. Face Jacket's young son would grow up piecing together the memory of a father gone too soon. Those of us who met him on trail knew what kind of soul he was—warm, hilarious, loyal to the bone, and someone who carried kindness like a second pack, handing it out to strangers without ever keeping score. He had the kind of spirit that made everyone feel a little more seen, a little more at home in their own skin. His absence was a rip in the fabric of our hiking community, and reminded us how fragile even the strongest among us really are. We were all lucky to have crossed paths with him.

The grief I carried for my trail friend opened me to other truths. For years, I had formed a habit of shutting people out and keeping certain longtime friends at a distance, not because they harmed me, but because their beliefs (and voting trends) offended me. Political and religious dissonance became excuses for me to ghost good people. I told myself I was protecting peace, and maybe I was justified, but it became clear to me that being a stranger to loved ones wasn't solving anything. It was time for me to reconnect with those I had become alien to. I began the toughest work of my life by overcoming my biases littering my ego.

On a recent visit to Texas, I reconnected with my old Catholic school friends, hoping to ease my Catholic resentment and learn to navigate our political differences peacefully. Friends I'd known since kindergarten hugged me and welcomed me into their hearts again as if I'd never left. We shared laughs, memories, and acknowledged our differences. We celebrated being together and something vital returned to my soul: grace. I was no longer the kid trying to make God proud, or trying to be straight enough, quiet enough, small enough. I was just . . . me. Wiser? Maybe. A little less angry? Definitely.

One of these lifelong friends, Greg, had wrestled with our Catholic upbringing like I had. We met up for breakfast burritos, and the conversation turned to things that mattered to us.

"So . . . you think of yourself more as a writer or hikertrash?"

I laughed because they weren't even opposite poles anymore. They were simply different sides of the same weird, wonderful map.

"You might as well ask me if I'm more of an inhaler or an exhaler," I said.

"So, both."

"Exactly. Occasionally I don't write or hike. Sometimes I just do nothing and watch Star Trek."

We let the silence sit. A silence filled with reverence, memory, and the quiet miracle of still being here. In that moment, Greg and I shared a sacred kind of humor, the kind that makes room for people, and heals. That's the kind I wanted to carry forward into every room, every story, and every life I wandered into.

After spending a decade in Albuquerque, a place that had cradled and tested me, I felt its edges soften. Even while soaring above the Duke City in a hot air balloon, I sensed Albuquerque no longer held me. My love for the granite face of the Sandia Mountains remained, but the magnetism had faded. The streets echoed with the laughter of friends who had since moved on. Their absence hollowed the city for me. I wasn't running away. I was answering the same call that had led me to trailheads and distant countries. It was time to find something new, and I took the first steps toward selling my home.

In November 2018, I crossed the stage to receive my Doctor of Management diploma. While the moment was victorious, and the title was real, so was the fatigue. The question lingered: Now what?

The doctorate didn't guarantee a dream job. After getting my diploma I spent several months searching for teaching jobs in Asia, eager to be out in the world for a while. When a teaching career didn't unfold the way I expected, I applied for one last contract in Saudi Arabia. I didn't want to teach students this time, I wanted to work with my hands, lift generators, and troubleshoot electrical circuits. I turned wrenches on F-15s for a year as I cleared my head and decompressed from academic rigor.

The fire from my time on the Camino and the PCT still smoldered. Even though I wasn't about to go on another long-distance hike, I was ready to sink my teeth into a new adventure. I felt a shift stirring in my life.

"Home's the most excellent place of all." —Neil Diamond

30

In 2020, I said ma'a as-salama to Saudi Arabia and moved to Whidbey Island, Washington. At the time of this writing, I've been in my home for five years, and I still feel like I'm in the honeymoon phase. Here, the trees rise like ancient sentinels, moss-cloaked and unbothered, as if they've been watching for centuries and still aren't done listening. The wind moves through them with the hush of reverence, the way a hand brushes through the hair of someone you love. From my front porch, I watch the Salish Sea sparkle and shift, reminding me again that some things aren't meant to be measured—only witnessed. There, in that flicker of tide and sky, I feel something trail-familiar. Not the ecstatic high of hiking the PCT. Not the spiritual thrum of the Camino. Something steadier.

An echo.

A stillness.

A knowing.

After working as a casino coin slot tech for minimum wage, then working at a catamaran manufacturing company for a dishonest employer, I lucked into a remote job that felt tailor-made for me: training Boeing civilians on F-15 electrical and environmental systems. It's a gig that lets me cash in on thirteen years of Air Force technical experience, flex my leadership muscles in a meaningful way, and still chase adventure when the moment allows. Some days I'm teaching from my laptop, other days I'm jetting off to a new country, soaking up culture, friendship, and worldly beauty between training sessions. It's the perfect blend of stability and freedom—proof that it is possible to find work that supports your lifestyle without dimming your spirit. This job won't last forever, no contract gig ever does, but I'm glad to have this job in my life until the day it runs its course.

I had wandered a long time—through faith and doubt, across mountains and borders, into and out of disillusionment—only to learn the lesson I never saw coming: the point was never the summit. Never the diploma. Never even the destination. It was the seeking itself—the hungry, holy pursuit of something real. Of truth, of connection, of purpose. I used to think I was looking for God, or answers, or some cosmic clean line to follow. What I was really doing was learning how to live with the questions.

In Saudi Arabia, I had money, structure, and security—but I was directionless. I watched the sun rise over Nassim Compound and the same sun set at the Red Sea while feeling like I was subcontracted out of my own life.

Then came the Camino de Santiago: that sacred walk cracked me open in gentle ways. It didn't demand my blood or adrenaline—it asked only for presence. I came face-to-face with my spirit, my heart, and something much quieter than ambition: peace. On the Camino, I stopped pretending I was above needing grace.

The PCT subjected me to wilderness without apology, heat that laughed at planning, and ridgelines that erased ego. It asked for strength—but also surrender. It was danger and beauty tangled together like roots I learned to step over without complaint. Somewhere between the early morning alpine starts and the desert's dry hush, I stopped fighting myself. On the PCT, I started listening.

It gave me inspiration for my trail afterlife, and guided me to my unexpected home.

On Whidbey Island, I stopped running and started rooting. I stopped chasing certainty and started letting my humor flag fly. Writing my dissertation was never just an academic exercise. It was spiritual integration. A realization that, at its best, humor isn't deflection—it's connection. It's how we say, "I see your pain, and I'm still here."

The world's still messy. The litter is still there. The old shame from dogma I didn't ask for. The resentment toward jobs that took more than they gave. The memories of nights under foreign stars, wondering if I'd ever find love. Now, I don't try to float above the mess. I walk through it. I pick up what I can—one crumpled bottle, one bitter thought, one outdated belief—and carry it a little further toward light. Not to fix the world. Just keep showing up.

People call me Chris. Doctor. Veteran. Author. Hikertrash. Sometimes I'm a leader. Sometimes I'm just a stranger with an extra granola bar and a headlamp. Beneath every title, I am Windscreen: seeker of wild trails and deep truths, and I still take the path that scares me enough to grow.

If the wind hits right, I swear I can hear the trail say: "You're doing it right."

And if I'm not, the trail will provide.

www.ingramcontent.com/pod-product-compliance
Lightning Source LLC
Chambersburg PA
CBHW070547130626
46556CB00001B/45